MW00564318

MARIKA CIFOR is assistant professor in the Information School and adjunct faculty in gender, women, and sexuality studies at the University of Washington.

CPSIA information can be obtained
at www.ICGtesting.com
Printed in the USA
JSHW011930010523
41116JS00008B/294

# *the* Morning Light, *the* Lily White

# the Morning Light, the Lily White

## Daily Dips into Nature and Spirit

### Katherine Hauswirth

SHANTI ARTS PUBLISHING
BRUNSWICK, MAINE

# The Morning Light, The Lily White
*Daily Dips into Nature and Spirit*

References to edible or medicinal nature finds in this book are meant to provide interest and perhaps inspire further research. I am not an expert on foraged or cultivated foods or medicines, and it is imperative to consult expert sources prior to using any substances in this manner.

For references to Native American peoples, their words and histories, and their uses of and relationships with a variety of substances in nature, I sought materials from people with Native ancestry whenever available, and, when not readily available, ethnobotany or archaeological research or other sources recognized as reliable. Unfortunately, some sources refer to a "Native" word or practice but lack information on the specific tribal nation(s) connected with the content.

This book was written on land once occupied by the Hammonasset peoples.

Published by Shanti Arts Publishing
Designed by Shanti Arts Designs

Cover image by izumikobayashi/1125891739/istockphoto.com
Interior image by pijama61/1097414896/istockphoto.com

Shanti Arts LLC
193 Hillside Road
Brunswick, Maine 04011
shantiarts.com

Printed in the United States of America

ISBN: 978-1-956056-64-8 (softcover)
ISBN: 978-1-956056-65-5 (ebook)

Library of Congress Control Number: 2022951393

*This book is dedicated to my brother John's memory. I wish we had taken so many more walks together. Also, to my father Mason's memory. You are the one who showed the world to my very young eyes. I think of you when I hear "This Is My Father's World."*

*It is also for my fellow "nature nerds" and encouragers—people who have read my newsletters, book, articles, and blogs; come to my talks with enthusiasm; and eagerly and humbly shared what they have noticed and learned—as well as the myriad "lovers of the world" out there whom I hope to someday meet.*

# Preface

When you read this book, I believe you'll see that I am curious about every aspect of nature. My curiosity often sends me to books, magazines, and websites to research what I see and find answers to my questions. Many of these resources are mentioned and occasionally quoted in this book.

There are several resources that are referred to over and over again because they are classics in the field of nature studies. I've listed these books and magazines below and encourage you to seek them out to learn more about whatever topic captivates your interest. There are also a number of websites listed below that are invaluable in providing up-to-date information and images that can carry the reader along on their journey to study the natural world.

## Books

Almanacs like this one, with an entry for each day, were more plentiful in prior decades. Here I list a few "oldies but goodies" as well as more contemporary finds:

Hal Borland and Barbara Dodge Borland. *Hal Borland's Twelve Moons of the Year.* New York: Knopf, 1979.
—*All Borland attributions in this book are to this source unless otherwise noted.*

Geoffrey A. Hammerson. *Connecticut Wildlife: Biodiversity, Natural History, and Conservation.* Hanover and London: University Press of New England, 2004.
—*I especially like referencing chapter 22, "A Naturalist's Calendar," where Hammerson lists his finds for each day of the year. All Hammerson attributions in this book are to this source.*

Mary Holland. *Naturally Curious Day by Day.* Lanham, Maryland: Stackpole Books, 2016.
—*All Holland attributions in this book are to this source unless otherwise noted.*

Edwin Way Teale. *A Walk Through the Year.* New York: Dodd, Mead & Company, 1978.
—*All Teale attributions in this book are to this source unless otherwise noted.*

## Magazines

*Connecticut Woodlands,* published by the Connecticut Forest & Park Association. https://www.ctwoodlands.org

*Emergence Magazine,* an initiative of the Kalliopeia Foundation. https://emergencemagazine.org

*National Geographic,* published by the National Geographic Society. https://www.nationalgeographic.com/magazine

*Northern Woodlands,* published by the Center for Northern Woodlands Education. https://northernwoodlands.org

*Orion,* published by The Orion Society. https://orionmagazine.org

## Websites

All About Birds, produced by the Cornell Lab of Ornithology. https://www.allaboutbirds.org

BirdNote at https://www.birdnote.org

Bird Song Id app, downloadable to mobile devices

Connecticut Department of Energy and Environmental Protection (DEEP) at https://portal.ct.gov/DEEP

iNaturalist app, downloadable to mobile devices, and website, https://www.inaturalist.org, a joint initiative of the California Academy of Sciences and the National Geographic Society

In Defense of Plants at https://www.indefenseofplants.com/mattcandei-asindefenseofplants; ecologist creator Matt Candeias also has a blog, a podcast, and a book of the same name, all accessed at the site.

Ladybird Johnson Wildflower Center's Native Plants of North America at https://www.wildflower.org/plants-main

Northern Woodlands' This Week in the Woods archive at https://northernwoodlands.org/this-week

USDA at https://www.usda.gov; their fact sheets and papers on plants and animals are chock full of information.

U.S Fish and Wildlife Service at https://www.fws.gov

# Acknowledgments

I deeply appreciate the inquisitive, thoughtful, and persistent review and betterment of my drafts by Christine Cote, Founder and Publisher, Shanti Arts Publishing.

I would like to thank Acadia National Park, the Connecticut Audubon Society's Trail Wood, and Denton Loving's Orchard Keepers Writers Residency for the opportunities that helped me to learn and gave me time to think and appreciate. All have some mentions in this book.

# Introduction

Poet Mary Oliver said, "Attention is the beginning of devotion." This turn of phrase embodies a credo for many who are drawn to the natural world and feel a reverence for and devotion to their experiences there. This book holds that credo with daily opportunities to pay attention to the natural world and enjoy a moment of contemplation, reflecting on the enrichment and meaning to be found in a vast array of creatures and happenings. Of the 366 days housed here (Leap Day included!), some share a walk, a sight, a sound, a smell, a taste, an encounter, a compelling fact or two, a moment of joy. Some days raise a question—something to ponder.

"The Morning Light, the Lily White" is from an old hymn called "This Is My Father's World." The words were written by Maltbie Davenport Babcock, a Presbyterian minister, and set to music in 1915. Babcock often took long walks along the Niagara Escarpment in the Lockport, New York, area, where he would relish the sight of Lake Ontario and its surrounding scenery. As he got ready to set out on his walks, he would tell his wife he was "going out to see my Father's world."

Babcock's reference to "my Father" represents a traditional Judeo-Christian perspective on God. But this collection goes down a wider path, with a focus on nature and how we connect to it. We come back from our time in nature feeling curious, filled, and inspired; we have enlivening and even ecstatic experiences as we interact with the world outside. All of us, whatever our traditions and history, can find fascination in the living world and acknowledge our longing for deep connection, a longing that extends beyond our own kind to the myriad elements of our swirling sphere, to the soil and the sky, to a nearly unfathomable range of plants and animals.

I hope this book helps you enjoy a simple but important practice of observing, constantly learning, taking time to wander and wonder, and being fed by the daily miracles found in even the humblest of rambles.

# WINTER

## December 21

### Holiday to Holy Day

Despite great efforts to simplify, each year holiday preparations mean many items piled onto my already overflowing to-do list. It's a matter of mathematics—more to do, but no extra time to do it.

Still, I challenged myself to brave the cold and walk for a while. I looked down a long, straight side street and saw the water at the end. My curiosity had a warming effect—I forgot my tingling face and fingers as I let the tree-lined block draw me toward the blue.

I looked up at the bare branches, taking in long-abandoned birds' nests and squirrels' dreys now exposed to the elements. I examined barks of this tree and that—some smooth, some wrinkled, some like alligator skin. I appreciated the older, craggy trees allowed to age with dignity and serving as homes to many a creature. I thought about how some trees hang onto their seedpods all winter, poised for the chance to drop them into the soft, fertile spring soil.

Soon I was at Founders Memorial Park, built on a former landfill and overlooking North Cove. The marsh and saltwater vista gave me a deep sense of contentment, and the sign about the park's bird life had me wishing I'd brought my binoculars. No doubt many had gone south for the season, but when they come back I will return, too, seeking a clapper rail or a salt marsh sharp-tailed sparrow.

The day was a tailor-made gift, better than any purchase. Simply stepping out, simply stopping to gaze and wonder, even in the harsh cold, even shoehorned between the myriad waiting tasks, revealed a world that's been waiting patiently all along.

## December 22

### Pileated Woodpeckers: Here through the Cold

While incessant drumming drives some folks batty, people mostly enjoy sightings of pileated woodpeckers. They impress with their out-sized presence and eye-catching color.

With the leaves down here in New England, they become much easier to spot. Matthew L. Miller, a birder writing for Cool Green Science, noticed they seem less likely to fly away when you observe them during these cold months. I'm not sure why—maybe they need to conserve their energy more, the better to deal with the season's scarcer food supply.

One thing they don't seem to do—huddle for warmth! Each pileated occupies its own roosting hole (fashioned, of course, by persistent drilling). In the spring that same hole may be used for nesting.

While the pileateds are here for winter's duration, yellow-bellied sapsuckers (another drilling and drumming species) migrate—as far south as Panama. They need access to readily available sap, hence the flight to warmer climes.

If you're lucky enough to spot a pileated woodpecker this winter, surely you have found a bright spot in the day. What other touches of color can you find in the mostly muted landscape?

## December 23

### Sips of Sambuca, Thoughts of Elderberries

Elderberry bushes don't look like much in winter. They are brown and twiggy; it can be hard to imagine the abundant white flowers and the generous reddish-purple to blue berry bunches that follow them in summer.

I haven't thought about these plants much in recent months, and an ad for an immunity supplement featuring elderberry brought them to mind. I was reminded of the Latin name for the family—*Sambucus*. This recalls a drink I haven't had in a long while. The sambuca I know—warm with a few coffee beans floating in it—is licorice flavored, but it can be made from licorice root or anise, and/or elderberry root. It's the European variety of elderberry plant that's typically used; this variety can be grown in the United States as well.

Elderberry offers so many gifts beyond its warm weather beauty. The University of Vermont Extension's Elderberry Project published a guide listing a host of the plant's uses: teas, tinctures, drinks—distilled spirits, wines, and cordials—baked goods, jams and jellies, dye/food colorant. The berries are in increasing demand due to their health benefits.

While all this is fascinating, mostly I like the way the plant looks in the warm seasons. I'm looking forward to the longer, coat-free days when I can come upon elderberry and recall some of what I learned. Maybe I'll sip some sambuca this Christmas and daydream about spring and summer.

## December 24

### All-Weather Hares with a Record to Beat

In Helen Macdonald's essay collection *Vesper Flights*, she notes that hares "are our fastest land animal." I assume she is writing about England, from where she hails. But that got me thinking—how fast do hares rate here in the United States? North American Nature, a site authored by mammalogist Bryan Harding, clocks hares at up to 40 mph. The North American pronghorn is at the top of the speed list—up to 96 mph! But it was the hare who bounded impressively across fields near Harding's home that got him researching the topic in the first place.

Hares don't burrow. They live out in the open, keeping simple nests on the ground. The depressions they make on the ground are called forms. Given the exposed nests, it's good the young are born nearly fully independent.

Like rabbits, hares eat and then retreat to cover. I wonder if that's what shot out from under our rhododendron the other morning. It was still dark, and our beagle Buddy flushed something fast out of the bush.

Here in Connecticut, we have snowshoe hares, also called varying hares because of their seasonal change in coat color. Their winter tracks are often a bit blurred, given the generous fur coating on their feet.

## December 25

### Herons with Backpacks

This winter's *Northern Woodlands* is chock full of interesting things— the perfect thing to read on a quieter-than-usual Christmas Day soaked in rain.

Cheryl Daigle's piece there on monitoring great blue herons grabbed my imagination. It started out talking about Harper, one of three herons wearing GPS transmitters to help gather data for Maine's Heron Tracking Project. Harper was tracked flying sixty-eight hours nonstop, most of it over open ocean! She went from Quebec to Cumberland Island, Georgia, on that flight. The solar GPS devices are carried by the herons in small backpacks.

Sure, the resulting data is fun and intriguing. You can even sign up to "adopt" a colony. But this is more than an entertaining exercise—these big, elegant birds are good indicators of how the environment is doing overall. Their position at the top of the wetlands food chain means they can tell us a lot about the state of that ecosystem at large.

## December 26

### Can Spiders be Social Butterflies?

I've been re-reading William Powers's intriguing book *Twelve by Twelve*, and at one point he writes about watching a complex, dimensional web with hundreds of tiny spiders on it.

I usually see spiders alone, except when they are tiny new spider babies that have just hatched and haven't yet parted ways. (Think of that final scene in *Charlotte's Web*).

But hundreds of spider species, across several families, tend to live in colonies. Most are tropical, but the US has its share of social spiders too. They can catch bigger prey with their bigger webs as well as maintain the webs more efficiently.

Once, in Tennessee, a massive web evolved by accident. New baby spiders, each with silk thread attached and primed to fly off, were grounded by harsh weather. This happened for so many tiny spiders at once that it looked like white sheets had been strewn about. It was temporary; they were simply all stuck in the same situation at once—like airplane travelers who can't go anywhere because of a massive storm.

Another time, in Dallas, Texas, a football-field-sized sheet of white silk became a bit of a tourist attraction. It sounds like that one was built purposely by a mass of sociable spiders.

Massive webs aren't inevitable when spiders decide they are going to work together—they are just more newsworthy! *Anelosimus studiosus*, known to spin messy webs in the undergrowth, are known to be fairly antisocial, but in colder areas they develop more of a tendency to collaborate.

## December 27

### Dune Life and Christmas Trees

When I was a kid, no one seemed to mind if I wandered the sand dunes on Long Island's South Shore beaches. Not that the dunes weren't at all valued; I remember an effort to deposit post-season Christmas trees to help prevent erosion. But these days, there seem to be more signs warning folks to stay off the dunes.

The jury seems to be out on the pros and cons of using Christmas trees as a line of defense against battering wind and water. On one hand, the trees help trap sand. On the other, storms can wash them away even when they have been staked and fastened together. This can amount to a cleanup nightmare and, of course, a failed anti-erosion attempt.

I didn't find any pro versus con discussions about staying off the dunes, however. In Connecticut, piping plovers and least terns are two threatened bird species that nest along the shoreline. And the diamondback terrapin, a small turtle, lays eggs in the sand in early summer. Pedestrians can disturb these creatures' nests. Plus, no matter the season, walking on dunes can damage and loosen beach plants that play a key role in holding these fragile mounds together and preventing erosion.

Watching where our feet go is a practice that goes well beyond preserving our own safety; many flora and fauna can fall victim to the misplaced human footstep. If that isn't enough of an incentive, a fact sheet produced by the Connecticut Department of Energy and Environmental Protection reports that "The defense mechanism of adult terns when intruders enter the nesting area is to dive-bomb and defecate on the offender."[1]

## December 28

### Imitating Nature: Ice as Insulator

Sometimes, in early spring, orchardists imitate nature when a threatening frost is on the horizon. They get their hoses out and spray down their trees, which at first seems counterintuitive. Wouldn't the water put the trees at more risk?

The resulting protective ice coating, which sometimes happens naturally after a winter storm, helps keep the protected buds at 32 degrees. Buds' natural structures, with overlapping scales and waxy or pitchy coating, can protect them from ice damage. This can be a tricky business, though; orchardists must constantly monitor the temperature and calculate the right application rates. Jeff Farris at Garden Guides advises it "isn't as simple as firing up a lawn sprinkler and letting it run all night."[2]

The concept of permaculture is all about learning from nature's cues. For example, the practice of planting "three sisters" together in some Native American cultures—corn, pole beans, and squash—imitates how, in nature, plants thrive in every available niche, often helping each other.

Biomimicry is the practice of adopting nature's wisdom into human life. We stuff our winter coats with down to keep warm like the geese. The inventor of VELCRO looked at burrs under a microscope and discovered the incredible stickiness lent by hundreds of tiny hooks.

The theme of being "inspired by nature" can sometimes be overplayed— all sunsets and grand vistas and not much attention to detail. But looking closely, even studiously, as we are out and about enjoying woods, fields, and bogs has much to teach us, in both practical and inspiring ways.

## *December 29*

# Beckoned by Art: The Call of Marsh Stones

As I shopped for last-minute stocking stuffers last week, the compelling visuals on the cover of the Marsh Stones of Hammonasset calendar drew me. Here was a set of stunning and novel images, and I flipped the calendar over to learn more. Photographer Michael Fanelli wrote, "It stretches our imagination to think that only 21,000 years ago coastal Connecticut was covered by a mass of ice over one mile thick. Ice flowed down from near the Hudson Bay, Canada, picking up debris and moving it thousands of miles. As the glacier advanced, it carried sediment ranging in size from boulders the size of houses, to gravel, sand, and microscopic clay."

Fanelli notes that none of the scenes he captured were retouched or digitally altered, and what he found was undisturbed—not rearranged for the camera. His images feature vivid greens surrounding more muted grays and browns. The stones nestled among the marsh vegetation have a patient and steadfast look, as if they have kept important secrets for eons. There's something about that juxtaposition—the soft against the hard, the growing against the unmoving—that beckons a meditative moment.

I generally prefer glaciers and geology in small doses; the slow drip of vast time can be hard to fathom. But the contrasting colors and textures in these images got me to think about vast time in a different way. What beauty it wrought! So much tumult as the glaciers moved through, but what they dropped or smoothed is still here for us to find and admire.

## December 30

### Otters Moving In

At her Naturally Curious site, Vermont nature writer Mary Holland reports that if you watch a beaver lodge closely, you might spot a stream of air bubbles as an otter emerges. You might see it pop its head up after a while. Otters are much more sleek-looking than beavers, and their comparatively thin tails look nothing like the beaver's characteristic flat "paddle."

But what are they doing emerging from a beaver lodge? Otters sometimes take over abandoned lodges, or even move into an occupied lodge. Beavers and otters don't compete for food, since the otters are all about fish and beavers only eat plants.

From a distance, the lodges look peaceful and cozy. Sometimes you can see steam coming out of the top during wintertime, roughly akin to the look of puffs from a chimney. This is a sign the lodge is occupied.

Horrifyingly, Holland reports that, occasionally, an otter will eat a beaver. Could the "cohabitation" be more of a hostage situation, the poor beavers under duress from their "guests" the whole time?

Not all in nature is cute and heartwarming. Reality can be harsh. In *A Walk Through the Year*, naturalist Edwin Way Teale wrote, "The red fang and the bloody claw are as much a part of Nature as the drifting cloud, the rainbow, and bird song . . . There are both the terror and the pain and the brightness and the beauty in Nature . . . Nature is not gentle but there are warm and gentle breezes. For even the most timid and hunted of creatures, there are moments of peace and natural pleasure."

## December 31

## Oh, For a Half-Earth

A giant of the naturalist/science world left us around this time of year in 2021. E. O. Wilson was ninety-two when he died. He was known for his expertise in ants, but his impact went far beyond these creatures' tiny worlds. His E. O. Wilson Biodiversity Foundation supports the Encyclopedia of Life, a worldwide effort to catalog every single species on the planet.

Wilson promoted the idea of "half-earth" in an article he wrote for *Sierra Magazine*: "Only by committing half of the planet's surface to nature can we hope to save the immensity of life-forms that compose it. Unless humanity learns a great deal more about global biodiversity and moves quickly to protect it, we will soon lose most of the species composing life on Earth. The Half-Earth proposal offers a first, emergency solution commensurate with the magnitude of the problem: By setting aside half the planet in reserve, we can save the living part of the environment and achieve the stabilization required for our own survival."[3]

The story of a childhood accident and how it altered the course of Wilson's life has been told and retold. He had a strong interest in studying birds, but a fish's fin nearly blinded him in the right eye. This is what led him to decide to study ants, since he could readily examine them up close with his left eye.

Before he even completed high school, Wilson had discovered the first fire ant colony in the US. Among other things, he discovered how ants communicate using pheromones. He promoted the term "biophilia"—love for living things.

Wilson also said, "When you have seen one ant, one bird, one tree, you have not seen them all."[4] A good reminder for us lovers of the natural world, or should I say, "biophiliacs?"—look closely! Keep noticing.

## January 1

## The New Year's Rose

On several New Year's Days running, with snow on the ground, I wandered into an outdoor nook between wings of my church where a small garden lived and found a rose blooming. How the find warmed me—a bright spot in winter, a promising omen for the freshly minted year! It was the rose that crystallized my tradition of a New Year's Day walk.

The rose fit well with an old German hymn sung in that very church, "Lo How a Rose E'er Blooming":

> It came, a flow'ret bright,
> Amid the cold of winter,
> When half spent was the night.

Dubbing my find a New Year's rose was not too far off. It was probably a Christmas rose, also known as a Lenten rose. Technically it's not a rose at all, but a hellebore. Hellebores are usually poisonous (so deer turn up their noses at them) and often hail from European meadows and woodlands.

This time of year makes New Englanders hungry for nearly anything green or indicating life. Roses are a special find, but we pay more attention to the mosses as their green hangs on through it all. We treasure the dormant buds decorating the otherwise barren trees, and only the birds appreciate the bright berries more than we do.

Here's a resolution to consider: A whole year of noticing and learning and appreciating creatures and cycles, what they bring out in us, and how we connect with them. This looking, this wondering, is a way of wholly giving oneself to the endlessly unfolding world.

## January 2

## Marvelous Marcescence: The In-Between Trees

American beeches' leaves shine brighter (less color competition!) in winter, seeming to hold the mid-morning light. How do they spread so successfully in a mixed forest? Their roots can sprout seedlings, often resulting in dense thickets surrounding older, undisturbed trees.

Trees hanging onto their dead leaves in winter is called marcescence. Theories about some trees' grip on leaves through winter include the idea that this is a defense against browsing creatures like deer. Another suggestion is that leaf buds are protected from desiccation by the retained leaves. Still another theory is that when they finally do fall, the leaves serve as a delayed source of nutrients or a moist mulch sorely needed by trees.

*Northern Woodlands* writer Michael Snyder explains that marcescent trees are likely on the evolutionary path from an evergreen-type tree to a deciduous (leaf-shedding) tree. Evergreens were our planet's earliest trees, but as various tree types branched out (yes, pun intended) and got creative, some learned to shed leaves seasonally. For trees, there can be advantages to either approach—winter nakedness or winter clothing.

Juvenile trees often keep their leaves, "learning" to shed them as they mature. But this doesn't mean marcescence is an unfavorable trait. Only big time will tell if these trees decide to become fully deciduous. In the meantime, their persistent winter profiles and illuminated presence lend beauty to our walks.

Maybe they can remind us that being "in between" is okay. Like the beeches, we may be gradually transitioning over time. We may look back and see advantages to a period when we were neither here nor there, just hanging on and figuring it out.

## *January 3*
### Fat and Happy Squirrels

On a walk around Boston Commons, I noticed that the eastern gray squirrels were especially plentiful, roly-poly, and tame. I'm not sure the hand feeding I witnessed is good for them, but it's easy to understand how the habit developed—humans and squirrels in daily, close proximity, with many humans caring about these alert and clever rodents.

While the human-squirrel bond may be especially cozy in Boston, the squirrels there have the same behaviors as their slimmer relations in other locales. In winter, when the branches are bare, it's much easier to spot their homes, called dreys. Sometimes they adopt a hollow in a tree, but often they build a drey of sticks and leaves in a fork made by branches. They are rich in real estate, building several dwellings. They move to a new drey "neighborhood" when fleas and ticks move in.

According to expert Robert Lishak, the reason their flimsy-looking dreys are so durable is that they are built while the leaves on the branches folded into the nest are green and pliable. After the leaves and stems die, they harden and become resistant to wind and rain damage.

Take a meditative moment to imagine life as a squirrel, viewing sunrise, sunset, and life below from your sturdy branch, scampering with ease to the ground and back up again. Tucking into your cozy, freshly constructed drey (before the fleas and ticks move in). Waking up to your bird alarm clock. Watching humans hurry by; wondering about their lives. In the case of the Boston Commons squirrels, hoping for a croissant. If your job brings you into some version of "the branch office," remember the squirrels' literal take on this phrase next time you head for work.

## January 4

### Cypress Knees: A Lovely Mystery

Cypress knees tickle me. They look like an assemblage of tiny, cloaked beings lined up and admiring the water.

Recently I spotted some at the famed and quite stunning Mount Auburn Cemetery in Cambridge. Besides its notable "permanent guests" and intriguing markers, this cemetery is a great place for wildlife, including birds that rest and replenish there along their migration route.

But I have always wondered: what are the knees *for*? I am not the only one! Volunteer Susan Higgins at the Lewis Ginter Botanical Garden in Richmond, Virginia, says all the theories thus far have been disproven, either by lab tests by or simply removing these appendages and seeing what happened.

Could it be they are there to stir our imagination and admiration? Maybe they want us to follow their "gaze" across the swamp or the pond—there is so much to see!

## January 5

### The Bright Side of Humanity: A Bird's Eye View

There's plenty of worrisome news about the status of birds these days. But in this moment, I'm thinking about the good things we do for them.

I couldn't determine when we humans first started giving birds suet, which is made of meat and fat and gives birds a bolus of heat and energy. But I did read about the first recorded feeding of wild birds by a sixth-century monk, Saint Serf of Fife, who tamed a pigeon by feeding it. While this is the first recorded wild bird feeding, I suspect it went on well before that. Folks noticed birds nibbling at berries, then set some out so they could enjoy watching the show. This entertainment would have fast become a habit.

Rachel Carson famously sounded the alarm when she learned that DDT was fatally thinning birds' eggshells. And I've written about other women, in England and New England, who many might call eccentrics, but, in essence, devoted their lives to birds. Most of us are not Rachel Carson or Cordelia Stanwood (a New England bird "eccentric" and researcher), but there is plenty we can do, much of it simple.

The Stewart B. McKinney National Wildlife Refuge's Salt Meadow Unit has an educational sign about leaving snags (upright dead trees) in place—they are favored homes for many birds. Places like our local, volunteer-run A Place Called Hope rehabilitate birds of prey. And then, of course, there are our feeders—seed and suet alike. What we offer in our backyards can be a lifeline.

In the face of discouragement, I read Tom Brown's *Guide to Healing the Earth*. He recounts his revered mentor's perspective: "The positive energy of each and every act of a caretaker is felt by the natural world. Each positive act sends a form of healing energy . . . in ever widening circles." As they say in some churches, "May it be so!"

## *January 6*

### Buried Treasure: How Many Snails Have We Walked Over?

My son Gavin's troop was busily digging out a spot for his Eagle Scout project's ramp when he handed me a snail shell from one of the shovelfuls of soil. It had some fleshy, moist matter within, and I wondered—could a snail that was under the dirt be alive? I realized I knew very little about these creatures, which are more ubiquitous than they may seem initially. I mean, how many snails do you typically see when you are hiking in the woods?

Whitelip snails are one of our local terrestrial (as compared with seaside) snails. The fact that they are nocturnal explains why we don't see them more often. The Trails of Freedom site says that humid, early morning conditions give us humans the best chance of seeing them.

I learned that, yes, snails will sometimes bury themselves in soil. They live mostly in the upper leaf litter of forests, old fields, and wetlands. They can also live in more disturbed habitats, even cities.

Snails need calcium for their shells, and when they are eaten, they pass this important nutrient up the food chain. But at least equally essential for some snails is the calcium needed to make love darts. Certain snails shoot love darts, which look like tiny arrows, at their intended mates. These may help with safe sperm storage.

What if you watched a snail shooting its love dart? What if you watched the receiver get pierced with something that might translate into new life? Would it remind you that every day holds the promise of the delightfully unexpected?

## January 7

## The Smallest Deer, In Winter Coats

White-tailed deer are the smallest North American deer species, and there is an even smaller subspecies of these creatures, called key deer, specific to the Florida Keys (and, sadly, endangered—there is a refuge just for them).

Winter in Connecticut means wardrobe changes for white-tailed deer. Their reddish-brown coats turn gray. This helps with camouflage. Their winter coats are also longer and thicker, absorb sunlight better, and provide amped-up insulation.

In cold months, deer seek areas with good browsing and protection from the elements. Cedar swamps make excellent deer yards. The yards become especially important in heavy snow, since the deer can collectively trample navigable pathways—snow makes it hard to run from predators.

They can remind us how, in hard and scarce times, we can go someplace safe together and "trample on" a problem collectively until we have forged a decent path.

## January 8

## Not Every "Evergreen" Is

"Evergreen" is a term sometimes applied indiscriminately to conifers (trees that produce cones). I wondered recently how I reached middle age without noticing that some conifers lose all their needles in winter, and even before that, they don't stay green. I was strolling my favorite cemetery when I found a bare tree sporting small, reddish-brown cones that sat upright, as if arranged on a twig shelf. I saw one like it again when I took the hill down to the marsh.

I was seeing eastern larches, or tamaracks. These trees' bluish-green needles turn gold in the fall, before dropping. Unlike many other conifers, the cones can stay on the tree for years after releasing seeds.

These trees are Disneyesque "Snow Whites" of the tree world—a magnet to a host of creatures. They provide nesting spots for veeries, warblers, and song sparrows. Red squirrels prize the seeds. Snowshoe hares relish new seedlings and porcupines consume the bark. I'm sure these creatures don't judge what Anne Krantz at the University of New Hampshire's Extension site describes as a "very twiggy, dead looking silhouette" in wintertime, or the "stick in the mud" of bogs.[5]

The tamarack is known to be a survivor, withstanding extreme cold temperatures. It grows to only fifteen feet or so in the coldest places, but in toastier environments it can reach sixty feet. Watch this spring for the new, light green needles that grow in spurs, leading to a lacy appearance at the height of the tamarack's summer beauty.

## January 9
### Color-Shifting and Gravity-Defying

They turn white for winter and can leap up to twelve feet—much higher than their rabbit cousins (two feet). Their huge hind feet help them leap and speed about in snow. The snowshoe hare's winter color change is triggered by lower light levels detected by their eyes and signaling the pituitary gland.

I remember an encounter with a hare at Acadia National Park. It let me get quite close, which isn't this creature's natural tendency. While rabbits tend to freeze and try to blend in with the scenery, hares are known to rush away to avoid danger. I admired the hare's long, powerful hind legs and its height. It seemed gargantuan compared with most rabbits I've run into.

Climate change is not a friend to snowshoe hares. The Pennsylvania Game Commission explains: "When a hare has a white coat and the habitat around it is brown, it is described as a hare in mismatch. In recent years, warmer weather has reduced the duration of snow cover thereby reducing the ability of a white hare to blend into its brown habitat. Mismatched hares are likely subject to increased predation rates."[6]

Time will tell if the hare can ride out its relatively new dilemma. Can you relate to being in a state of mismatch, recognizing a moment when something that had served you no longer worked?

## January 10

### Stick Hoarders and Huddlers

My friend watched a beaver retrieve a stick from its cache the other day. Famous for being perpetually busy, beavers endlessly collect and store troves of sticks underwater. These become their food supply on even the coldest days of winter as they retrieve these sticks from under the ice.

Like many of us, beavers get fatter for "sweater weather." Also, beavers' tails store fat and then shrink during winter as the fat gets used. These characteristics, together with huddling with other beavers on sleeping platforms inside their lodge, make for a cozier existence as cold winds blow and ice thickens outside. Muskrats sometimes pile onto the huddles as well.

If it's been snowing, look at the top of a beaver lodge to see if the snow on top has melted. If it has, the lodge is likely occupied. The body heat and breath from the residents will have risen to melt the snow. You may not get close enough to see and hear it, but there is likely cuddling, gnawing, and squeaking within this snug home.

## January 11

### Early Birds: When Will We See Our First Return Migrants?

Reading an old journal entry, I was reminded that I spotted an osprey at Pratt Cove one January day. This startled me, but there was no doubt in my mind. Had this one been especially eager to fly back from the Caribbean or South America, leaving all peers behind?

I read up a bit more on ospreys. Osprey expert Charles Clark explained in the *Day* that male and female ospreys migrate separately, making the inevitable quip about how separate vacations might support their habit of choosing a single mate for life.

An article in *EarthSky* says, "Bird-banding data in North America shows a spring migration pattern that's become progressively earlier with each of

the last five decades."[7] It seems the data is mostly about songbirds, but it seems to make sense that it might apply to other types of birds.

I don't know how to feel about this because it's not clear how it will all turn out. I like to think birds are adapting to our changing world in ways that will help them, but only time will tell which species succeed. I do know that my heart will skip a beat when I see the season's first osprey, before stopping to wonder if it's too early.

## *January 12*

### Gutter as Wildlife Refuge?

A gutter segment up near our roofline has sprouted an interesting collection of plant life—mosses mixed with some leggier specimens. Maybe some birds helped plant them.

If you Google "animals in gutters," the first thing that comes up is what a nuisance they are, and no doubt they are, especially if you are a company that deals with keeping gutters free-flowing, or a pest control service, or if the upper reaches of your home have been overrun by one creature or another.

Squirrels and birds build nests in the intended channels. Raccoons use gutters as base camps for prying roof shingles off to gain attic access, according to one pest control site. Roof rats are found in some parts of Connecticut, and they like to climb gutter downspouts to get to their "room with a view."

Of course, no one wants their gutters to become the animal equivalent of Grand Central Station, particularly if it means water going to all the wrong places. But it's interesting to wonder how many animals have been traversing, resting, or raising families in the gutters over the years.

Starting a terrarium I can peer down into is preferable to squinting up at our overgrown segment of gutter and wondering about the mix of plant life within. But there are tons of sites recommending gutter gardens— that is, in gutter materials not being used to channel water away from the house! There are also many sites promoting downspout gardens, which make the best use of the water descending through the gutter network.

## *January 13*

### Invisible, Crucial, Magical

While the days are gradually getting longer now that Winter Solstice has passed, darkness still comes early. Sometimes my contact with nature is limited to a good read, giving me things to think about next time I get outside. Tim Folger's 2020 *National Geographic* article, "Saving the Great Lakes," is distressing in many ways, with details too vast to summarize here, but it's a story of we humans being poor stewards of our world. We fail to take the welfare of other creatures into account, and the welfare of these creatures is so intertwined with our own!

The piece isn't without hope. Farms have adopted anti-pollution practices. Scientists are studying myriad challenges, like algal blooms and invasive creatures. Articles like these, though worrisome, can spark more action.

Diatoms are a surprising star of the piece. They are not, as today's title suggests, entirely invisible, of course, but you need a microscope to see them. These algae, with rigid cell walls made of silica, are of astonishing, gem-like beauty, and Folger's description of "a kaleidoscopic variety of shapes" is apt.

It's diatoms in the waterways of the world that make about half our atmospheric oxygen, and our waterways need the oxygen from the diatoms as well. Diatoms are also eaten by zooplankton. The worry? They appear to be shrinking over time. The ripple effect of this problem will be huge. It is attributed to climate change.

I noted the article's wry aside that "diatoms don't get much press"—so here is my small part to share these crucial beauties and their unequivocal importance. And, yes, the problem is daunting, but there are many efforts underway to reverse the damage. Most policy recommendations for the Great Lakes apply to many areas facing a similar threat.

What better time to learn more and do more about the state of our natural world than the freshly minted new year?

## January 14

### Cold, Refreshing Spring

Today found our family in Cold Spring, New York, a village on the Hudson. The wind whipped off the river; the temperatures were single digits with the wind chill. But even so, we were bundled up and enjoyed a brisk walk along the coast, where we picked through driftwood and marveled at the abundance of spiky, otherworldly-looking water chestnut seedpods, sometimes called devil's heads, that had washed onto the beach. Water chestnuts, introduced in the 1800s as exotic ornamentals, have unfortunately become quite the invasive species, choking our rivers and spreading at alarming rates.

I'm not sure whether the next two sightings should be taken as signs of the havoc that climate change is predicted to bring, but, regardless, they made me feel hopeful about spring coming. We were treated to the spectacle of two sparrows mating alongside the curb—cute, fascinating, and shocking all at the same time. I looked up house sparrows, and sure enough, they sometimes begin mating as early as January. And then we saw an osprey on an aerie. According to the state's Department of Energy and Environmental Protection, they aren't supposed to return from southern hunting grounds until March. Then again, perhaps there are some early birds in every crowd.

It's good to be reminded that other creatures are busily living their lives in the elements even when our instincts tell us to stay where it's warm and dig in deeper beneath the blankets.

## January 15

### Deep Dive: Fish in Waterfalls and Anti-Gravity Fish

Tom and Gavin, husband and son, have just been in the Catskills, and Kaaterskill Falls—one of the tallest waterfalls in the eastern states—was a big highlight. Ice everywhere made the hiking an exercise in watching their footing, with the slick steps being a special concern. They saw some people preferring to climb on hands and knees!

The thaw feels a long way off, but looking at their photos got me thinking about the role of waterfalls in creatures' lives. What about the fish at the top—can they survive a big drop like Kaaterskill?

Vandana Gupta at BBC's Science Focus site reports that more than 90 percent of fish survive the steep Niagara Falls drop. But that's a smooth shot. A waterfall that drops over rocks, like Yosemite Falls, means certain death to all but the tiniest of fish.

First, I found myself writing about fish while looking at pictures of ice. Now, I am sitting in my chilly room, and my thoughts turn to Hawaii, where there are five species of waterfall-climbing fish, according to Alison Nugent at Massive Science. These fish grab the rockface behind the water with their pelvic fins, using suction. They have been found as high as 422 feet up the waterfall. 'O'opu, as this type of fish is called in the region's Native tongue, has long been part of Native Hawaiian religious ceremonies. They may be at risk due to changes in the climate.

## January 16

### Owl Envy

I have been obsessed with the idea of spotting an owl in a tree for quite some time now. I am a morning walker most of the time, which means they are sleeping as I walk. Still, every dark hole in every tree is a target for my binoculars.

*Central Park in the Dark* started this obsession. Author Marie Winn describes coming upon a sleeping saw-whet owl roosting in the Shakespeare Garden: "You can scan a tree with your finest binoculars and swear there's no owl there. Only if you know an owl's in a certain tree . . . will you continue the excruciatingly careful, inch-by-inch examination necessary to know that a certain bump on a branch is actually a perfectly camouflaged sleeping saw-whet."

I was jealous when I read Mary Oliver's piece "Owls" in her stirring essay collection, *Upstream*. She apparently saw owls everywhere, routinely. What gives? I am also jealous of her writing prowess! Take this swoon-worthy prose: "And I search in the deeper woods, past fire roads and the bike trail, among the black oaks and the taller pines, in the silent blue afternoons, when the sand is still frozen and the snow falls slowly and aimlessly, and the whole world smells like water in an iron cup."

Time in nature can be time in faith. Faith that we will learn something and that we may encounter a surprise. Faith in quietude and in cycles and in the mundane noises. Faith that we will return to this spot, and also find new ones. Faith that goes deeper than just mastering the trail; the kind that Emily Dickinson described so famously and well. She wrote, "instead of getting to Heaven, at last," we are "going, all along."[8] In many ways, walking shoes can be our pearly gates right here on Earth.

## January 17

### Mullein in Winter: Washed-Out Oasis

Mullein isn't the prettiest plant, even in full bloom. Still, it has appealing yellow flowers and a circle of happy bumblebees in warm weather, and it can grow to impressive, eye-catching heights—up to ten feet!

First-year mullein plants are low rosettes with fuzzy leaves. The rosettes can look battered and drab in winter months and are easy to miss.

Edwin Way Teale made an inventory of mullein hibernators. He likened those fuzzy rosette leaves to "a stack of woolen blankets" with tiny springtails and spiders nestled between.

Birds are clever about food sources, especially when they are scarce, but Teale reported he'd never seen mullein rosette leaves disturbed or bitten into. It's nice to learn that even the tiniest beings can find a warm home to wait the winter out.

## January 18

### Winged Stories in Snow

If you've spent any time in fresh-fallen snow, no doubt you have noticed tracks. The chunky treads from human shoes, dog pawprints, and if you are lucky, the imprint of a deer's cloven hoof or the splayed "hand" of a raccoon.

We might miss the stories birds sometimes leave, though. A video by Woodland Classroom points out subtle marks in the snow, sometimes just faint lines next to an indentation where the bird has landed or taken off. Sometimes it's easy to notice the tiny "rake" imprint of the wing edge, but the bird's body—so very light—doesn't leave much of a dent.

On the Great Divide Trail Association site, Jenny L. Feick says if you see a print with three narrow toes forward and one at the back, these are characteristic of perching birds like chickadees or jays. Out west, white-tailed ptarmigans prefer walking over flight, to conserve their energy. They roost in snowbanks and stay quite sedentary in winter. Their tracks can play tricks! Feathered feet can leave prints that look like those of small mammals.

In nature, as in the human-made world, things are not always what they seem.

## *January 19*

### Still Waters: Vernal Pools in Winter

Alex Wells, on The Vermont Center for Ecostudies site, told me something interesting: fairy shrimp eggs must both dry out and be exposed to winter temperatures if they are to hatch in spring. Vernal pools, also called ephemeral pools, have a seasonal period in which they dry out. If you ever had Sea-Monkeys® as a kid, you had a sort of brine shrimp, a fairy shrimp relative. They are marketed as creatures who "magically" come alive when you add water.

In addition to fairy shrimp, egg cases for dragonflies, damselflies, caddis-flies, mosquitoes, daphnia, and other insects are deposited in vernal pools in warmer months, stocking up what will be spring's food pantry. When amphibians such as wood frogs and marbled salamanders move into the vernal pools to breed, they will have plenty to eat. Some amphibians over-winter in the pools. Tadpoles can overwinter under ice, as can marbled salamander larvae.

Sadly, a winter thaw can trick some creatures into returning to the pool too early, only to freeze when cold temperatures return. A recent paper in *Journal of Hydrology* found that vernal pool species are likely to diminish with climate change. Some species—wood frogs, spotted and marbled salamanders, fairy shrimp, among others—are obligate, which means they must breed in these pools. The Northeast Climate Adaptation Science Center is mapping climate change-resistant pools.

There's an oft-quoted recollection by children's television icon Fred Rogers: "When I was a boy and I would see scary things in the news, my mother would say to me, 'Look for the helpers. You will always find people who are helping.'" While the changes in our world can be scary, we find scientist helpers all around us, using their smarts to monitor and advocate for a host of creatures. What can we do to, in turn, to help them?

## January 20

### Behold the Hoop Pole

There's a Hoop Pole Hill Road the next town over, and a Hoop Pole Road in Guilford. North Carolina boasts a Hoop Pole Creek Preserve. There's a tiny town named Hooppole in Illinois. In Mount Vernon, Illinois, the local high school's yearbook is called *The Hoop Pole*. What gives?

Mount Vernon's town site says many tender, young saplings were grown there and used for barrel staves. Jack Sanders at the Naturegeezer website about Old Ridgefield, Connecticut, explains: "Hoop poles were a well-known and valuable commodity that many local farmers harvested from the wild to earn extra cash. Hoop poles were long, straight rods, cut in the woods from ash, hickory, hazel, and white oak saplings or from bushes that had been specially pruned for the purpose. While they might be cut in spring or fall, farmers often processed them in midwinter, when they were less busy."[9]

So, roughly this time of year in the 1800s, farmers would have been soaking these saplings to make them more pliable, perhaps flattening them for barrel staves, even prepping them for use in ladies' hoop skirts. They could be used for temporary flooring, to help roll heavy things, or to make butter churns. Baskets were made from the saplings as well.

I wonder if we humans did enough damage to alter the course of our forested landscape specifically with our hoop pole enthusiasm—so many young trees that never got to grow up! These days, of course, we have different concerns, like immense quantities of never-disintegrating plastic, so we don't have to make our own barrels and baskets. And some of our butter is in plastic; churning is now merely a quaint concept for nearly all.

In my neck of the woods, saplings can be "a dime a dozen," but this history makes me see them differently. How very interwoven they once were in our lives!

## Catalpa Trees: Much More Than Ornamental

In *The Book of Noticing*, I confessed a moment of amateur naturalist worry. My first instruction as a writer in residence as I pulled into Trail Wood, former home of Edwin Way Teale, was to pull around and park by the catalpa tree. Would I be revealed as an impostor and sent home if I admitted I didn't know which tree that was?

Like so many things in nature, once I knew what a catalpa was, I saw them everywhere, including several in and around local Fountain Hill Cemetery. Even the most basic beginning naturalist can readily identify the tree by its enormous pods; it's also called a cigar tree or Indian cigar tree, and sometimes a fish bait tree.

What purpose do these distinctive pods serve? Mark Gelbart's blog told me the catalpa may be an "anachronistic" species—no modern animal disperses the contents of its long, tough "cigars." Most often the tree is used as an ornamental shade tree, and while its pods are its most widely recognized feature, its showy white flowers with yellow and purple markings inside are a treat to behold in May or June. They smell good too!

Where does the fish bait moniker come in? Some folks plant the tree to attract the catalpa sphinx moth. It lays eggs on the tree, and the resulting caterpillars eat the leaves. Fish love these caterpillars, I am told. I also learned that the yellow-billed cuckoo bird loves the caterpillars as much as some fishing enthusiasts. Anglers, set your alarms. You know what they say about early birds!

*January 22*

## Earthworms in Winter

Did you ever wonder what happens to earthworms in winter?

Most of them roll up into slime-coated balls and take a very long nap. For other types of earthworms, their final act is to lay eggs in cocoons that stay in the soil until conditions are right for hatching. They die in the leaf litter not long after the cocoon is formed.

Earthworm cocoons, which look a bit like miniature lemons, are created on the surface of the worm's body as a slime tube during mating and then slide off the worms, pulled over their heads like a discarded sweater. They can hold as many as twenty eggs, according to which species they are.

There's a whole world of both holding patterns and regeneration going on in the soil beneath our feet, even when it looks barren and lifeless.

## *January 23*

## Teakettle or Cheeseburger? Certainly Not Germany!

I didn't realize when first setting out to identify birds by sound that there are so many sounds—per bird! Take the Carolina wren. There are songs, calls, and "other sounds" listed on the All About Birds website. Under "other sounds," I learned that males sometimes purposely slam into objects with an audible whirring of the wings; this "drumming" is a response to intruders. In Florida, the males prefer palmettos for their slamming targets. For vocalizations, the site lists "a large repertoire of calls, including loud repeated rasping, chattering, and a rising and falling *cheer.*"

Calls serve many purposes—to warn, to locate young, or to instruct. (Familiar migrating Canada geese calls indicate, "follow me," according to MassAudubon). Songs, on the other hand, are most often sung by male birds and signal breeding availability and establishment of territory. I'm not sure I could pick any of the Carolina wren's calls out from the canopy. But I do know that when I hear "cheeseburger, cheeseburger, cheeseburger," that's a male singing his song. Of course, others don't hear the siren song of "cheeseburger." They hear "teakettle" or even "Germany."

I loved hearing the "cheeseburger song" during my workday recently, which led me to look out at the backyard suet cake. There was one lone Carolina wren flying to and from it, a quiet flurry of rusty-looking topside plumage with telltale stout body and long tail feathers pointed up. These birds, unlike many other songbirds, sing year-round.

How welcome, to be called away from the workday by the sight and sound of a modest, but heartwarmingly melodic, wren.

## Deer Visits and Winter Browse

My sister Linda, her husband Randy, and their neighbors in Vermont get frequent visits from a lone—and somewhat odd-looking—deer. He has a burro-like appearance. Linda says he seems stunted, compared with the others. I looked up mule deer simply based on his appearance—but mule deer are a western species. Maybe this guy is just an unusual-looking white-tailed deer. And my theory is that he is a guy, since, generally, the males are loners.

My sister is worried about this one. Her husband nixed her idea to take him in on a cold night, and it is also illegal to feed deer in Vermont. But it's hard not to melt under the gaze of those bright black, inquiring eyes. Maybe it's anthropomorphizing to perceive him as a lonely guy, but even my heart strings are being tugged, and I've only seen the photo my sister texted!

This deer, let's call him Don, seems especially curious, peeking into windows and such. We wondered if helping him with winter browse is okay. The National Deer Association says the best thing to do if Don seems to be struggling to eat is to help him access more browse—buds and twigs of woody plants.

By late winter—especially if it's a harsh one—there may be little left. March can be the toughest month. The Association adds that if you prune trees or shrubs, you can leave the pruned limbs in piles, a kind of twiggy buffet. In the Northeast, the white-tailed deer's top browse choices are greenbrier, blackberry, and dogwood. In the Southeast, however, Japanese honeysuckle and Alabama supplejack are top choices, along with greenbrier.

## The Long Winter with Cordelia

I've learned to be hardier for winter walking, with the help of long johns and a wealth of layers. But now that I'm eager to layer up and get out, I'm not supposed to bear weight on my foot. I am impatient about this, but also relearning the lesson that there is always something to notice, something to ponder when I'm in the right mindset.

Only with my binoculars can I discern a duo of song sparrows below the feeder—they blend in so well with the leaf litter! They are hopping about, sporting those handsome striped heads.

I turn towards my new friend Cordelia Stanwood. Well, the book about her, anyway. I bought *Beyond the Spring*, by Chandler S. Richmond, during our family visit to her home, Birdsacre, in Ellsworth, Maine. I am so glad to be learning about this kindred spirit who died at ninety-three, about a decade before I was born.

Richmond, who based much of what he wrote on the voluminous papers Cordelia left behind, described how she reunited with the world after a long illness: "One day while looking down the long hill below the house she had become aware of the rugged peacefulness of what she saw: the flat smoothness of snow-covered fields on either side of Card's Brook, the lazy blue smoke curling up from the chimneys in town, the purple outline of the hills in Dedham silhouetted against the rosy tints of late-afternoon sky. Suddenly she felt as if a great weight had been lifted . . . and when a gull sailed majestically through the golden rays of late sunshine she had smiled and whispered to herself, 'Oh, world, you are there after all. You haven't changed. It is I who have been away, and you have been waiting for me all the time.'"[10]

On these quiet days, I like to imagine Cordelia's reawakening as she looked out over the snow. The possibility of this deep knowing that Cordelia had, that the world is always waiting for us, is there for us every single day. We just need to rise and meet it.

## *January 26*

## No Ordinary Sparrow

It's not an especially common occurrence, but if you are viewing a large grassland or dune close to the coast and think you are seeing an "ordinary" sparrow, you might want to look again. There's a chance you may be seeing a Lapland longspur on a comparatively warm winter "vacation" in North America.

During breeding season, these birds make their home in grassy spots along the Arctic tundra. On this continent, we can see them hanging around with birds like horned larks and snow buntings, pecking about for seeds scattered by the wind.

Folks have spotted these birds at the Milford Point Coastal Center and at Hammonasset Beach State Park—both favored birding spots. But they also seem to like an airport down in Stratford—no doubt plenty of weeds and seeds there too.

The males look different when they are back on the tundra: yellow bills, a mostly black head, and a patch of rusty color at the nape of their necks. We aren't the only ones who don bright new "outfits" when spring arrives.

## January 27

### Everybody Huddle

Many birds puff up in the cold, fluffing their feathers against the chill. Like us, they seek shelter to stay warm, and they can shiver, too, to bring up body heat.

Geese grow extra layers of fat for winter, and many water birds preen with oil, keeping a coat between their feathers and the frigid water.

Of all the strategies birds use to stay warm, huddling is the most endearing to me. Herb Wilson at the Maine Birds site reports that a British gardener found sixty-one common wrens (similar to our winter wrens) huddled together in a tiny nest box after a cold night. It seems to be the small birds who huddle most.

The popular Bored Panda entertainment website posted thirty images of birds huddling, snuggling, or cuddling—chose your verb. Many of the photos hint at birds banding together against the cold, but in others they look perfectly warm—maybe they just like each other! I particularly like one photo that looks like some sort of Gothic drapery—swallows are all pressed together in vertical formation against a house—they look like crows in the photo as their darkest feathers are showing.

Could some of this huddling in fact be cuddling for affection? The birds, of course, can't tell us, but I read a piece in *Nautilus* by Brandon Keim on the concept of love among birds. It said, "Part of the reluctance to talk of bird love is rooted in our misgivings about our own love's biological underpinnings: Is it just chemicals?" Science has been cautious not to anthropomorphize, with the concern that it will taint our observations of nonhuman creatures. But the Keim piece includes an ornithologist's remark: "there's no reason to think that we humans have some brand-new thing" when it comes to emotions."[11]

## January 28

## Crimson Clusters

It's a treat to turn a corner in the mostly muted winter landscape and come across a holly tree or bush. These pops of color, red berries among spiky leaves, have been recognized by humans as something special for eons. Holly festoons many a Christmas card, but Druids brought the boughs inside their homes long before Christmas existed. They believed holly enhanced fertility and drove witches and bad luck away. As time went on, holly bushes were planted bordering the home.

The pretty fruits are deemed poisonous to humans and their pets (although some sources argue that they aren't as toxic as once thought). But many birds thrive on them. Migrating flocks of small birds like cedar waxwings and American goldfinches are thought to be the best dispersers of the plant. Bees, wasps, ants, and night-flying moths help to pollinate the white flowers, which bloom between April and June. Only female plants produce berries, which, technically, are not berries. They are drupes—a fleshy fruit with a stone in the center, like a cherry.

Guess where HOLLYwood got its name? Some say the captivating California holly (aka toyon) inspired it. According to Lisa Cahill at TreePeople, Los Angeles passed a law in the 1920s preventing collection of the plant, which had become immensely popular as holiday decor. Others disagree with the Hollywood name origin story, but, regardless, California holly was named the official native plant of Los Angeles.

## January 29

## When Bobwhites Were Plentiful

In a 2012 column for the *Day*, Robert Tougias recalled a childhood bobwhite encounter: "They flew in all directions, swirled around me, then spiraled upward into a vortex. Sunlight gilded their speckled breasts and turned their brown wings golden as they ascended, through falling snow, into the cold ether."[12] He said the memory lasted a lifetime, wistfully reporting that we can still, at least, see them on Cape Cod. Sadly, it seems their decline may have escalated since Touglas penned his story. Native populations in Connecticut are said to have likely extirpated—vanished from the state.

A few years back, I ambled toward the water here in Deep River. Behind a row of houses, I heard a few birds calling back and forth. The damp morning air seemed to magnify the sound. What was I hearing?

Quick research clearly defined the northern bobwhite call. Their song, sung mostly by unmated males, is distinctive. I never did determine who decided the spaced, whistled syllables sounded like "bob white"—maybe a guy named Bob White?

Here and there we read stories about creatures thought extinct or extirpated that have been rediscovered. And sometimes humans have forestalled what seems inevitable. A massive campaign to put up bluebird nest boxes helped keep eastern bluebirds in this region. For the bobwhite, a National Bobwhite Conservation Initiative is active in twenty of the more southern states.

We humans can keep our ears open for bird calls, but also for opportunities. What, specifically, can we do today to help our fellow creatures?

## January 30

### Puffed Up Zenaidas

I've met a couple of women named Zenaida and learned recently that they share the name with the mourning dove—*Zenaida macroura* is the scientific name. The dove's "last name" means long-tailed, and its first name is after ornithologist Charles Bonaparte's wife.

It's not long tails or Bonapartes I think of when I hear these birds, though. Their familiar, throaty "coos" have graced every neighborhood since my first suburban New York home. In each place I have admired their iridescence as they lift off in a certain light. As with many birds, the males boast more color than their mates, sporting slight blue coloring on crowns and napes and a pinkish wash over breasts.

They are infamously sloppy nest builders, sometimes losing eggs through the gaps as a result. They can fly at up to 55 mph. And they are immortalized as turtle doves in the "12 Days of Christmas" song, forever preceding the lone partridge in its pear tree.

North of the freeze line the birds change their behavior in winter, forming small flocks instead of pairs. That explains the seven I saw in the cemetery tree, feathers plumped up against the cold. Most of these winter residents may be males, more apt to stay behind when others migrate as they are eager for a head start on claiming good breeding territory. Sadly, some of these intrepid doves are prone to frostbitten toes, as their species hasn't yet spent enough time in colder weather compared with other birds like black-capped chickadees.

## January 31

### Stones Sprouting, Part 1

I browsed a site on native ground covers and found myself drawn to the stonecrop listing. I liked the idea of stones "growing a crop," so to speak. The site featured wild (also known as woodland) stonecrop, or *Sedum ternatum.*

Learning more at the Lady Bird Johnson Wildflower Center's Plant Database, I was surprised to see a big list of stonecrop varieties, from Allegheny stonecrop to Wright's stonecrop. Narrowing my list to Connecticut, I learned that we have Allegheny, ditch, roseroot, and wild types. The wild kind looks most familiar—one of those plants I have walked by and wondered about.

I like how this plant is described as "rock loving." It's typically not thought of as edible or medicinal to humans, although the Plants for a Future site says the woodland type's young leaves can be eaten. But the species' nectar and pollen attract various kinds of bees, wasps, and flies. The Gardens with Wings site says butterflies, including the variegated fritillary, use the woodland type as a host, and it is a nectar plant for the fiery skipper.

Also, the eastern chipmunk eats the woodland variety's roots. How often do I see a chipmunk running along a stone wall? Next time I spot this frequent New England occurrence, I'll see if I can spot some stonecrop in the vicinity too.

## February 1

### Stones Sprouting, Part 2

What do stones sprout? Of course, stones don't literally sprout, as yesterday's and today's fanciful title might imply. The more accurate question to ask is what colonizes stone and why?

Robert Krulwich wrote a great NPR piece on moss, and it starts, "Sometimes the quiet ones surprise us."[13] Yes, over time, the pretty, green, innocuous-looking moss that finds its way onto stone will break the hard substance down, first to smaller pieces, eventually to topsoil. Typically, no one worries about this much, even for human-made structures, because it takes so long.

Lichens can also wear down stone over time, as any trip to an old cemetery will tell you. (It's hard to gauge how much of a role lichens have, as opposed to other factors like weather erosion. In fact, some argue that lichens can have a protective effect on tombstones).

Rock tripe is one of my favorite lichens, and come to think of it, I haven't noticed it on my cemetery walks. This might be because it likes high elevations, large surfaces as in cliffs and boulders, and moisture. This type of lichen was reportedly boiled by Washington's troops for food at Valley Forge. Smooth rock tripe, one of the thirty types, is a staple for elk in Canadian arboreal forests.

## February 2

### Winter Loungers: The Northern Water Snake

I like watching the glossy, dark northern water snakes in the pond in warm weather, but I haven't ever seen one in winter. Not a surprise, since they are brumating (staying quite still, but not in the full, deep sleep of hibernation).

They stay close together in winter, in a cluster called an aggregation. As I walk, I think about how they might be aggregating anywhere—tree hollows, deep under the leaf layers, in a muskrat mound or beaver lodge, in an earthen bank, in a vole tunnel. Wherever they are aggregating, they are good hiders. They will intermingle with other snake species while brumating and come out occasionally for water or food. They don't need to eat much since they are using little energy.

Around March, the snakes will come out of their cozy winter spots and become more active. Breeding will start around April. Some snakes lay eggs, but northern water snakes have live births, usually about twenty young, but up to fifty at a time! Babies are a half foot or foot long and immediately independent.

Sometimes it doesn't look like there's much going on in the winter land-scape, but it can be heartening to contemplate what lies beneath, just wait-ing to reemerge.

## February 3

### Forest Princesses and Moss Misnomers

The first kind of clubmoss I learned about was princess pine, also known as ground pine. These tiny, evergreen "trees" grace the otherwise brown forest floor even during the harshest phase of winter. Clubmoss is the common, overarching name for Lilliputian delights like princess pine, ground cedar, and shining firmoss, although the term "moss" is as mis-leading as the term "pine." It seems these types of plants eluded catego-rization for quite a while. The *Adirondack Almanack* says they were once thought to be closely related to ferns and so referred to as "fern allies," but we have since learned that this isn't technically the case, either.

Little "forests" of these plants provide protective cover for ground-nest-ing birds, and in picking one you can damage many of its brothers and sisters, since they grow via an interconnected root system. Also, only a minute percentage of the spores that puff out of the "clubs" (or in some cases from specialized leaves) will generate a plant. This can take up to twenty years, which explains why experts strongly advise us to resist the urge to bring one home. Climate change and human over-picking have put these beauties at risk. Years ago, clubmosses were more popular in wreath making, and their highly combustible spores were used for flash photography.

In ancient times, these miniatures weren't miniature at all; they evolved to be small. Back then the landscape was swampy, dominated by these plants and some scarily giant insects like dragonflies with two-foot wingspans. Whether we conjure up fantastic visions of this Jurassic Park-worthy scene or simply gaze down appreciatively at these filigreed, feathery kingdoms of green, these plants adorn our walks even at winter's height. If you are lucky one spring day, you might spot an ovenbird nestled in one of these perfect verdant groves.

# February 4

## Saving Mice

Today's entry in Edwin Way Teale's *A Walk Through the Year* delights me and has me again marveling at Teale's "Snow White" or perhaps "Dr. Dolittle" quality. He had a knack for finding the smallest creatures, or perhaps they found him, knowing he was a friendly presence.

The entry recounts two instances where Teale saved a mouse caught off guard. The first, a meadow mouse, got stuck unprotected when snow drifts iced over. It must have popped out to forage and then couldn't get back in, back to its more protected place. The other incident had a white-footed mouse cowering against a large, plow-created wall of iced-over snow. Teale poked holes so they could scurry back whence they came.

When I typed "types of Connecticut mice" into my search engine to learn more, most entries were about getting rid of "pests." I understand. We had an awful invasion of house mice beneath, and even in, our stove and did finally resort to the unpleasant business of traps. But there are so many small rodents in the wild—foraging, taking shelter in tiny crevices, not doing humans any harm, and being an important part of the ecosystem. For example, white-footed mice eat gypsy moth caterpillars. In turn, they are preyed upon by snakes, owls, bobcats, weasels, and foxes.

At the Connecticut Wildlife website, I found a welcome relief from that pest-oriented viewpoint. One entry is about the white-footed mouse, but it also names its cousins: the meadow-jumping mouse, the deer mouse, the woodland-jumping mouse (jumps up to eight feet!), and the ubiquitous house mouse. And then, of course, there are voles, sometimes mistaken for mice at a casual glance. I had a memorable vole encounter once, but my role wasn't as noble as Teale's. It didn't need my help, but I failed to resist the urge to bend down and gently touch it. Next time, my hand will stay in my pocket.

# February 5

## The Forest Has Ears—Wood Ear Mushrooms, That Is!

The last time I saw a wood ear mushroom, it was in a delicious salad at our local Taste of China restaurant. Here they seemed exotic, prepared just right with greens and oil. But they grow locally, and I've spotted them here and there.

Wood ears have a rubbery or springy texture (yes, like ears!) and can dehydrate and then rejuvenate after rain. They don't mind cool weather, into early winter and again in early spring, after overwintering and rehydration. In warmer climes you can find them in mid and late winter too. They grow in clusters and fold easily, again like ears. They like elder trees, especially.

These mushrooms have a legend and nickname attached, and here I'll quote professor of biology Tom Volk from the University of Wisconsin: "The common name Judas's ear comes from the legend that *Auricularia* formed its ear-shaped fruiting bodies as a curse on the tree on which Judas hanged himself . . . Judas was the apostle who betrayed Jesus for thirty pieces of silver. Obviously, someone had an overactive imagination when seeing an ear on a tree and thinking of Judas. However, the intriguing name has stuck, even with the normally stuffy taxonomists. In fact *Auricularia* means ear and the epithet 'auricula-judae' means 'the ear of Judas.'"[14]

It's been said that Judas hanged himself on an elder tree (also called a Judas tree), so I can see how someone with both Bible and tree knowledge (and a fanciful tendency) put the two together.

On a much lighter note, wood ears are a reminder that some sustenance can be found even in the bleak winter landscape.

What other forms of sustenance (sights, smells, textures, sounds)—the kind that can feed the spirit—can we find outside?

## *February 6*
## Woven Wonder, With a Wiggle

Last week I wrote about the unimpressive nest-building skills of the mourning dove, with eggs poised to slip through to the ground. This past weekend I got to see the opposite end of the nest-building spectrum. Walking through a stubbled field at Trail Wood, a Connecticut Audubon property in Hampton, Connecticut, I came across a blown-down nest that looked almost like a woven ladies' pocketbook. Something tickled the circuits in my mind to make me think this could be a Baltimore oriole's nest, and I was delighted when a picture online validated my guess.

The female does the weaving. It takes her about a week to weave long grasses into a pouch, often interlaced with other finds like fishing line or ribbon. The nest I found was about six inches long. What impressed me more than the shape or "stitches" was the feel of the thing in my hand—so stretchy and surprisingly sturdy. Diane Taggart at the Fire Island and Beyond website gives a great description of the layers involved: first an outer bowl is woven using elastic animal, plant, and/or human-made fibers. Then, spring-like fibers form the next layer. Softer fibers are used to line the inside.

The best part? When the nest is finished, the female wiggles around at the bottom to sculpt the final shape. Wouldn't it be great to spy on this "construction site" with binoculars?

## February 7

### A River Runs . . . Under It?

A tour guide at the Mark Twain House in Hartford pointed out a patch of parking lot and explained that a river once ran there. Hog River, later renamed Park River, got its original name from hog farms abutting the river. Later, when industry boomed, the river grew rife (and ripe!) with pollutants, along with human and pig waste. Some of the river was rechanneled; some was buried altogether.

Nine miles of this river are now hidden, but it remains above ground at the University of Hartford campus, through the city to the University of Connecticut Law School campus, and on to Farmington Avenue. When water levels get low, you can get to the (still stinky) underground parts. There was once a canoe tour of the underground section, but liability concerns sank that boat (so to speak).

All this came to mind when I read about Parisians' efforts to resurrect the Bievre River, which feeds into the Seine. *Bievre* is French for "beaver," and these creatures were once a common sight where culverts now lie. There's a verb for such efforts: daylighting. The Earth Law Center says, "Daylighting can create new habitat for plants and animals, potentially reduce flood risks, and create new 'green corridors' through urban areas."[15]

I learned that the Saw Mill River in downtown Yonkers, not too far from here, was daylighted, with great hopes to bring back habitat for muskrats, snapping turtles, and other creatures. A new park was made, fish and eel ladders installed. Salamanders, snapping turtles, and egrets returned. Folks are hopeful that more New York rivers and streams will see daylight again, with Yonkers as an inspiration.

## February 8

### Ubiquitous, Hardy, Well-Traveled: The Gull

Gulls were part of the atmosphere where I grew up on Long Island. Not so much around my house, but circling the hills at the dump and always present at Jones Beach. They stood in loose clusters and watched the Atlantic, sometimes looking stoic and profound and sometimes shrieking like maniacs. They soared and dived overhead and scarcely minded us humans as they scavenged our leavings of French fries and sand-laced hot dog buns.

A line of them greeted me at Deep River's town dock the other afternoon, and as one friend pointed out when she later viewed my photo, "one of these things is not like the other." I admire birders who can tell the gulls apart, and I am determined to learn more. A checklist of Connecticut birds by the Connecticut Ornithological Association lists seventeen species of gulls, although seven of these are marked with asterisks, meaning they are rare here.

Greg Hanisek at the Connecticut Audubon Society site says, "Gulls as a group are known for some monumental wandering."[16] We have records of the slaty-backed gull and the Kamchatka gull coming all the way from northeastern Asia. A US west-coast gull, the glaucous-winged gull, has been found in Europe.

I was amused to find several people inquiring on the Internet about "seagulls so far from the sea," and "why do gulls like mall parking lots so much?" "Seagulls" is a misnomer; these birds are simply gulls and can live inland quite contentedly. As for the malls? It's simply that there are many opportunities for food, from what humans throw away to the insects in grassy medians. Plus, gulls like open areas from which they can survey the scene and also take off easily. They can use their super sharp eyes to scan a vast area and zoom in on tasty morsels.

Have you ever wanted to be a "monumental wanderer," like the gull? Where would you go if the sky held no limits?

## February 9

### Tale of the Overwintering Foundress

My friend Laurie, a fellow Master Naturalist program alum, shared an endearing tale on Facebook and gave me permission to share it.

Laurie found a slow-moving wasp indoors. She noticed the wasp was stumbling. She expected her to die.

Wanting to help, Laurie soaked a paper towel in sugar water and let her lick it up. She watched her unfurl her long proboscis to drink. Adult wasps only eat nectar, but they feed caterpillars to their young.

Laurie learned that she had a northern paper wasp on her hands—likely an "overwintering foundress." Typically, foundresses sleep through winter, then wake up in spring and start a nest. The eggs they lay in the nest house the next generation of worker wasps who will emerge ready to keep building.

But mild winters can throw these creatures off their game! They wake too early and in many cases are doomed to wander in search of food, eventually dying. Laurie made careful efforts to help her wasp friend literally "chill out," cooling her down gradually so she could go back to her overwintering state for a while longer.

I feel connected to this tiny wasp and hope she fares well. There is something magical to me about overwintering, about all those "tucked in" animals waiting for spring.

## *February 10*

### Maligned and Marmorated

I posted an action shot for my newsletter readers of a brown marmorated stink bug who moseyed on after a few poses against my hand, my sweater, and the desk. Laminated wood made a flattering background for his intriguingly decorated back. The bug had a bluish tip on his body, and a handsome, stripey edge. "Marmorated" means having a veined or streaked appearance, like marble.

Imagine going through your life known as a stink bug. Imagine Googling yourself to mostly find lists of ways to kill your kind off. And, on top of that, just about everyone finds you frightfully ugly.

Through the cyberstatic, I can hear my naturalist friends tsking at me, saying, "Why so sympathetic?" The brown marmorated stink bug is an invasive species from Asia that loves to eat vegetation, including, potentially, farmers' and orcharders' livelihoods.

But taken as an individual and not a "hoard of invaders," this gentle bug (and in this case "bug" is a scientific term—an actual type of insect!) with a tender way of walking brought some interest to my day. I admired his "shield" (shield bug is another moniker for this type). I learned these bugs don't breed in our homes and are in diapause (a hibernation-like state) in the winter, which explains this guy's slo-mo navigation across my workspace. And he didn't stink at all—they emit an awful odor when feeling threatened. Or when someone decides to squash one.

I am not alone in my sympathy for these creatures. In a piece for Medium, C. M. Barrett went so far as to talk about seeing God in a stink bug. Call me crazy, but I get that. And another write-up by Sarah Taddeo and James Johnson in *Democrat and Chronicle*, mostly maligning the bugs, inadvertently slipped in a nonhorrified sentence: they "just want a warm window where they can sun themselves."[17] Don't we all?

## *February 11*

## Bird's Nest Fungi: A Miniaturist's Delight

For this nature find, it is necessary to lean in and peer closely. Sitting on some decaying wood is a little assemblage of what looks like a bunch of minuscule birds' nests, each with its own set of "eggs." Autumn is the favored time for these finds, but they can be spotted all year in damp, shady spots.

The "nest" is the mushroom's fruiting body; the quarter-inch "eggs" are spore-producing structures. These tiny structures wait for a storm, when raindrops will splash into the nest and force the eggs out. Later, the eggs will dry and release their spores.

This is one of so many examples in nature with a compelling aesthetic and architecture. The fluted "nest" looks shimmery and sculpted; the cache of eggs also catches the light and draws the eye. I feel the same way about the comparatively gargantuan southern magnolia fruits, which look like cones studded with small berries. The base of the stem looks hand tooled; the eye-catching architecture remains appealing long after the berries have been eaten by squirrels, opossums, turkeys, and quail.

What in nature has you leaning in and peering closely?

# February 12

## Gumball "Machines"

The spiky "balls" that fall from the sweetgum tree (actually seedpods) are a source of fascination, especially to children, who love to pick them up and hurl them around.

Each pod contains multiple seeds, and unlike somewhat similar sycamore fruits, they keep their shape and stay hard even after the seeds within have dispersed.

Many birds are adept at cracking the pods open, including goldfinches, purple finches, sparrows, mourning doves, wild turkeys, northern bob-whites, and wood ducks. Squirrels and chipmunks get in on the feast too.

This tree is a larval host plant for the stunning, enormous luna moth, and extracts from several parts of the tree are incredibly medicinal, including being a precursor to the antiviral drug Tamiflu®. And yes, the resin is sweet and chewy as the name implies; several sources say the tree is so named because of the several Native American tribes' (Cherokee, Choctaw, and others) practice of chewing the gum.

A *Hartford Courant* article by Peter F. Sleight calls this tree "a cursed beauty," with star-like leaves changing color in the fall with an effect of "billowing flames," and the "curse" being those many spiky balls. Sleight writes, "We accept the thorns of roses because the flowers are so beautiful. Is it possible to accept the seedpods of the sweetgum?"[18]

This leads to thoughts of the thorns and spiky occurrences that sometimes poke annoyingly into our day-to-day lives. Are there opportunities to accept these, knowing something beautiful might be connected with them?

# February 13

## Junco Snow Party

The seasonal influx of dark-eyed juncos came down to Connecticut from farther north a couple of months ago, but somehow this Tuesday, with an official "snow day" called for the schools, they seemed especially fitting guests at the feeder. They are, after all, called "snowbirds" because we see them in winter when they've come south to avoid even colder temperatures up north.

It's always puzzled me why they are called "dark-eyed." Aren't most birds dark-eyed? I learned that the name distinguishes them from yellow-eyed juncos in southwestern states, reaching from Mexico to Guatemala as well.

Whatever the color of their eyes, both types are sparrows. I've never seen the yellow-eyed variety, but I treasure the soft gray of the dark-eyed's backs and their pale underbellies and tail feathers, and how they seem to take polite turns at the feeder, rotating into and out of a nearby shrub. I learned today that females can be much browner than males. The ones at the feeder all looked gray to me.

There are about thirty-five sparrow species in North America. I know the snowbird, and I'm pretty sure I know the chipping sparrow by both its stripey look and persistent trill. When I heard "Old Sam Peabody-Peabody" this past summer, I know I was hearing a white-throated sparrow, but would I know if I saw one, if it didn't give itself away with music?. How heartening to think of a lifetime learning the rest!

## February 14

## Is That Love?

There's an old Squeeze song called "Is that Love?" The singer lists a bunch of bad or indifferent lover behaviors, all the while repeating the title's question.

I thought of the song when I read wildlife interpreter Krystle Smith's column called "Nature's Valentines." Smith wrote, "Organisms in nature form relationships not based on love, but rather survival."[19]

She went on to write about commensalism, mutualism, and parasitism. In commensalism, only one party benefits. Mutualism means both creatures benefit. Bees get nectar from flowers, but at the same time they help spread the flowers' pollen around. And parasitism sure doesn't look like love! Brown-headed cowbirds don't bother building their own nests. Rather, they put their eggs in other birds' nests, sometimes kicking out the other birds' eggs.

I'm not sure that creature relationships are never motivated or touched by love since, for the most part, we can't understand their language. We can flip the tables too; might we humans sometimes be driven mostly by instinct in our various "love" relationships?

## February 15

### Westward Expansion

I treasure reveling in and learning about the local Connecticut landscape. But I am grounded again, waiting for my foot to heal. I bring an old book to the stationary bike, multitasking by reading and sweating simultaneously. As I pedal, I embark on a mental trip out West.

In *Wandering Through Winter*, Edwin Way Teale writes about the American travels that he and his wife, Nellie, took over a season, starting in California. The ground they covered in the first third of the book is so rich with compelling creatures and scenes! They searched for pupfish (also known as desert sardines) in Death Valley and marveled at the different species that evolved over time in their separate, mineral- and salt-rich pools. They watched the Christmas morning sunshine illuminate mistletoe that hung among clusters of ironwood trees.

In that era—the book was published in 1957—Teale would have gathered reams of hard copy notes and canisters of film to be synthesized later into his Pulitzer-winning book, most likely doing the bulk of this work in his home back east. I can imagine him rereading his notes, again "feeling" the grit on his face and "seeing" the haze of the sandstorm that preceded his and Nellie's first glimpse of the White Sands, which had only been a national monument for a couple of decades when they stood there admiring the gleaming gypsum sand.

Teale wrote, "There is more to the out-of-doors than a schoolroom, and much has been lost when the sight of a hermit thrush stirs in our consciousness merely the scientific name *Hylocichla guttata*. The simple enjoyment of universal nature, with no other end in mind . . . has its importance. And fortunate indeed are those who know this enjoyment to the end of their days . . . In this speeding, modern world, an increasing number of people are realizing that just to stop, just to enjoy nature has its own significance."

## February 16

### For Peat's Sake: The Miraculous Life of Sphagnum Moss

There are more than 350 species of sphagnum moss, and typically, it grows in thick, dense clumps and often in bogs. It can become so thick and dense that it forms a "bog mat" strong enough to support several moose! On the other end of the creature scale, tons of microscopic beings live in sphagnum, especially in the bog environment, providing food for creatures higher up the food chain.

Peat moss is sphagnum moss, but sphagnum moss is not necessarily peat moss! In other words, peat moss comes from the plant, but it is its dead and decayed form that settles at bog bottoms. Harvested peat is used by gardeners to "amend" soil; it hangs onto water and nutrients and can benefit plants that love acidic environs. But Matt Candeias from In Defense of Plants writes, "Peat moss is not a sustainable option for gardening on any level . . . the mining of peat moss is an incredibly destructive industry . . . harming not only sensitive habitat but some of our largest carbon stores on the planet."[20]

During WWI, communities in North America and the UK held "moss drives" and were instructed to drag collected sacks to hard ground and then to "dance" on them to pound the water out. Its absorbent and antiseptic properties in the face of cotton shortages are said to have saved many lives.

Scientist and writer Robin Wall Kimmerer wrote about dancing on sphagnum moss in *Gathering Moss*: "I am standing quietly on the surface of an earthly Drum, my feet supported by the floating Sphagnum, responding to the smallest movement, rippling under my shifting weight. I start to dance. In the old way, heel and toe, in slow tempo, each footfall rippling across the bog and answered by the returning wave rising to meet my step . . . It too is dancing deep beneath me, sending its energy up to the surface . . . I feel the power of connection with what has come before, the deep peat of memory holding me up. The drumbeat of my feet calls up echoes from the deepest peat, the oldest time."

## February 17

## Still Waters in February: They Really DO Run Deep

Fountain Hill Cemetery's pond changes dramatically over the seasons. In the thick of summer, I see northern water snake trails through the dense water lilies, and some years I've been fortunate to watch muskrats making their own, wider trails, diving down here and there to get tasty vegetation from below the surface.

As colder weather sets in, I watch the green growth disappear, the pond once again becoming a blank slate. Gone are the turtles that sunned themselves on the log. Gone are the bullfrogs and green frogs that sang their "jug of rum" (bullfrog) and twangy banjo (green frog) songs into the summer evening. Sometimes the ice makes interesting formations, but as I scan the water there is little life to see in February.

I marvel, however, at what I imagine in the mud at the bottom. Aquatic frogs hibernate in the water. They need to be near oxygen-rich water, so they typically lay on top of the pond's mud or, at times, are partially buried. They may even take a "stretch break" and go for a swim now and then. Turtles, on the other hand, slow their metabolism so much during hibernation that they can fully bury themselves in mud and make do with the minimal oxygen supply there.

There you have it: the shallow, still pond runs deep with possibility and promise. I rest my case.

## February 18

### Winter Doldrums Redeemed: The Promise of Skunk Cabbage

I've had a bad case of winter doldrums, a predictable February happening for many New Englanders.

I looked up doldrums. I've never seen it used without the word "winter" before it. It turns out that the nautical use of the term refers to a belt near Earth's equator where ships get stuck in windless waters.

I think of those stranded, antsy sailors on ships described as maddeningly "becalmed." In this state, they must have forgotten that, while their ships were mired in some purgatorial saltwater loop, there was rich life thriving below the surface: octopuses coming up with clever hunting schemes; crabs moving into new and colorful shells; glittering schools of tiny fish; and enormous, prehistoric-looking deep-sea creatures encrusted in barnacles.

It helped me to apply this metaphor to my restless take on February, trudging through snow to refill the bird feeder, wondering when the snow will melt so I can park my car where it belongs and take an easy-stepping walk. Like the "becalmed" sailors I imagined stuck somewhere near the equator, I sometimes forget how much is happening below the surface: mice who pop out from below the snow to forage or wasps that overwinter below bark, later awakening to create new life. Mycelium networks, those thin, white mushroom "threads," are busy under the forest floor as I write.

And today, I looked it up, to be sure: yes, dreary February is the month when skunk cabbage first flowers around here. The flowers come first, inside the plant's hooded part. They make heat, which helps melt snow. Early flies and carrion beetles find and pollinate the flowers. In early spring, young bears may eat the plants.

Soon, all of this will begin to emerge—the wasps, the mushrooms, the skunk cabbage. The doldrums will feel relentless, and then, one day, we will glide across the unimpeded landscape, seeing all the emerging wonders and thinking that winter seems so very far away.

## February 19

### Is There Anything Good about *Phragmites*?

Today's title comes from a fact sheet on *Phragmites australis* (also known as common reed) from the Fish and Wildlife Service (FWS). Let's start and end with the more hopeful things, with the problems in between.

FWS says several bird species have been found nesting in these copious plants, which I saw so often during our family's three-day trek to and around upstate New York. Red-winged blackbirds and some wading birds nest in the stuff, and yellowthroats, marsh wrens, salt marsh sparrows, and least bitterns roost in it. And maybe it can be viewed as a friend someday, at least in some places—FWS notes it might help offset problems with sea-level rise due to its high rate of production, slow decay, and the fact that it stays right where it falls.

Now the problems: this nonnative plant crowds out native wetland plants; this in turn crowds out native animals. It is so dense that many creatures can't penetrate it, and over time it raises the surface elevation of the marsh, making it even harder for native plants to thrive. Even *Phragmites* that appear to be dead can in fact be viable for regrowth.

Scientists are working away at this problem. It turns out both salt and sugar may be helpful. Some studies have noted less growth when sugar has been introduced. Early in *Phragmites'* campaign to take over, restoring full tidal flow into the area may help control them.

Should we chow down on the stuff? A page by John Kitsteiner at The Temperature Climate Permaculture site says many parts of *Phragmites* are edible, in various forms, and a sugar can be extracted from it. Of course, we'd be at the table for quite some time in our efforts to eat the problem.

## February 20

## Quoth the Parrot: "I Don't Belong in This Poem"

According to Poe enthusiast Christoffer Hallqvist, Edgar Allan Poe considered using a parrot instead of a raven in his famed poem "The Raven." Good call, Edgar. Ravens are dark as night and have a reputation as bad omens. Parrots work much better with the Jimmy Buffett vibe—hardly ominous.

How did the raven get to be a bad omen? Well, these days we sometimes find them gathered in morbid "parties" around roadkill. But for centuries they were known to follow humans, having learned that they might find a good meal as a result. This was much more noticeable and creepy to humans (and feasible for the birds) before we drove cars. The birds followed wagons, sleighs, hunting parties, etc.

In this part of "The Raven," Poe seems of a mixed mind about this glossy corvid's purpose: "Prophet!" said I, "thing of evil!—prophet still, if bird or devil! . . . " This makes sense from the point of view of Haida (Pacific Northwest Native American) lore, as described by the American Museum of Natural History. In Haida stories the raven is portrayed as a powerful figure who transformed the world, but also as a trickster who brought light to the world by stealing it. He dropped some as he flew, and that became the moon and stars.

The trickster lore makes sense: these are clever birds. They tag team when they raid seabird colonies; they are known to wait in trees while ewes give birth so they can snatch the freshly newborn lamb. Famed naturalist Bernd Heinrich tested raven smarts by dangling meat from a long string—clearly not a situation found in the wild—and the birds quickly figured out how to work the string, efficiently reeling in their suppers.

However, ravens also love to play, somersaulting in the air! They've been seen flying upside down. Young ravens drop sticks and catch them in flight. So, let's NEVERMORE stereotype them again (There, I said it. The poem's insistent meter drove me to it).

## February 21
### The (Dia)Pause that Refreshes: Ladybug Naps

When we first moved into our house, we were greeted with a spate of ladybugs who hugged the warm, bright windows.

These were likely Asian ladybugs who had emerged from diapause (basically, insect hibernation). They were released in many states to combat aphids. They likely also came over to the US on freighters. The Asian (versus native) variety has a penchant for buildings. Native species prefer old tree trunks and rocks as cover for overwintering.

I see mixed reviews on the Asian variety. Some complain about their yellow, smelly fluid emissions (if disturbed) or tendency to bite. Sometimes, they get into grape harvests. Their contribution to wine is not tasty. Other sources present Asian ladybugs as relatively benign. A Connecticut Public Radio piece by Charlie Nardozzi says many die over the winter from our homes' dry heat, or from lack of food if they wake up too early.

Those who survive winter go on to emerge, mate, and eat aphids. This is true for both Asian and native types. In fact, the story goes that farmers in the Middle Ages prayed to the Virgin Mary for help when their crops were being destroyed by aphids. Ladybugs (called lady beetles in the UK) arrived and saved the day, and were hence called "Our Lady's Beetles."

Cornell University, with several other groups, is sponsoring the Lost Ladybug Project, to help figure out how and why the North American ladybug species composition is changing. Some native ladybugs have become rare, and in other parts of the world, some types are booming and widening their range. Folks contributing to the project are encouraged to send photos. I like looking at these photos, imagining these ladybug encounters, and seeing these contributions to citizen science cheers me.

## February 22
### Nevertheless, We Persisted

The wind howled, and at times, the snow looked like a glistening white tornado. I was surprised that the dark-eyed juncos were at the feeder. I wondered if the birds have a heightened instinct to feed when a storm is blowing, or about to blow—the same instinct that drives us humans to rush out in determined droves to get our bread and milk.

Have you ever held a bird? They are remarkably light; many have hollow bones. But the juncos didn't stop feeding when the wind picked up or when the flakes came down thicker. Nor were they blown off course. They seemed unperturbed, perhaps even content, to be in the snow and eating their seeds. I mused as I watched, noting how their design must—despite its fragile appearance—allow them to coexist with the wind, even master it.

Dark-eyed juncos don't grab my eye the way red-bellied woodpeckers and cardinals do. But I admire them. As I watched the birds ride out the squall with uncommon grace, I was reminded of a friend's favorite T-shirt, which reads: "Nevertheless she persisted." The words have a political history, but they take on a softer tone when I apply them to the juncos in the yard. Nevertheless, they stayed near the feeder. Nevertheless, they dined heartily. Nevertheless, they are there to greet me daily. I have come to appreciate their steadfastness.

Steadfastness can be underrated—we humans bore easily. What do you see in your world today that is ordinary, perhaps nearly ever-present, but something you can count on, something to perhaps look at with fresh eyes?

## February 23

### Go Figure: Tree's Blemish, Woodworker's Prize

The way tree burls produce a contorted grain is called "figure." When you see a burl on a tree, it's not often pretty, although it can be fun to imagine the kinds of creatures represented by the ungainly shape. Yesterday I spotted one that resembled a climbing bear.

I wonder if the tree perceives the burl as a burden. It is, after all, formed by injury or disease. Although very often it renders no perceptible harm.

It's clear woodworkers and decorators love the swirled wood grain patterns that come from burls—and each is unique. Treehut, a woodworking company, calls them "ugly on the outside, but magnificent on the inside."[21] In a *Northern Woodlands* piece, Joe Rankin calls them "surprise packages."[22] There is no way to make a burl happen, and this makes them even more prized. Unfortunately, this results in the occasional crime by burl poachers seeking a quick buck.

## February 24
### Stalking the Wild Marshmallow

How many of us, when we toast marshmallows over a campfire, are thinking about marsh botany? Usually, I'm thinking about how burnt is too burnt and how sticky my fingers are becoming. But there is a botanical story here! Here's what *Encyclopedia Britannica* has to say: "Marsh mallow, (*Althaea officinalis*), perennial herbaceous plant of the hibiscus, or mallow, family (*Malvaceae*) . . . has also become established in North America. The plant is usually found in marshy areas, chiefly near the sea. It has strongly veined heart-shaped or oval leaves . . . pinkish flowers, borne on stalks . . . The root was formerly used to make marshmallows, a confection."

Connecticut is one of about fifteen states in the US that have common marsh mallow plants growing wild. Aha! A new plant to seek, with a nod to Euell Gibbons who wrote *Stalking the Wild Asparagus* and other tasty foraging reads. My mission? To find a salt marsh (not too hard around here). The pinkish flowers bloom from August to October, so that won't help me now. In the meantime, I can seek grayish, velvety, heart-shaped or oval leaves. Whether I find it or not, I will savor being out there, looking and learning.

## February 25
### American Coot: The Pleasures of a "New" Bird

Watching the ducks at the end of Essex's Main Street gave me great pleasure. The ice had melted into rough rectangles, and I watched them hop the geometry, dipping their beaks down into the water between shapes. One extracted a morsel of river-wracked greenery.

It became clear that ducks ice skate. It seemed a natural thing, that their oversized, rubbery feet were gliding as they moved. I wondered if they took any special pleasure in this winter mode of ambulating.

The general impression of "a bunch of ducks" gave way to seeing them individually. Then I had a "one of these things is not like the other" moment. One of the "ducks" didn't seem to be a duck at all. Or was it a duck with unusual coloring—all black, except white in the beak area?

I was seeing, for the first time, an American coot. Besides the coloring, it had a small head, scrawny legs, and a chicken-like body and feet. It was hanging out with ducks, as American coots are known to do.

American coots are also called mud hens, and they belong to the rail family. *Encyclopedia Britannica* has the following definition of rails: "Any of 127 species of slender, somewhat chicken-shaped marsh birds, with short rounded wings, short tail, large feet, and long toes, of the family *Rallidae* (order *Gruiformes*). The name is sometimes used to include coots and gallinules, which belong to the same family, but coots and gallinules are far more ostentatious. Coots and gallinules flock like ducks, swim in open water, and waddle conspicuously on shore. By contrast, rails are secretive birds, hiding among reeds at the water's edge by day and uttering their calls mostly at night."

I have a special place in my heart for "secretive birds" in this entry. The lower chance of spotting a rail makes it that much more intriguing.

## *February 26*

## Not Just Any Old Mushroom: The Polypores

Gavin has a collection of these hard, knobby things that never seem to disintegrate or change much, unlike the many other varieties of mushrooms that are soft, sometimes even mushy, and often edible.

University of Wisconsin biology professor Tom Volk writes that these types of mushrooms are in for the long haul—they recycle the nutrients and minerals in wood and release them over a very long time—even up to several hundred years on a single, large fallen tree.

The professor says it used to be simple. "Polypore" just meant a pore-covered fungus that didn't really look like a typical mushroom. But now scientists have identified all kinds of polypore subtypes.

Some look like shelves, others look like horses' hooves. Some make great tinder for a fire, and beyond that there are a lot more uses for these hard mushrooms than you might imagine. One that grows on birch is nicknamed "razor strop" because it's great for sharpening knives. My favorite type is the "artist's mushroom," which makes a great natural canvas. People have made fiber from the polypores as well. This list goes on!

## February 27
### Happiness on Wings

Word has it that a playwright first coined the term "bluebird of happiness" in 1908. But the roots of pairing this bird with a cheerful mood go back way more than a century. According to the website titled Native Languages of the Americas, in Iroquois mythology, bluebird song drove off the destructive demigod who represented winter. Naturalist Amanda Bancroft writes that bluebirds as a symbol of happiness were found on oracle bone inscriptions dating back to the Shang Dynasty in China, 1766–1122 CE.

There are three bluebird species in North America. Here in Connecticut and other states east of the Rockies, we have the eastern bluebird. Western states have western and mountain bluebirds.

There's something about seeing these flits of blue that lifts the heart, so it makes sense that legends, plays, and songs (think "Over the Rainbow") have framed the bird so positively. I remember being in an otherwise drab office space one day and feeling so enthralled to see bluebirds coming and going around the eaves near my window. It was the males who caught my eye; as with so many bird species they are the gender that boasts more color.

My heart lifts more when I am reminded how the bluebird nest boxes so many humans put up have worked to keep our eastern bluebirds here. For a while, they were driven out by more aggressive tree cavity nesters like house sparrows and European starlings, since cavity real estate was scarce. What else can we humans do to help struggling birds?

## February 28
### Dark Ponds in Winter

Every year there's a part of me that wonders if spring will ever arrive. Then I reassure myself. Last week I saw emerging skunk cabbage off the red maple swamp boardwalk as well as a pair of house finches checking out materials from an abandoned nest on our porch pillar. They will start breeding in March.

Before these heartening signs emerged, I read my the winter issue of *Connecticut Woodlands*. A piece called "The Afterlife of Leaves," by biology professor Declan McCabe, stirred my imagination. It renewed my admiration for how cleverly and efficiently the natural world works.

McCabe writes of the fall leaves that end up in our ponds, lakes, and rivers, "The accumulated leafy piles provide most of the food base for everything in fresh water ecosystems, including bacteria and fungi, insects and other invertebrates, and fish."[23] Eventually, this nutrition works its way up the food chain, including to us humans.

He explains that when leaves first find a body of water, they are of little nutritional value and can retain tannins and even toxins (substances useful in repelling leaf-eaters when the leaves are still on the tree). Then, these dark, leathery forms convert into something the water creatures can eat. This happens gradually, first with the chemicals leaching out and then with bacteria and fungi going to work on the leaves. Invertebrates like crayfish, sowbugs, and various insects then jump on the bandwagon and shred the leaves. After that, fish eat the invertebrates. So everyone gets a turn at the buffet (even if that means being on it!).

So often, things are so much more than they appear. Our "dark mirrors" in the woods are teeming with life, even as a cap of ice seems to forbid activity. The cold and dark of winter can prime us to be perhaps disproportionately excited when we are reminded of the earth's covert preparations for spring.

## February 29

### Leap Day Gender Switch

Stephen Wood at the History Channel site says Leap Day is often associated with flipping gender roles. This goes back to an Irish legend in which St. Patrick designated Leap Day as a day when women could propose marriage to men.

This role reversal pales in comparison to the world of nonhuman creatures. The male striped maple tree can become female when under stress. Several fish species (e.g., clownfish, hawkfish, sea bass) can change gender, as can frogs and bearded dragons (the latter while in the egg, due to temperature shifts).

Remarkably, in some cases we have only recently learned of these shifts, or of the reasons behind them. This begs the question: what else will we come to learn about the goings on in the nonhuman realm? The capacity for surprise is never-ending.

## March 1

### Foul-Smelling Connected Fruits

*Symplocarpus foetidus*—that's the scientific name for skunk cabbage. *Foetidus* means "foul smelling;" *Symplocarpus* means "connected fruits." The compound fruit is basically connected ovaries.

The unusual look and smell don't exactly make this plant a gardener's favorite, but Anne Baley at Gardening Know How points out that it has the dual benefit of attracting pollinators while repelling mammals—preventing raccoons and squirrels from sidling up to the planted "buffet."

The Lake Forest College Environmental Studies site points out the plant's ecological importance: its deep roots make damp areas more stable, helping keep the soil permeable and preventing erosion; insects like to eat the large leaves; and it occupies land that might otherwise be taken over by invasive plants, since many other native plants don't like such saturated areas.

The plant has gone up a notch in my estimation now that I know my favorite poet Mary Oliver wrote about it in her poem "Skunk Cabbage." She wrote as only she can about how, in the woods, each death contributes to new births, and how sometimes the "ugly" things are what pave the way to new life.

## March 2

### Ivy League: For the Birds

Sunday found Tom and I in Portsmouth, New Hampshire, enjoying the mild day and snapping photos. Old buildings festooned in ivy caught my eye. Otherwise ordinary structures gained an enchanted look from the climbing plants. I think the picturesque variety we saw is Boston ivy.

It's said that the term "Ivy League" used to refer to prestigious colleges may well be referring to this plant, which tends to like the sorts of walls those hallowed halls offer. I think it's the blue berries that hang on through winter that make these vines extra attractive. We humans can't eat them, but for birds they are high-calorie foods, rich in sugars, fats, and antioxidants.

Boston ivy isn't what horticulturists call a "true ivy." (True ivies are in a different genus altogether—*Hedera.*) It comes from Asia, and while it is technically considered invasive, it succumbs rather easily to native vines. The Boyd Nursery Company also notes that the special sticky property of this climber lets it effectively glue itself to buildings without causing damage. Their website notes that researchers have studied the ivy's incredible adhesive capabilitie and gives a thumbs up to this plant's energy saving capabilities, effectively shading buildings in summer while allowing them to absorb heat in the winter after its leaves fall.

## *March 3*

### Seventeen Days to Mourning Cloaks?

The question mark in the title hedges my optimistic bet, but the hopeful statement preceding it is something I need.

I'm tired of winter. The latest batch of snow combined with some physical challenges make me long for the comparative ease of spring walks.

I idly watched the feeder this morning, happy to see the cardinals and sparrows well fed. Predictably, a downy or hairy woodpecker (they look a lot alike) clung to the metal suet cage while pecking down his breakfast. But I was antsy for something different.

Nature books are a solace when it's difficult to linger outside. I flipped open Mary Holland's *Naturally Curious Day by Day*. At the start of each month, before the engaging photos and write-ups of what we can watch for each calendar day here in the Northeast, Holland includes some longer pieces on interesting creatures and occurrences for the month. How my heart lifted when her first piece for March was about mourning cloak butterflies!

I doubted her for a moment, glancing out at the snow. How could these fragile creatures belong in this month? I read that they overwinter as adults and emerge from behind loose bark or some other crevice in early spring. Technically, early spring (Day 1!) is March 20 this year, so technically that could happen in seventeen days. The male will perch in the sun, waiting for a female to come by. Mating will commence, and the resulting caterpillars will live in a communal web until summer. The chrysalis looks like a spiky, rolled-up, weather-bleached leaf. How many of these "leaves" have we all overlooked?

The butterflies, like me, often emerge a bit tattered after winter. They are drawn to tree sap. I will be watching for them eagerly. Listening, too—they often make a loud click when they fly off from where they have been resting.

## March 4

### Rose Hips in Winter

Walking near Essex dock, I noticed an abundance of old, brown rose hips on the plants lining the Connecticut River Museum's lawn.

Writer Amber Shehan calls roses "the gift that keeps on giving"— blooms in the warmer months, medicinal hips in autumn and winter.[24] Foragers praise them for their vitamin C boost and make teas and jams from their harvest.

The hips didn't look at all enticing, and an experienced forager confirms that, yes, they can go bad, leaving the unwise eater nauseous or even with a little "buzz" from fermented samples. The practice is to pick them while still robust and dry them out before use.

The invasive multiflora rose can still produce fresh hips well into winter, when other plants have long stopped fruiting.

Some folks are allergic to this family of plants. And the itchy, hairy seeds must be removed before consumption; if you don't know how to prepare rose hips, you may fall prey to what many describe as "itchy bottom disease." I am going on the assumption that the birds, squirrels, rabbits, and bears who consume them don't suffer this uncomfortable fate.

## March 5

### Beavers in Spring: Habitat Creators

My area is checkered with wetlands, and every now and then we see a dead beaver on the side of the road. No doubt that beaver had been on a mission, looking for tasty plants to gnaw while also in the process of building or repairing its dam.

These creatures' impulse to build is irrepressible, and articles on beaver nuisance abound. For example, beavers may perceive a road's culvert as a big hole in need of "fixing." The beaver works hard to plug the hole, and the more persistent and skilled the beaver, the more the chance of significant flooding. I learned there is a Connecticut Beaver Initiative meant to assist property owners in nonlethally resolving beaver-human conflicts.

What is all this tireless building about? An article by the Toronto Zoo calls the beaver "the wetlands guardian." Dam construction isn't simply about beavers making themselves an appealing neighborhood. The resulting pond is a friendly habitat for birds, reptiles, amphibians, and insects. Also, the beavers' work helps improve water quality, and flooding can benefit the soil via nutrients.

Over time, the dam area gets tapped out; beavers have used the resources there to a hilt. The area gradually becomes a "beaver meadow." The beavers have gone, but they helped create an area built on rich sediments, a crucial cog in the forest ecosystem.

## *March 6*

### The Early Bird's Vacation

I did a summer project for my Master Naturalist program. For a few days in August, I got out before dawn and ventured only as far as the lawn chair in the front yard under the twin Norway spruces. There I sat and waited for the dawn chorus to begin. I took notes, made recordings, got rained on, and treasured the whole project, observing who sang first, how many sang, and what variety came to visit.

I had to use the Bird Song Id app to help me, especially because it was too dim to use the birds' appearances to help discern who was who. I was surprised to learn that the first singer in my neighborhood was often the scarlet tanager. To me, this has always seemed an elusive species. An article by the Menunkatuck Audubon Society describes the male's song as a "raspy rendition of the American robin's song. *Jeeyeet, jeeay, jeeoo, jeeyeer* is tirelessly repeated, over and over. The female will sing, but more softly."[25] The male perches quite high in the treetops, so he's been more difficult to spot compared with the birds that frequent our porch and yard.

The scarlet tanager song is pretty; words can't quite do it justice. Right now, that song is being heard in much more exotic locales. These birds migrate to Central and South America for the winter, their trip triggered by seasonal changes in daylight. This age-old pattern, however, may not serve them as plant growth and food sources change with the climate.

This spring, now that I know their song better, I'll be on "safari" with my binoculars, hoping to spot the male's flash of red or the female's olive and yellow. The tanagers and I share the practice of early rising—that and the impulse to winter somewhere warm.

## March 7
### Spring, Seeds, Sponges, and "Ramping Up"

Today, with a high of 59 degrees, folks have their car windows down. They are walking around without jackets. I see broader smiles. There is nothing like that first preview of spring.

It's not all balmy weather from here. After Friday, we'll be back down into the 40s most days, with some chilly nights. I can recall some blustery and dank Easters and Mother's Days, and that annual happy relief when Memorial Day comes, knowing the warm weather will finally stay for a stretch.

In the meantime, we are cheered by the local nurseries' signs proclaiming: "The seeds are here!"

My latest intrigue is the prospect of growing loofah sponges. These gourds are edible when quite young, but they get quite large if left on the vine. Mature gourds are tan and dry, and the seeds shake inside when rattled. After some soaking, the skin can be stripped off and the inner fruit can be rinsed free of seeds and pulp. Voila! A usable sponge or three! Some gardening blogs say this could even work in my relatively chilly zone if seeds are started early indoors and I am blessed with a lot of luck! Maybe another year.

For a less effortful project, I want Gavin to show me where he found a long-abandoned squash patch in the state forest—likely a forgotten homestead. Even better, I want him to show me how to find wild ramps; the chance for that is only about a month away! The 3 Foragers, a local phenom, gave me a chuckle with their blog: "It's that time of year when Facebook is flooded with photos of ramps, requests for recipes, foodie blogs are trying to out-blog each other about their rampi-ness, and conservationists are preaching about sustainable harvesting."[26] They advise not to pick more than 10 percent of any large patch of ramps—assuming you are on land where picking is permitted!

## March 8

### Woolly Bears and Tiny Spiders: Where Have They Been Sleeping?

When was the last time you saw a woolly bear caterpillar? Did you see it in the fall and stop to assess its color? Legend has it that a wide rust-colored band predicts a milder winter, and more black color means a more severe winter. Catherine Boeckmann's 2020 article in the *Old Farmer's Almanac* pretty much debunks this, although she says the color might tell you about what happened the previous winter.

Did you ever wonder what kind of moth the woolly bear turns into? The resulting Isabella tiger moth is quite pretty, a beigy to orangey affair with some dotted decor.

I wasn't especially thinking about woolly bears or tiny spiders recently, until I read Edwin Way Teale's 1953 *Circle of the Seasons*. Gosh, he would have been a fun person to take a walk with. He spent one day harvesting abandoned long-billed wren nests so he could see what creatures were overwintering in them. (Note for birders: I think Teale was writing about marsh wrens, which used to be called long-billed marsh wrens.) Most winter sleepers in his nest collection were "pale, straw-colored little spiders."

He also wrote about rolling a log to find three hibernating woolly bears, aptly described as "little black and red-brown doughnuts." They will be weaving their felt-like cocoons this spring, preparing to turn into Isabella tiger moths. The moths are active only at night, and I don't think I've seen one close up. Something to look for when the porch light draws moths closer.

## March 9

### March Micro-Expeditions

Gavin needed an early ride to school. The fact that we were unusually ahead of schedule was miraculous in and of itself, but it got more miraculous. The brief drive entailed rapt looks through the windshield at the pale, full, setting moon; the burning orange of the rising sun through the trees; and a fox (they really are quick!) running across Warsaw Street. He was so fast as to be a bit of a blur; I might have thought he was a lovely, low-slung hallucination if Gavin hadn't seen him too.

This preview boded well for my pre-work walk near Pratt Cove. I pulled my turtleneck up, zipped my coat higher, and looked out at a muskrat lodge, a modest, tan structure made of sticks. It doesn't compare to the "mansions" beavers can construct. No obvious signs of life there, but I wondered about the muskrat family who might be inside.

I trekked up to Fountain Hill Cemetery. The crows were out in full force, cawing insistently and swooping about. I got within twelve feet of a pileated woodpecker who was busy doing some serious, high-decibel damage to a cedar. He saw me but seemed conflicted about leaving his construction project until I inched much closer. I'd seen his characteristic rectangular holes many times, some on this beleaguered tree, but this was my first time seeing him in action here. (The males do most of the excavating.)

His holes, in addition to being nests for his own brood (the average clutch is four per nest), can provide shelter for many others: swifts, owls, ducks, bats, and pine martens. Nature sure has a thoughtful sense of economy.

## March 10

### Frigid Water Craft Collective

One summer, our Master Naturalist class spent a Saturday mucking around in a stream, pulling up a slew of creatures to ID in an awed kind of catch and release. Caddisfly larvae were among the many finds. I was impressed that our teacher could spot what looked to me like a remnant of a twig or reed and recognize it for what it was—a larva that had fashioned its own case.

I researched whether some of this case-building goes on in wintertime. Indeed, it does. This intel is especially interesting to those who fish. The Catch and the Hatch website is about the tasty morsels fishermen can gather to tempt their targets. It drives home the point that fishermen do well to study entomology. Expert fly tyers imitate the real insects to fool the fish.

My friend George sent a video from Red's Fly Shop. In it a man breaks open a small, dark, waterlogged "stick" to reveal the substantial caddisfly larva inside. This man's shop makes fishing flies that imitate the larva's silhouette, attracting rainbow trout. If this larva's well-crafted case hadn't been so rudely destroyed, he would have eventually made his way to shore and hatched to live a brief life as a flying insect. The females lay eggs on vegetation just above the water, starting the cycle over again.

Caddisflies spin silken thread to help build their cases. What each species uses to embellish its case can help naturalists identify its type, although the larva can change the case as it grows and in accord with local materials. That's where these insects' craftsmanship comes in—the flies tack on seeds, pieces of plants, snail shell pieces, tiny pebbles, and even other, smaller species' cases.

## March 11

### Conk-la-ree!

This past Sunday was the first time I heard it this year—the sound of a male red-winged blackbird who had returned to the cattails in the marsh. When he and his cohorts flew up to a nearby tree, I found it hard to spot their flashes of red. But putting the song and the silhouette together, I got my joyous confirmation of spring being sprung.

I enjoy Journey North, a program that tracks migration of all kinds of creatures. It is based in the University of Wisconsin-Madison Arboretum. I've consulted the site for monarch travel patterns. It's fun to look at the map and see when the first red-winged blackbird sightings were reported in our area. Someone in New Haven saw a red-winged before March 1. I wonder if it was in the Quinnipiac River Tidal Marsh about a half hour away—an important landing place for birds.

So where have the blackbirds been? Somewhere down south in the US, according to Journey North. There are also nonmigratory red-winged blackbirds that stick to the western states and to Central America. Of those who migrate, the males return north ahead of the females. They are famed for their spring song: *Conk-la-ree!*

This species' nests are tucked into the marsh and are more elaborate than they may look on the surface. All About Birds says, "One nest picked apart by a naturalist in the 1930s had been made by weaving together thirty-four strips of willow bark and 142 cattail leaves, some 2 feet long."[27] An inexperienced birder might not recognize the female sitting on the nest as belonging to the same species as her strikingly handsome male spouse. Females are a subdued, streaky brown and have been likened to sparrows.

## *March 12*

### Bumper Crop of Tree Circles

What joy—enough snow melted that I could foot the mile to town without fearing the need to dive into tall snowdrifts should two cars come down the narrow street simultaneously! There they were—a bumper crop of tree circles where before was only the slightest hint. Tree circles are the initial areas of melt that appear around the bases of trees, revealing the dark, warming earth beneath.

As I walked, I felt sorry for those in eternally temperate climes because they can't experience the happy release that comes with the long-awaited start of spring thaw. It's a tenuous joy because there may be more snow, but maybe that makes the first moderately warm moments even sweeter.

I thought of my favorite Robert Frost poem, "My November Guest."[28] Here's a small piece:

> Her pleasure will not let me stay.
>     She talks and I am fain to list:
> She's glad the birds are gone away,
> She's glad her simple worsted gray
>     Is silver now with clinging mist.

Frost's words serve as a reminder that some part of me loves and welcomes the coldness and barrenness of winter. It is a time for hunkering down and thinking about things and venturing into inner space, and there certainly is a quiet beauty to the world laid bare. But it gets old for most of us—to the point where "familiarity breeds contempt" starts to ring true!

How lovely to see the world waking up as I am, again alert to what's going on beyond the confines of my snowy street. Long live tree circles, their widening embrace, and their eventual disappearance as all the melt goes underground to bolster the trees' deep source.

# March 13

## The Cartoon Bird

I haven't seen many pileated woodpeckers around my stomping grounds lately. Then again, I don't run into them all the time, the way I do crows, sparrows, wrens, and the like.

An Audubon Society source tells me they are not considered migratory birds, although an increase in the winter population has been noted in southern New England and southern Canada.

Pileated woodpeckers are the largest Connecticut woodpeckers, and I've seen them referred to as crow-sized in more than one place. Well, maybe my local crows are puny, or maybe it's the odd, colorful appearance of the pileateds, but they seem way larger than crows to me. I am always impressed when I come upon one—they look so solid and bright. Even hearing their rapid-fire drumming (performed by both males and females) or coming upon their trademark rectangular holes grabs my attention.

But, oh, the sight of one! That grand red crest, sported by both genders, is eye-catching. Both genders sport a "mustache," too—black for females, scarlet for males.

I couldn't rest until I looked up Woody Woodpecker. An NPR piece told me that the type of woodpecker Woody was modeled on was a matter of speculation. Writer Julie Zickefoose confirmed that the unmistakable Woody laugh was based on the acorn woodpecker the inventor heard while honeymooning in a California cabin. But Woody looks more like a pileated. Artistic license is the cartoonist's prerogative. (By the way, the cartoonist's wife voiced Woody's laugh).

# March 14

## Thirsty Plants, Thirsty Pollinators

In 1982 Connecticut had a 100-year storm. In Ivoryton, dams gave way; first the dam at Bushy Hill Lake and then the one at Clark's Pond. In the *Hartford Courant*, Charles Stannard described how the contents of the two ponds merged with the already overflowing Falls River "in a four-mile path of destruction that wrecked three smaller dams, several bridges, and more than two dozen homes."[29]

Today the same area boasts the placid, six-acre Millrace Preserve. The Millrace trail crosses Falls River at several spots, and I walked there on a relatively balmy day that promised to melt most of the lingering snow. It was mucky in spots with rare slippery patches of ice. Water, water everywhere—the river, the mud, the dirty mounds of snow, the evaporating ice. Walking the Millrace is a reminder of when water was everywhere in an out-sized way, tearing down structures, threatening lives.

Someone planted an array of young trees and shrubs by the water, still wearing their nursery tags. For now they look like bundles of twigs. But the buttonbushes will bloom in fuzzy white balls, and their leaves will go copper in the fall. They will welcome butterflies. The swamp azaleas, also called clammy azaleas for their sticky corollas (rings of flower petals), will grow white, sweet-scented flowers and attract a variety of pollinators, including hummingbirds. Willows will be mostly pollinated by the wind, but bees like them too.

These plants are great for muddy, mucky areas. They drink water eagerly, making the path prettier and drier underfoot while pleasing the creatures who dine on them. It pleases me, too, to know that some thoughtful folks restored—and continue to steward—this once-decimated, once-neglected riverside plot, encouraging new life and new appreciation.

## March 15

### Overcaffeinated Ducks

Overcaffeinated ducks—that's what the wood frogs of early spring sound like to me. At first it seems exactly like the "conversation" you overhear in any duck pond, but then you realize they are talking way too fast.

My FrogWatch USA training told me that wood frogs are often the first frogs to raise their voices in spring, although a lot of people think spring peepers talk first. If they inhabit the same pond, the peepers' high-pitched calls can drown out the wood frogs' calls, which don't carry as far.

Why are they called wood frogs? Simply put, they spend a lot of time in the woods. They reside, frozen, under the leaf litter in wintertime, kept alive with a sort of natural antifreeze.

The National Wildlife Federation says wood frogs are the only frogs that live north of the Arctic Circle, so clearly, they are a hardy bunch.

Vernal pools are their favored breeding place. Have you spotted their egg masses? They are gelatinous-looking, multi-spotted affairs, each "spot" a tiny frog to be. The masses are often deposited in communal rafts, with each mass numbering up to fifteen thousand eggs.

## March 16

### Sassafras Time

Even the most amateur naturalist can learn to identify sassafras, owing to its three distinctive leaf types. I like how Penn State's Virtual Nature Trail site describes them: a three-lobed "ghost"; a two-lobed "mitten," both right- and left-handed; and an un-lobed elliptical "football."

I wondered if I'd be able to ID sassafras minus its telltale leaves. Then I remembered how the bare plants have candelabra-type branching. Brian Edmond at the Grow Native site describes a "dark, corky bark" in winter. When in doubt, there's always the plant's smell. Many say the leaves smell like Froot Loops cereal, while the inner bark and roots smell like root beer. Root harvesting is best in February or March when the sap is concentrated in the roots.

Sassafras tea has long been used as a tonic for a variety of ailments, although some now warn against its use because of its potentially poisonous ingredient in larger doses: safrole, which may have a link to cancer. We live in a different world now with so much information and so many options at our fingertips. But I admire the old ways too, when plants were often the best medicinal option and no part was wasted.

The USDA page on sassafras notes that numerous tribes used sassafras. The historical uses by Native peoples seem limitless: root infusions to ward off fever, diarrhea, rheumatism, and measles; poultices rubbed onto stings, cuts, bruises, and injuries; a decoction from new sprouts to treat nosebleeds; pith from branches to treat burns. Leaves were used as a food spice and thickener; and something called "filé," made from ground roots or leaves, is still used in Cajun foods such as gumbo.

I'm not a fan of root beer or of tea that tastes like root beer, but I am still fascinated by the harvesting and brewing process, and the resulting fragrant, reddish sassafras tea. To me, it smells like spring is coming soon.

## March 17
### Dripping with Color: A Chickadee's-Eye View

In *The Forest Unseen*, biology professor David George Haskell wrote about Carolina chickadees; they "live in a hyperreality of color that is inaccessible to our dull eyes." He explained that the birds have an extra color receptor that detects ultraviolet light, and their color receptors also have tinted oil drops that act as filters, increasing the precision of their color perception. Ultraviolet perception helps these birds find food; it reflects off wild grapes and some caterpillars and beetles, things we humans easily overlook when we scan our surroundings. We might notice them if we watch closely, but they won't jump out the way they do to the chickadee.

I wondered if this was true of our local black-capped chickadees too. Writing for The Audubon Society, Emily Silber confirms that the ability to see ultraviolet color is shared by all birds, leading with the headline "When You're a Bird, the World Always Looks Psychedelic."[30] Ultraviolet perception also helps birds see each other differently; while we humans often can't distinguish male versus female birds, studies have shown that ultraviolet perception makes it a no-brainer for our avian friends.

I like how expert Laura Erickson, at the *For the Birds* radio program, puts it: "Birds can see and often hear things we cannot perceive at all. It's exciting to look at our elegantly plain little chickadees—such simple black, gray, and white birds—and realize that there is much more than meets the eye— at least our eye."[31]

## March 18
### So Much to Offer, Even Grounded
### (Don't Forget the Pollynoses)

A powerful storm sheared a huge part of our backyard red maple. It will be a big job to chop it up, and I'm glad that hasn't happened yet. The limb is not entirely separated from the tree, and I was treated to a closeup look at the stunning male blossoms yesterday.

I don't know if this tree can continue to thrive, but I was impressed with how much it still has to offer at this point. The Lady Bird Johnson Wildflower Center says it's of special value to native honeybees. The cecropia moth, a giant silk moth, favors the tree as a home for its offspring. These moths will stay tucked into their cocoons until around June. Rosy maple moths also like the red maple. Squirrels eat the buds. Did you know red maples can be a source of syrup too? More red maple sap is needed to yield the same amount of syrup, but an experienced sugarer says he can't tell the difference between the syrups.

And then there is the beautiful, red, fringed blossom worthy of wonder. The blossoms don't get as much praise as the fall leaves, but that's likely because we don't get to see them close up as often. The female flowers are bigger and make the fruits, which are winged samaras. As kids we called them helicopters because of how they spun to the ground, or pollynoses because we'd split open the base where the seed lives and stick the natural adhesive to our noses.

I'll be interested to keep watching this fallen limb and see how long it can go in its compromised state. My next task is to walk its length, looking for cocoons.

## March 19

### Snowdrops: Naturalized Woodland Citizens

My friend Terry and I got out for a walk in today's mild air. When we started a path through a wooded area, she spotted them first—snow-drops! They appeared in random patches along the walkway. How much the human spirit craves and delights in bright new growths after a long winter! We oohed and aahed, taking photos of these diminutive clusters and wondering aloud when we might see the first daffodils.

I felt a bit puzzled when I looked up snowdrops. They are not native to the US and most sites describe planting snowdrop bulbs. But surely no one planted these quite random patches we found yesterday. I have found simi-lar clumps in quite random corners of other woodlands.

Writing for Penn State Extension, Martha Murdock explains that the plants have naturalized widely in the US. According to the USDA, natural-ized plants are nonnative plants that don't need human help to reproduce and maintain themselves over time. Gardeners sometimes use the term "naturalize" differently, meaning they will informally scatter bulbs to make it look like the plants randomly appeared in those spots.

I was reminded that ants can play a role in spreading these beauties. Each seed has a small appendage called an elaiosome, which is rich in fatty acids. The ants are attracted to the elaiosomes and take the seeds into their nests to help feed developing larvae. However, the actual seeds remain undisturbed, and we can thank the ants for planting them in new locations.

Snowdrops and snowflakes are often confused. Snowdrops appear much earlier, so I am pretty sure that's what we were ogling. But in April, if I see a similar (but taller) flower, I may well have a snowflake on my hands.

# SPRING

## March 20

## Muskrats (Not) Jitterbugging

If you're a child of a certain era and you contemplate muskrats long enough, the surprising and silly hit song "Muskrat Love" will pop into your head. It managed to hit number four on the Billboard charts in 1976 with the help of duo Captain & Tennille.

There is not one scientifically based lyric in that song. The muskrat I saw last evening was not jitterbugging at all, or shimmying. But, despite the lack of dance moves, he lifted my spirit.

Muskrats, like us, spend a lot of time inside when it's cold. I learned that what I have been referring to as muskrat "lodges" in the marsh are often called "push ups." These domes, fashioned from aquatic vegetation over a hole in the ice, serve as feeding shelters when muskrats are gathering food far from their more substantial home lodge. In warmer weather they build feeding platforms: rafts to rest on while they chow down on vegetation or meat, which may include mollusks, turtles, and fish. Meat is consumed when vegetation is scarce or if there has been an aquatic "baby boom."

Breeding starts in March, and females signal their availability with mouse-like squeaks. I heard no squeaks from where I stood but admired my aerial view of the sleek dark ovoid with a tail as he or she pushed into the reeds.

On his site devoted to muskrats, aficionado Bob Arnebeck says, "For me a muskrat demonstrates how eternal spring can be. It shows me the way to green life no matter how dark the winter season. Of course, it must briefly go where I dare not follow into the cold dark waters of the frozen pond, but what it brings up so often startles with still green life."[32]

Here's to the muskrats enjoying some down time on their rafts after a season of gnawing through ice. Watching them glide, dive, and resurface is a happily mesmerizing affair. I wish them warm waters and many cat-tail feasts.

## March 21

### Yellow Eyes Watching Us—Worth a Climb in the Brambles

Tom and I left the wide path at Hammonasset Beach State Park for an odd clearing. We walked through the brambly area and wondered if there had been a house or barn there once. Thorns from multiflora rose bushes jabbed at me, and we stepped over and under a host of vines. Parts of the thicket were too packed to even consider traversing.

Suddenly, a large, dark shadow rose and flew over Tom's head. A great horned owl landed in a nearby tree and positioned him (or her) self to watch us. That deep furrowed brow! Those quizzical and somewhat angry-looking yellow eyes!

I marveled at the swivel of his (or her) head and made a fool of myself by transmitting a barred owl call—the only owl call I can muster—so motivated was I to converse.

The Wildlife of Connecticut site told me that the great horned is the largest and heaviest owl in North America. And my barred owl call was a faux pas; great horned owls are major predators of this species so don't likely enjoy dialogue with them.

To find an owl, follow the focus of other birds, especially crows, making a big ruckus. Crows will put up a big fight when the great horned tries to kick them out of their nest, unrelenting in their harassment until the owl flies off for good.

## March 22

### Here Come the Pussy Willows

A month ago, the silver-furred catkins of the pussy willow appeared. Now that it is early spring, the flowers will start to open. The yellow flowers are tiny and close-packed, without petals. But they make up for this modest aesthetic with a wealth of golden pollen, an important source of early-season food for creatures such as honeybees and tiny mining bees.

Pussy willows also serve as a host for a range of hungry butterfly and moth larvae, including the mourning cloak and eastern tiger swallowtail butterflies, and the cecropia moth. Hummingbirds are known to use the fuzz from catkins to line their nests.

Willows take root easily, likely owing to the salicylic acid they contain that serves as a natural rooting hormone. The *Grow Forage Cook Ferment* blog says you can use water that willow cuttings have been rooting in to help other plants grow roots as well.

Native Americans, typically in more western regions, used willow for centuries to make baskets. In the East, sweetgrass use was more common. Ben Marks at *Collectors Weekly* says the railroad boom starting in the 1890s spawned an absolute tourist craze for these baskets, which makers modified over time to be more appealing to nonNative buyers.[33]

## March 23

### The Voice of One Crying in the Wilderness

If you grew up going to church, you likely recognize today's title as being associated with John the Baptist. It popped into my mind when I thought of this week's seasonal firsts.

I am using the term "wilderness" loosely. But when you've been dealing with cold weather, a pandemic, and your guest room being transformed into your workplace, even a short jaunt away from the pavement is a comparative jungle adventure.

I haven't yet heard the year's first peeper chorus. I was, however, rewarded for a long walk at the cemetery by hearing a peeper singlet, or maybe couplet, singing from the pond. Was it the first time a frog spoke from the pond this year? Most years my first notice of peepers is of a virtual symphony—no way to distinguish a lone voice. Typically, I'm driving home some spring evening, car windows closed against the still-present chill. As I drive past a local marsh, I can hear the peepers in concert. I roll down the window and stop the car if I can, savoring—at long last—the undeniable confirmation of spring.

But who is that peeper who first starts the singing? Kurt Heidinger at biocitizen explains that these frogs have evapotranspirative skin; thus, they are "especially sensitive to the slightest changes in temperature, humidity, chemistry and other things we don't have words for, including that feeling that we also get when spring arrives. There is, for example, a new kind of sunlight that appears out of the gray slush and slog of the late winter months . . . "[34] Maybe that peeper who sings first has especially fine-tuned skin. Maybe the combination of warmth and light in his corner of the pond translates into the earliest burst of "spring fever" in his bunch, with that impulse to announce his vernal awakening to the world or, more accurately, a receptive female.

## *March 24*

## Mourning and Healing, Waterside

The weeping willow's long, flowing silver-backed leaves and drooping branches have a way of stirring emotions. Monet fashioned ten weeping willow paintings thought to symbolize the mass tragedy of World War I. Many tombstones, especially from the Greek Revival period, feature this tree. Raindrops flowing off the cascading limbs are said to look like tears.

Weeping willows came to America from China by way of the trade route to Europe and then by our nation's early colonists. While their beauty is prized, they also spark strong opinions and even disdain among gardeners. Steve Bender's column in *Southern Living* has a vehement tone, saying the only good place for this tree is by the water, with nothing else around. He cites aggressive, shallow root systems; wood that breaks easily in storms; and the tree's tendency to invite insects and pests as reasons to impose solitary confinement. Also, weeping willows are known to be uncommonly thirsty.[35]

Looking more closely at cemetery lore, I learned that the tree has a remarkable ability to regenerate even after significant damage, connoting resurrection and eternal life. Cuttings that have lain on the ground unattended for months can grow into new trees. They can even grow when planted upside down.

It's nice to think that these sometime symbols of mourning are also healers and renewers. They are often the first tree to grow in a disturbed site, and the bark produces salicylic acid, used to make aspirin.

Many of us warm to childhood memories of climbing a willow's accessible limbs and being rendered "invisible" by its fluttering, long strands. Writing about weeping willows leaves me with the desire to seek one, book in hand, and hide away for a while with my back against its trunk.

## March 25

### Needles Return to the Stitching Tree

Walking around in the colder months, it's hard to overlook the tamarack, also known as the American larch. Unlike other cone-producing trees (conifers), the tamarack loses its needles but hangs onto a collection of small cones, which makes it stand out in the stripped landscape.

There seems to be agreement that "tamarack" derives from a Native American word, but there's more than one theory about which word. Is it the Algonkian word for "snowshoe wood" or the Ojibwa word for "swamp tree?" There does seem to be agreement that tamarack roots were used to stitch together birch bark canoes. (And, by the way, "Stitching Tree" is a nickname I made up. I don't think anyone else uses it!)

There are some good specimens at Chatfield Hollow State Park, and I'll be watching for their needles to return soon. In the fall, they turn a bright yellow before falling.

Kathy Bernier at Off the Grid News refers to this species as the "duck-billed platypus" of trees, defying easy categorization. Besides having both deciduous and conifer qualities, Bernier adds that the wood is not quite softwood and not quite hardwood.[36]

## March 26

### Pausing to Peer

I have a predilection for peering into upright, hollow snags or downed trees. When I walk with friends, I see I am not alone in this. What might be inside? What or who carved this space out?

Usually, I find the holes empty. Still, I relish the possibility that I might see something, like the gray treefrog that Edwin Way Teale found singing in one such hole. And I recall how John Burroughs wrote about an owl he found, pretending to be asleep in the hollow of an apple tree. I enjoy pileated woodpeckers' impressive rectangular openings. Maybe I'll find one with the hungry heads of chicks poking out.

Holes provide great clues. I think I have seen a yellow-bellied sapsucker from a distance and assumed it was a downy woodpecker, although the

Connecticut Audubon Society tells me sapsuckers are larger and stockier. I've seen their telltale bore holes, made in rows to extract sap. They carve two kinds: deep round holes for sap probing and shallow rectangular holes to aid sap flow. Hummingbirds time their migration with that of the sapsucker, so they can take advantage of their feathered friends' tasty excavations.

This is the time of year when male American woodcocks engage in their elaborate courtship ritual. Each spring Patti Laudano gives a presentation on this at the Stewart B. McKinney National Wildlife Refuge, which maintains appropriate habitat for these birds. She leads her charges outside at dusk, and we watch the dimming outline of the woodcock as he performs his song and dance. There, I was reminded to look for characteristic probe holes in the soil made by the woodcocks' exceptionally long beaks as they pull up worms.

Oh, and then there's that quite large hole at the base of a local cemetery tree. Sometimes coyotes will inhabit such a hole, and I have seen coyotes not far from there. Here's to peering and wondering, a happy pastime for many a naturalist.

## March 27
### Who Is Your Loneliness Bird?

Many decades ago, in an entry marking this same date, Edwin Way Teale recounted a story of a friend who worked at a lumber camp one summer. As he lay on his bunk there, he wondered about a bird he could only hear. He never saw it. It would be the first sound he heard at dawn, and he'd often hear snatches of its song into the evening. I'm not sure if it was because he was lonely or because the bird sounded lonely, but he came to call it the Loneliness Bird. It came to light later that it was a white-throated sparrow.

The white-throated sparrow's song has been described several ways, including "Oh, Canada, Canada, Canada" and "Poor Sam Peabody, Peabody, Peabody." I am from the Peabody school, since that is what I learned first. And, yes, I do think the song, while so sweet and emblematic of spring, also has a twinge of loneliness.

My own Loneliness Bird is the mourning dove. I recall hearing the doves cooing when I was a small child, particularly in early morning hours while I was still rousing from sleep. There is a loneliness in that call, but there is also the sound of home.

## March 28

### Quaking Aspens and Pocket Gophers

Greetings from Colorado! Gavin, Tom, and I went to Admitted Students Day at Gavin's chosen college—Fort Lewis. He has chosen well—thirteen hiking trails on the campus, which sits atop a mesa.

What a treat to walk the Animas River trail and see a mix of familiar and unfamiliar goings-on in nature. Canada geese and mallard ducks were swimming and sunning alongside a pigeon-like bird in the shallows, one I've never seen in Connecticut.

At first I called the quite straight, white tree trunks "birches," more common in my neck of the woods. But quaking aspens are among the major tree species in Colorado, while they don't even make Connecticut's Top Ten list for native trees. They are not quaking now. The "quaking" describes the trembling of the leaves in light breezes, and trees here are not yet in full leaf. One way to tell birches from aspens, especially when you don't have leaves to help you: the bark of the birch peels back, while the aspen does not.

Refreshing my knowledge on quaking aspens—the most widely distributed tree species in North America—felt good. Random facts along the way were a fun bonus. For one thing, the National Wildlife Federation states, "A grove of quaking aspens in Utah is the largest known living thing on Earth. Nearly 50,000 stems protrude from a single root system. The entire organism covers over 100 acres and weighs 6,000 tons."[37]

Also, it was amusing to read that these trees, with their incredible reproductive powers, may be curtailed by tiny pocket gophers! The National Park Service says that, in abundance, these critters can chew roots faster than they can grow back.[38]

## March 29

### Ducks in Trees—Wood Duck Love Is in Season

A man with a spotting scope told me there were wood ducks swimming back and forth in Pratt Cove, just past the swans and the heron. For the life of me, I couldn't see them. Given the color of the male, it should have been hard to miss them.

Male wood ducks are our most colorful ducks. Here in Connecticut, they have only recently returned from wintering in southern states. The ducks return in pairs, having coupled up before their flight north.

Wood ducks nest in tree cavities, but they don't have the ability to create their own nesting spot. They will use what they find near the water. Also, they don't transport materials to the nest but use what's right on hand near the nest site.

There are far fewer naturally occurring tree cavities than there once were, and that's where humans have come in handy. Wood ducks are happy to use nesting boxes, and provision of the boxes has helped the birds make a comeback. They were in danger of extinction for quite some time. By now, some clutches have likely already been laid, and in thirty days they will hatch. It will be another two months or so before the ducklings fly.

Wood ducks can congregate in wooded swamps in groups of up to two hundred in late summer or early fall. Wouldn't that be something to see?

# March 30

## Tongue Trees and Apples on Oaks

A remnant of stored information surfaced today when I was able to identify an alder tree by its male catkins and female cones. Its location alongside the lake at Bushy Hill Nature Center made sense—they love the water.

There was a branch I couldn't reach and couldn't see too clearly, but something about the cones looked amiss. Could I be seeing some galls? According to the Trees for Life website, galls are "the bizarre lumps, bumps and growths that develop on plants after being invaded by some very unique organisms. Galls appear on over half of all plant families and have a range of causes, including viruses, fungi, bacteria, insects and mites."[39] The alder tongue galls I saw were caused by a fungus that affects the alder's cone. Typically, they don't do much harm.

Galls go unnoticed until you start looking closely. "Apples" that seem to "grow" on oak trees are homes for a particular kind of wasp larvae. The parents inject eggs into oak leaf veins, and the resulting reaction has the leaves shapeshifting into green spheres. Once the wasps mature inside their green "incubator," they chew their way out. As with the alder tongue galls, there isn't much harm to the tree, and the wasps aren't harmful to humans either. Later the oak gall turns brown and drops to the ground. I have a goal of finding one that hasn't already been abandoned. Each one I pick up has a telltale exit hole.

Galls can be a fun game of, "one of these things is not like the other." If you scan a tree and some lump or bump or alien-looking life form stands out, you may have found a gall.

## March 31

## All Through the Night

I was thinking about robin commentary as dusk sets in and other bird "bedtime" sounds our chilly group listened to at a recent woodcock watching event. It was only after the other birds said their last piece for the day that the male woodcock launched into his elaborate courtship ritual.

Curious about birdsong at night, I did some research. Melissa Mayntz, at The Spruce, lists twelve birds that sing at night: the eastern whippoorwill, the hermit thrush, the American robin, the killdeer, and others, including, of course, owls. Robins may be "tricked" into night singing by light pollution.

I also found a Q and A on All About Birds. The sleep-deprived questioner asked what could be done about a bird that sang all night right outside his window. The answer? This was likely a northern mockingbird, more specifically a young and as yet unattached male. Or it could be an older male who lost his mate. The site advises, "the best way to shut him up is to entice a female mockingbird to your yard too." The Q and A page ends with a riff on Robert Frost's poem, "A Minor Bird," in which the last lines suggest there is something wrong with the desire to silence birdsong. Instead, this alternative is suggested: "Because of course there must be something right about wanting a decent sleep at night."[40]

## April 1

## Color from the Inside Out (or Birds Dipped in Wine)

A hasty glance made me think I saw a sparrow at the feeder. Then he turned, showing off a gorgeous flush of red chest and head. The male house finch was a pleasure to see, a bright spark in a still subdued landscape, in a way more compelling than the male cardinal who is so obvious about his red feathers!

The male house finch derives his color from the plants he eats. Females prefer the redder males. These birds used to be considered western birds, until in 1940 someone released a few on Long Island, New York. They have been breeding in these parts ever since.

I like how *Bird Watcher's Digest* describes the males, as having a "dipped in wine" look.[41] A toast to these springtime feasts for our eyes, some of whom have returned north from warmer areas recently. Others stay put year-round.

## April 2
### Painting Winter Away

Gavin's favorite part of his school bus ride was spotting the basking painted turtles on a roadside pond. Basking must have seemed a distant memory for the painted turtles when winter had them residing in muddy pond bottoms. But now, at long last, the early spring sun beckons, melting the ice and illuminating the logs we see them pile onto.

The scientific name for the eastern painted turtle is *Chrysemys picta*. *Chrys* conveys "gold," referring to the yellow or yellow-orange coloration around the face and on the shell, not to mention the yellow underside, called a plastron. *Picta* derives from the Latin *pictus*, which means "painted."

Male painted turtles' breeding behavior has been described as friendly or even charming, as sometimes the males stroke females with their long foreclaws as a kind of "foreplay." However, a 2020 study found that, when this strategy doesn't work, males turn to aggressive behaviors.[42]

## April 3
### Songs (or Quacks), Then Silence

If you weren't acquainted with wood frogs and you walked on a hillside above an obscured vernal pool, you might think you had come upon a chorus of hyperactive ducks. When breeding season is at its height, this "ducky" sound is the male's breeding call, and the sheer number of wood frogs ready for love can swell the sound to an absolute cacophony.

I wrote in *The Book of Noticing* about the ephemeral nature of vernal pools. These modest dips in the landscape fill with water for a discrete period long enough to allow creatures like the wood frog to breed. Some of these creatures are obligate vernal pool users; wood frogs, spotted salamanders, and fairy shrimp, for example, must have this type of environment to breed. The lack of fish gives the offspring a chance to make it past infancy.

The breeders at vernal pools are seemingly ephemeral, too, completely "disappearing" into the forest once they have left the water. Even expert eyes are unable to find them. Their loud communication ceases, and they blend in. In a 2011 article for the *Pittsburgh Post-Gazette*, Keith Berven, an associate professor of biology, is quoted as saying: "The only time you will see them is during that brief period when they reproduce . . . The rest of the time, this frog is out in the woods and undetectable. In my studies, I've had as many as 100,000 juveniles leave the pond within a couple of weeks. You would think you would have trouble avoiding stepping on them, but they assimilate to the forest so well, you just don't see them, ever."[43]

Seize the moment—find a vernal pool! You will find that the frogs go silent as you approach. Hang around a while and the concert will resume.

## April 4

## Familiar, Conspicuous, and Rocking the Style

The All About Birds entry about northern cardinals gave me today's title, which refers to the hard-to-miss males: "They're a perfect combination of familiarity, conspicuousness, and style: a shade of red you can't take your eyes off."[44] The females, while pretty in their own right, take a visual back seat to their mates' brilliant hues. Females are more of a pale brown, with reddish tinges in a few places and a rosy beak.

I find other red or reddish birds much more difficult to spot. I've seen a scarlet tanager here and there, but never at the feeder! They gravitate to forested areas. Purple finches, also a treat for the eyes, are more subtle in their coloration.

There's an aspect of the northern cardinal song that reminds me of those complex car alarm "songs" that seemed to be all around in the eighties. BirdNote has a more flattering description: "pure whistled tones."[45] Because both the male and female sing, you can enjoy recordings of their call-and-response "duets." Her replies are a bit softer in tone.

So far I have never spotted a cardinal nest. The female does most of the building. She uses her body and feet to make a cup shape, which has four layers: a leafy mat over coarse twigs (and sometimes bits of trash), then a grapevine bark lining topped off with grasses, stems, rootlets, and pine needles. Cardinals like to nest in dense foliage— unlike the robins in my rhododendron!—which explains why I don't spot them.

## April 5

### Shy Great Blues

It happened again yesterday. I stopped to scan the marsh, telling Buddy to "stay" and repeating the command as he continued to pull on the leash with all his might. At the sound of my insistent voice, a great blue heron rose like a specter from prehistoric times and glided away.

This is so often the pattern—I am lucky enough to come across one of these magnificent birds and then it flies off, even when I keep quiet and am relatively far away. These birds, and larger water birds generally, are sometimes called "shy pokes." Some say the "poke" part of the term refers to the defecation they leave as they make haste into the sky.

I hit the territorial "sounds" button on the All About Birds great blue site and heard an ungainly sort of croaking that at one point sounded like an old car engine straining to turn over. So far, I have only witnessed these birds being completely silent.

I enjoy trying to sneak up on great blue herons as they stand, stat-ue-like, waiting to pounce on a tasty fish or frog. Sometimes I do get a minute of watching before the bird takes off. Coming upon a heron-ry—a colony of their nests in trees close to wetlands—would make for a banner day. Although, would l then be watching hundreds of them instantly fly off?

## April 6

### The Humble Minnow

According to scientist Brandon Peoples at the *Fisheries Blog*, not all small fish are minnows, although I'm sure many of us don't know the difference between, say, a golden shiner, highscale shiner, or true shiner—all minnows—versus a mudminnow, mummichog, or silver-side—all not minnows.

Most native North American minnows belong to a family of freshwater fish called *Leuciscidae*, but to make things more confusing, some nonminnows have the word "minnow" as part of their common (nonscientific) name!

Greg Bohn at Northland Fishing Tackle frames minnows as "the first choice [for bait] in spring from ice-out through spawning time."[46] Surprisingly, they say small minnows can attract more fish than bigger minnows in early spring. Earlier in the year, minnows are said to make good ice fishing bait too. A determined fisherman or woman can drill through the ice, lower a trap baited with enticing bread, and hopefully catch some minnows in short order!

Anglers aren't the only ones after minnows. Birds and other fish eat minnows, so they are considered high in ecological importance. One type, the goldfish (*Carassius auratus*), is the most popular pet fish, and some have been released into waterways. Unfortunately, these introduced goldfish, should they manage to become well established, can wreak havoc on the lake or pond's natural ecosystem. These tiny pets can grow to four pounds and their feeding behaviors stir up mud and sediment, contributing to harmful algae blooms.

## *April 7*
### Toasted Marshmallows Already?

In early spring, it's heartening to peer at trees and bushes looking for buds. If you do this long enough, you start to notice something unusual or unexpected. You start to wonder things like: "Is it just random chance that this otherwise bare tree sports just one leaf?" Or, "Why did this leaf curl up so tightly?"

In the case of the Japanese maple in my front yard, the lone leaf remaining from last year is housing some kind of cocoon. I'm watching to see what emerges. I have found curled up leaves that are in fact woven together, by some tiny creature that sewed the formation for protection.

Keep an eye out for "toasted marshmallows" as you do your survey of the burgeoning spring foliage. These odd appendages feel like Styrofoam, but with a little less give. They have swirls reminiscent of the paper that some wasps use to house their young, but it's easy to tell that these are not wasps' nests.

These "marshmallows" are praying mantis egg cases. The Chinese variety they hold will spring from their case by the hundreds and, once grown, may even go on to eat hummingbirds on occasion! This type of mantis, initially introduced as pest control, is not well loved all around. They have been described as indiscriminate predators, as quick to eat beneficial creatures as they are to eat pests.

Making discoveries while out walking can feel like winning the lottery. They offer a chance at joy and fascination with what Darwin described as "endless forms most beautiful and most wonderful."[47]

## April 8
## Tangled Webs: Decorative "Duct Tape" or Deathtrap?

Even the most casual observer is likely picking up on birds preparing their nests these days. I've watched finches sorting old fibers from a long-abandoned nest and a robin carrying some sort of grass or shoot as it flew away. Yesterday I saw an osprey on its man-made platform in Pratt Cove; has it added many sticks to last year's pile?

We've all likely spotted bits of human-made materials in birds' nests—bits of plastic wrapping, twine, or torn pieces of tarp. It makes me wonder how intentional the decor is. Did some glint of the material catch the bird's eye, perhaps appealing to its sense of style, or was it a random choice?

Biologist Nancy Flood has a Baltimore oriole nest made entirely of fishing line[48]—an irony, since microfilament can be lethal for birds, hopelessly entangling them.

Spider web silk can be another double-edged sword for birds. Birds known to retrieve pieces of webbing to help their nest materials adhere include hummingbirds, vireos, kinglets, and gnatcatchers, according to the National Audubon Society. Besides being sticky, it has the added benefit of being stretchy and resilient.

In a macabre twist, I found an article in the *Wilson Journal of Ornithology* by Daniel M. Brooks about birds that get caught in spider webs.[49] Brooks says birds looking for spider silk are unlikely to get caught in the stuff. It's birds flying direct flight paths in the understory that can sometimes run into trouble as this is where orb-weaver spiders build. Researchers reported about fifty-four species of birds in twenty-three families trapped in webs, with hummingbirds of nine different species topping the list. There were some happy endings when humans came along and saved them. But, while birds are not on the spiders' list of favorite foods, some chowing down—euphemistically termed "opportunistic predation"—did take place.

## April 9

### Can't Live on Sauce Alone

This week Gavin harvested baskets of garlic mustard, an invasive herb that's easy to find. It's also sometimes called poor man's mustard or sauce-alone. Last year he made a pesto with the stuff. This year he's experimenting with dehydrating it for flavoring purposes.

It's not a bad-looking plant—generous, shapely leaves, and minute white and yellow flowers that will come around May. Green Deane at Eat the Weeds says one garlic mustard plant can produce up to eight thousand seeds, and the germination rate is close to 100 percent. It seems to have come from Europe to Long Island, New York, in the 1860s and spread west from there. Deane theorizes that when deer—who have proliferated in recent decades—eat the surrounding native plants (they prefer them to garlic mustard), it gives these invasives a chance to take over.

This isn't a food source we could live on, and if we did for some reason want to eat it in copious amounts, we'd have to consider its cyanide component! Some people react badly to it, even in quite limited amounts. Our family has been fine with this once- or twice-a-year treat in small doses.

David Taft titled his *New York Times* piece about it "Evil, Invasive, Delicious," which ends with the friendly reminder to pull it out by the roots as a way to give native woodland wildflowers a chance to shine.[50]

## April 10

### They Never Left, and They Are Not Mute

I found myself wondering about swans the other day. I didn't see them all winter, and yet I read that they don't migrate as many geese do. Here in Connecticut, we have mute swans, and they don't tend to travel any great distance. Also, they're not mute! Their sounds are described as "a hoarse, muffled trumpet or bugle call"[51] that doesn't carry very far. If you live around here or grew up around mute swans, and perhaps on some occasion got too close, you have probably heard them hiss too. They are known to be aggressive, especially if they think their chicks are threatened.

The Department of Energy and Environmental Protection had an answer about where the local swans had gone this winter, which seems obvious now: "After freeze-up (usually early or mid-December), most swans are forced into coastal areas or major river flowages where open water is available."[52] So, the small, inland waterways closest to me likely froze out these regal residents' access to aquatic vegetation, the staple of their diet.

If you've thought these birds have an exotic look, you are right. They were imported from Europe and Asia, transplanted here for decorative reasons. Initially captive, some escaped and started feral populations that continue to reproduce. In fact, scientist James MacDonald referred to them in JSTOR Daily as "the poster child for a harmful species protected by public goodwill."[53] Apparently, their overgrazing destroys the food supply that native waterfowl need.

I do feel goodwill when I see them, especially after I didn't see their graceful forms for much of the winter. Their association with fairy tales and ballets probably doesn't help the cause of those who are suggesting they make a lovely menu addition.

## April 11

## Buttercups = Little (and Sometimes Dangerous!) Frogs

I saw the first buttercup of the season today and was later surprised to learn that there are more than six hundred species in this flower's genus, *Ranunculus*. *Ranunculus* means "little frogs." Huh?

It makes sense, at least to a point. The name alludes to how native buttercup flowers grow abundantly along streams, as do little frogs. But it is a generalization; my find was nowhere near the water.

Since there are so many species, I should not be surprised that many stunning buttercup types look nothing like what I consider to be the iconic buttercup—small, low-lying, yellow. The Persian buttercup is a dreamy, orange bloom that florists favor, a bit reminiscent of a rose. White water and yellow water buttercups are aquatic.

The Plant ID app on my phone told me the specimen I found was a fig buttercup, also called lesser celandine. Seeing it filled my heart; it was one of the many, happy proofs on yesterday's sunny walk that spring is undeniably here in the form of abundant curbside and woodland flowers.

Home Stratosphere says, "It was once believed that the yellow color of butter comes from cows consuming large amounts of buttercups, but since these flowers are toxic to cattle, this is not true."[54] Buttercups are also toxic to dogs, cats, horses, and humans. In fact, some humans get skin blisters from simply touching certain types. This surprised me. They look so sweet and harmless!

## *April* 12

## Hunting Umbrellas

Blooming pink magnolias are turning my head. As a kid I had decided these were "tulip trees." I wasn't completely off-base; the trees commonly known as tulip trees are in the magnolia family. But tulip trees have mostly yellow, and yes, even more tulip-like blossoms than the typically lower and wider pink magnolia varieties, such as saucer magnolias and others that can survive here in the North. Tulip trees can grow quite tall, so often the flowers are not fully appreciated, unlike the showy, bounteous magnolia varieties that are the stars of our yards.

What does this have to do with umbrellas? Well, not every kind of magnolia can grow abundantly in the Connecticut climate, and umbrella magnolias are a variety you'd typically expect to find farther south. But I learned that we have a champion umbrella magnolia in Branford. In a 2013 *Hartford Courant* article, Peter Marteka says the Yale School of Forestry used the forests around Lake Saltonstall in the 1920s as a giant outdoor laboratory, planting both common and lesser-known species, including what turned into our champion tree, which is listed on Connecticut Notable Trees.

Let's imagine we can get to Lake Saltonstall. What would we see there? First of all, there's not just the champion tree; there's a grove of them. They have huge leaves that block out ground vegetation. The *Courant* article says some of the trunks look like huge, twisted corkscrews, with the beech-like bark bulging out here and there. And the flowers? Six to eight inches of creamy white. The way the leaves cluster at the end of the stem gives the plant its common name—umbrella. I think I might invest in a

Regional Water Authority permit that will let me get to that spot. For now, I am enjoying imagining time in a grove of umbrellas.

## *April 13*

### Dappled Fawns in Dappled Light

Tom found a charming old book for me—the 1903 *School of the Woods* by William J. Long. Over the decades since the popularity of this writer/minister, some have questioned how many of his works contained made up or misinterpreted animal facts. And I noticed he liked to call animals by what he termed "Indian names," like "Unk Wunk" for porcupine, with nearly no discussion of the Native peoples that were here first. He said these names were from the Milicete Indians, which I think translates to the modern term Maliseet.

Still, I appreciate Long's love of woodland creatures and illustrator Charles Copeland's detailed sketches. The first chapter is about noticing brown "mold" under roots of a fallen tree flecked with white and yellow in the sunlight. Only gradually does he realize he has found two fawns.

In Connecticut, right now, there are quite a few does about to enter their final month of pregnancy. Fawns will arrive late May to early June. Yearlings typically give birth to one fawn; older does often have twins, sometimes triplets. Does hide their young well, and the fawns' natural coloring helps tremendously. *Northern Woodlands* columnist Susan Shea recounts walking right by a fawn in the ferns just three feet off the Appalachian Trail. Her dog didn't smell it. Doe moms lick their newborn fawns clean, and the fawns' scent glands are not yet well developed. Fawns instinctively stand still when frightened. Their heartbeats and breathing slow to a crawl.

Does nurse their young on relatively rare visits, and wildlife rehabbers are too often brought perfectly healthy fawns by folks who feel they have been abandoned. When in doubt—if for some reason the fawn looks ill or injured, or the mom has not come back even in response to the fawn crying—best to call an expert rather than move the animal.

# April 14

## Underworld Underdogs

It's discouraging when I start to research a creature and top search results focus on how to destroy them. So today I write in defense of moles.

Gardeners, they do not eat our bulbs and roots. They eat beetle larvae (grubs), other insects, and earthworms. Here in Connecticut, eastern moles (or common moles) do well in the relatively loose soil. We also have star-nosed moles, who like wetter areas. The star-nosed variety are good swimmers, so their diet includes aquatic insects too.

Contrary to popular belief, moles are not completely blind. Relatively recent science has determined that their detection of light, even through permanently closed eyes, helps control their body clocks, orienting them to time of day and season.

While they're not likely to win any beauty contests, these creatures are incredible diggers. A study by University of Massachusetts and Brown University scientists found that moles appear to "swim" through the earth with a powerful stroke aided by shovel-like paws, exerting a force up to forty times their own body weight.

So how about some sympathy for the much-maligned moles? At Hobby Farms, Karen Lanier writes: "Keep in mind that these natural predators are maintaining your grub populations while aerating your soil."[55] And they work hard for their food. They must eat incredible amounts to keep their metabolism going. Moles cannot take a vacation from digging.

I don't mind the tunnels that pop up in the lawn; it's intriguing to think about the underground "swimmers" who made them. I'm with Ken Catania, a wildlife biologist who studied star-nosed moles. Mary Beth Griggs's *Popular Science* article surrounding Catania's work calls the star-nosed mole "an engineer of the swampland . . . providing an underground superhighway for other mammals, including several different species of shrew and weasels, to enjoy." Catania said, "How all those animals are interacting is an unknown, fascinating question, because they're all using these same tunnels . . . I would love to know what's going on down there."[56]

# April 15

## Daffodil Escapees

The daffodils that interest me most are not the appealing clusters in our gardens, although I appreciate their bright presence. Those that catch my eye are the random yellow faces dotting uncultivated roadside spots or rocky hillsides in the woods. What is their back story? It seems unlikely someone planted bulbs here.

Most of us plant bulbs to produce garden daffodils, and this makes good sense, since daffodils planted from seeds can take up to seven years to bloom! When daffodils spread by bulb division, this is asexual reproduction. The plants are cloning. Sexual reproduction among garden varieties is not frequent because many highly bred specimens have lost their pollen-attracting features. Urban Pollinators says wild daffodils, however, can be pollinated by honeybees. I also learned that squirrels will sometimes dig up and replant bulbs! They don't eat them because daffodils are toxic to many creatures, including humans.

Ants can also play a role in spreading fertilized daffodils. Matt Candeias at In Defense of Plants explains that ants are attracted to the fatty structures (elaiosomes) attached to daffodil seeds. They bring the seeds back to their nests where they remove and eat the elaiosomes, giving the seeds a nice chance to thrive in the ants' nutrient-rich trash heap called a midden.

Human landscape disturbance can unwittingly help spread these plants. And, of course, there is always the wind to help with pollination and seed dispersal.

A random daffodil may have a long history. A piece in *Grit* by Mary Carton follows a devotee of flowers at abandoned homesteads who transplants heirloom finds. Steve Eisenhauer's column at Natural Lands describes daffodils deep in the woods at a New Jersey preserve, a remnant from a house that burned down eighty years ago.

# April 16

## Plight of the Salamander

Connecticut boasts twelve types of salamanders, although, sadly, half are either endangered, threatened, or of special concern.

Salamanders are known for their smooth, slippery bodies. Glands under their skin secrete mucus, keeping them moist. While they must lay their eggs in moist places, most of their adult lives are spent in forested areas. I'll never forget the childhood delight of tipping up a large stone to find a salamander nestled below. They also favor living quarters under fallen logs or burrowed underground.

What can we do to help the salamanders? First, leave them alone, says the Connecticut Department of Energy and Environmental Protection (DEEP). As a child, I didn't follow this rule. I must have picked up and admired hundreds of eastern red-spotted newt efts (salamanders in their terrestrial stage), holding some captive. DEEP also says we can help by promoting stewardship of vernal pools and other important salamander habitats. And our yards matter; forget the manicured lawn! Leave the leaves where they fall. Avoid herbicides. Consider building a brush shelter, which can be a magnet to all kinds of creatures.

## April 17

## Circles in the Sun

A wise person told me it's good practice to look for circles or spirals in nature if you feel the need to center yourself. This week I admired the beauty and symmetry of botanical rosettes.

Since ancient times, the rosette has bloomed in art. According to what you read, it can symbolize kingly authority, God's love, protection of the home, or love of the earth or the sun. Artwork reflecting rosettes includes grand tile work and stained glass. I looked up the Notre Dame's famed windows, and they survived the awful 2019 fire. They are called rose windows, not rosettes, but a rose by any other name . . . could be a rosette!

As I started to read up on these fanning marvels, I was sorely tempted to steal another writer's title. Blogger Anita Sanchez wrote "Basal Rosettes: Life in the Flat Lane." She explains how the generous circle of leaves hugging the ground provides advantages: crowding out the competition, catching rain and directing it toward the roots, and resisting damage even when walked on or disturbed. The spread of the leaves is an ideal design for absorbing maximum sunlight. Sanchez further points out that some plants with rosettes have a two-year lifespan. During the first year, the plants gather as much nutrition as they can. Then they are ready to shoot out from the ground the following year with an early start on competitors.[57]

Whatever we choose to read into the design, the rosette's spiral draws us in. I treasure its generous unfolding, and its broad acquaintance with the earth as it gazes skyward, a way of being I'd like to emulate.

## April 18

## Flanked by Gold

It was everywhere as I ran my errands, creating a thick border between my neighbors' plots, prettying the concrete foundations of highway bridges, broadcasting brightness from many a yard. Maybe the overcast day plus the height of this shrub's season made the forsythia shine in an extra compelling way. Jonathan Safran Foer already used the title, but if he hadn't, I would have called today's entry Everything Is Illuminated.

How many times have I walked or driven by forsythia and not given it my full attention? For the first time, I wondered how birds experience this shrub. Sally Roth at *Birds & Blooms* counts forsythia as a good choice for "birdscaping," as it provides appealing shelter. Catbirds, mockingbirds, and cardinals nest in forsythia, which compels me to peer more closely, past the blossoms and into the plant's tangled depths.

Birds see more colors than we do! With this enhanced perception, I wonder how they perceive the generous gold blossoms from the vantage point of their nests. Their fledglings are offered the promise of a marvelously illuminated start in life.

When I think of birds eating, I typically think of seeds and fruits. But a quick Google search comes up with headlines like: "Birds Eating Flower Buds," "Why are Birds Eating my Flowers?" and "Birds Eating Buds—Help!!" Landscape designer Darcy Larum at Gardening Know How says finches and cardinals are fond of munching on forsythia flowers. Birds sometimes eat buds in early spring because their preferred fruits and seeds are not yet available. Typically, this doesn't do much damage to the plant.

## April 19

## Smelling the Water

Unlike Buddy, my beagle-mix walking companion, we humans most often lead with our vision. Of course, we appreciate a good scent, and scents carry rich meaning because the way they are processed ties in with our memory center.

The scent of water and waterside aromas may seem more nebulous than, say, lilacs, but it's got a stronger role than it seems, at least in our sub-conscious. I remember driving home to Long Island after a trip to West Virginia and being flooded with the scent of salt air, something I hadn't realized I'd missed deeply until I experienced it again.

I love the scent of low tide because of the childhood beach memories it stirs. But Luis Villazon at the BBC's Science Focus describes it as a stale, sulfury smell, and I've heard it called worse than that. Bacteria digesting dead phytoplankton make the smell, and the chemicals we smell at low tide are sex pheromones produced by seaweed eggs to attract the sperm. And then there is the "iodine" smell of the sea, caused by chemicals produced by marine worms and algae.

What about the scent of rain? A *Smithsonian* piece by Joseph Stromberg swam into my news stream and explained how the chemical compound geosmin causes the scent of fresh rain. A particular type of bacteria uses this compound to attract tiny springtails, who eat and distribute it. This bacteria type, *Streptomyces*, is very important to the antibiotic-making process. Maybe we humans instinctively know that the scent of rain is associated with recovery?

My next walk may be a "smell walk," following Buddy's lead. I do this on occasion and it's a marked change from leading primarily with eyes and ears. Who knows what our noses might help us discover?

## *April 20*

### Blue Jay Ditch- and Grave-Diggers

I take great pleasure in Mary Holland's book *Naturally Curious Day by Day*. Yesterday's entry caught my eye: blue jay nests are underway this time of year, and they like to line their nests with rootlets. They'll travel quite a way to pull them up from recently dug ditches, newly felled trees, and even freshly dug graves. Rootlets are sometimes called hair roots. They are very small, analogous to capillaries versus major blood vessels. Small bits of paper, cloth, string, or other visually interesting tidbits are often nestled among these soft additions to the blue jay nest.

Nesting runs from March to July, and eggs need only about eighteen days before they hatch. The babies will hang around for about another three weeks after that. By then, they will have their feathers and can fledge.

# April 21
## Spring Bubbling Up

Driving by one of the white pines next to the road, I spotted a mound of "soap bubbles" near the base. If I didn't know better, I'd say that some of the lather from my kitchen sink chores had managed to float off, aiming to hitch a ride curbside.

The spittlebugs are here! We have up to sixty kinds in the US that feed on plant juices and for the most part do little harm. Froghopper insect nymphs benefit from the foam we see riding grasses and other plants; it hides them from predators and keeps their systems moist. They make the bubbles by eating more juices than they need, then pumping air into their excretions by abdominal contractions, mixing in some glandular fluid.

The insects dive into the foam to hide, holding their breath. They must poke their abdomens out of the bubbles to breathe.

Some call the spittle unsightly or gross, but I find it fascinating. When they mature, the fragile insects within will have the ability to "leap tall buildings in a single bound." Well, not really, but the height of their jumps, considering their size, is magnificent—up to two feet. Entomologist Richard Zack at Washington State University calls them insect superheroes. At the very least, they excel at hide and seek.

# April 22
## Hepatica and the Doctrine of Signatures

Buttercups are not simply those little yellow flowers often associated with the name. There are more than six hundred species in their genus, *Ranunculus*, and *Hepatica* flowers are among them.

My nursing background helped me know that the name *Hepatica* must have something to do with the liver. The name *Hepatica nobilis*—the much-loved, diminutive, and often blue forest flower—translates to "noble or notable liver."

I wondered, "Why would someone make the association between leaves and an internal organ? How many people know what a liver looks like?" I thought of the brown slab of liver and onions I ate growing up. Have I ever viewed a plant and thought, "That looks like a liver"?

We are centuries past when *Hepatica* was named, sometime in the 1700s, and at the time, the Doctrine of Signatures was an important principle. The Indiana Native Plant society explains, "The ancient Doctrine of Signatures stated that plants treated whatever human body parts the leaves resembled. Because the leaves were of similar shape, form, and color to the liver, many early herbalists believed this plant could treat various liver ailments."[58]

Carol Gracies from the New York Botanical Garden says *Hepatica* was harvested in copious quantities in the 1800s, so much so that it was put at risk. It made its way into patent medicines peddled by "snake oil salesmen," but recent studies haven't found the plant to do anything for the liver. Gracies insists it deserves a prettier name!

It is the first true wildflower to blossom in the Connecticut/New York/ New Jersey area—if you don't count the early skunk cabbage bloom. Hail to these tiny blooms that keep shouting spring out to us!

# April 23

## Lilliputian Soldiers

The wood on our deck railing and mailbox is sprinkled with tiny, red British soldier lichens, named for the redcoats or Tories from the Revolutionary War era. It's fitting that I noticed them around the time of Patriots' Day in Massachusetts, which I have learned is a fairly big deal in that state. The company I work for, based in Massachusetts, hosted a series of employees reading Henry Wadsworth Longfellow's patriotic poem, "Paul Revere's Ride," in which the redcoats were chased down the lane.

Lichens are part fungi, part algae. The green parts of the "soldiers" are the algae, which do the photosynthesis work. The red parts are the fungi, which throw out spores for reproduction. But British soldiers can also reproduce by splitting apart and getting carried to new places by the wind, animals, etc. They are fragile, so they tend to favor crevices where they can shelter from the elements a bit; hence their starring role in our weather-beaten deck railing and mailbox.

The only human purpose I see listed for these "soldiers" is as decor in a terrarium. Hummingbirds sometimes use lichens in nest building; I wonder if these little pops of color sometimes make it into nests of hummingbirds.

The scientific name for British soldiers—*Cladonia cristatella*—literally translates to "crested mountains," a perfect, if ironic, name for these tiny specimens. It's fun to get down to their level and watch these bright structures "tower" over their substrate. Maybe the mites walking through are craning their necks, wondering what's at the top of these gargantuan growths.

## *April 24*

## The Turtle and the Mayapple

I learned that mayapple germination works best if the seed passes through a box turtle first! On a walk through a garden at the Goodwin State Forest in Connecticut, my guide pointed out that mayapples are just the right height for these creatures.

Arlene, from Hemlock Hill, not far from me, sent pictures from her lawn with the announcement: "Mayapples are up." So far, they're just some rather droopy-looking clusters, but Arlene hopes to send me more pictures when they bloom and then when the apples appear.

Janet Marinelli, writing for Brooklyn Botanic Garden, discusses how gardeners can support box turtles, who, according to the article, "increasingly find themselves marooned in a sea of suburbs."[59] I may have to plant some of the foods they can't resist. Besides mayapples, they like elderberries, blackberries, and summer grapes. And they like leaf litter and, of course, moisture. We have plenty of both here.

Marinelli noted that meeting up with an eastern box turtle "almost always leaves a good impression." True. Have you ever met a box turtle you didn't like?

Arlene said a ton of mayapples sprouted and have been sprouting ever since from just one that a friend supplied more than thirty years ago. Maybe she had some help from saurochory. Not to be confused with sorcery—although it can seem kind of magical—saurochory is the dispersal of seed by reptiles.

## April 25

### Lowly or Holy? A Fresh Look at Earthworms

Jay Griffiths wrote a piece in *Emergence Magazine*, "Dwelling on Earth," that was full of worm surprises for me. For one thing, Darwin wrote "The Formation of Vegetable Mould, Through the Actions of Worms." Not a super tantalizing title, but Darwin was trying to demonstrate worm intelligence. From his observations, he inferred that worms form judgments about different leaf shapes and make decisions about how to best drag leaves to plug their burrow openings based on a thorough assessment.

Worms are essential to soil. Griffiths says it well: "The worm, softly rubbing through terra mater, passing through the soil and passing the soil through itself, turns soil into bright actuality, transforming the dark and turning earth and turning death back to life, the lovely holy worm."[60]

It's not often we hear "worms" and "holy" together. But if you think this adjective goes overboard, it's worth knowing that earthworms increase food crop yield by about 25 percent. They are greatly endangered by herbicides, chemicals used all too often by farmers and casual gardeners alike.

Griffiths also points out how we typically praise what is above—Her Royal Highness, heavens above, etc.—and disdain what is below—lowest of the low, the depths of despair, being "soiled," etc. When I read about all the amazing goings on underground—the mushroom mycelia, the network of roots, the mass of tiny overwintering insects, our prodigious earthworms, and other creatures that burrow, all with very specific and helpful roles—I see a good case for praising the ground beneath our feet for all its unseen industry and benevolence.

## April 26

### Wake-Robin, Nodding Off

Yesterday was a much-needed break out into the sunny, warm day. Gavin and I rode with Tom on a work errand, knowing the People's State Forest was nearby. We were rewarded with a long, streamside walk, starring green frogs, polypore mushrooms, and red trillium.

Trillium is also called wake-robin, and I like that name better. "Trillium" refers to its three leaves and three petals, but "wake-robin" tells a spring story about how these flowers show themselves when the robins do. The flowers can be either upright or nodding, and most we saw were nodding.

Ruth Smith's piece in the *Berkshire Eagle* told me to "stop to see—but don't smell—the trillium," explaining that other names for the plant include stinking Benjamin, stinking Willie, and wet-dog trillium.[61] The forest smelled fine yesterday, as we weren't close enough to pick up the odor. The smell makes sense, since carrion flies are one of trillium's main pollinators.

The Connecticut Botanical Society's vascular plants checklist names six types of trillium in the state. Looking for the other types, besides red trillium, will be a fun spring pursuit.

## *April 27*

## Dandelion as Geometric Divinity

Dandelions are popping up everywhere—in conversations as well as on our lawns. My sister has a dandelion salad recipe to try, and my friend shared an annual family tradition of fried dandelions.

And then there's dandelion math! Someone posted a picture of nine dandelion snapshots titled "The Geometry of Dandelions." These humble blooms are so stunning with their radiating facets and the light shining through. As with the surface sameness of snowflakes, if you look closely enough, each is different.

Geometry is not my strong suit. In high school, I found little obvious relevance for the subject in day-to-day life. But I may have to rethink that, thanks to dandelions!

Benedetta Palazzo's' article at Eniscuola Energy & Environment explains, "the plant kingdom has a curious preference for particular numbers and for certain spiral geometries . . . these numbers and geometries are closely related. We can easily find the numbers of the Fibonacci sequence in the spirals formed by individual flowers in the composite inflorescences— the complete flower head of a plant—of daisies, sunflowers, cauliflowers and broccoli."[62]

The ratio, also called the Divine Proportion, is instinctively pleasing to the eye—notice the way a dandelion or the swirls in a snail shell are constructed. And symmetry serves a real purpose. In "The Perfection of the Snail," another piece at Eniscuola, Tiziana Bosco explains that symmetrical structures provide several advantages for living organisms: they are stable, compact, homogeneous, and interchangeable, and they can be easily and efficiently reproduced. Spheres also disperse less heat. However, symmetrical forms are almost never perfect. Each four-leaf clover leaf is not exactly equal to its neighbor.[63]

These things we see go so much deeper than a pretty bloom or snail or starfish. There's another layer of existence that is much cleverer than what we could have dreamed up.

# April 28

## Cemetery Friend

Today's cemetery stroll had me leaving Buddy waiting with his leash tied to a railing so I could get closer to a black vulture who was weaving between the tombstones. I wasn't sure if Buddy might see the bird as tasty prey, although it would have made for an ambitious and out-sized meal.

I approached slowly and gently and was surprised that the bird didn't take off even as I got within four feet or so. I got some lovely photos but was concerned. Was this bird not flying off because it couldn't? I contacted the birds of prey rescue and rehabilitation center—A Place Called Hope. I explained that the bird seemed fine other than not flying away—walking well and pecking at the ground. S/he seemed alert to his/her surroundings, including me!

It never occurred to me that these birds are ground nesters, and this was the likely explanation for my new friend hanging around. All About Birds says these birds lay their eggs directly on the ground and often nest in caves, stumps, or abandoned buildings. They favor rocky ledges and roosting near the water, so the cemetery's rocky elevation above wetlands made perfect sense. Mom and dad black vultures take turns at twenty-four-hour nest-sitting shifts. The birds typically subsist on carrion but will sometimes eat live prey as well. I was surprised to learn that these birds are closely related to the stork family!

It was hard to walk away from this unexpected contact, and Buddy was sure straining at the leash, hoping to get closer. Hopefully, there is a clutch of new life somewhere nearby. It's not far from where I once watched a snapping turtle dig a hole to lay her eggs.

# April 29

## Wahoo! The Winged Bush

If you've walked around woodlands enough, you wouldn't need to see a photo to know which bush Cathy Heidenreich at the Geneva (New York) Arboretum Association is describing here: "No other shrub in the East has those thin, blade-like corky ridges on the four sides of its twigs."[64]

If you catch winged euonymus (*Euonymus alata*) at the right time in autumn, you will be treated to a show of brilliant red to translucent pink foliage, hence the nickname "burning bush" or "winged burning bush." Common plant names get confusing, though, because other varieties of this type are also called burning bush, as well as wahoo. Winged euonymus is called winged wahoo by some.

Why wahoo? One of our native species of burning bush was reportedly used as a strong purgative or laxative, which could make anyone react with a wahoo, I suppose.

UConn's Plant Database says this plant has invasive tendencies thanks to hungry birds who really like its red berries and drop its seeds liberally as they travel.

A European cousin of this plant that has been introduced here, known as the spindle tree (*E. Europoeus*), is also sometimes called wahoo or burning bush. It has a host of known uses besides possibly making humans go WAHOO! Its wood makes a high-quality charcoal for artists. And back before plastic and other modern materials were so ubiquitous, the wood made skewers, toothpicks, spindles for wool, pegs, knitting needles, and pipe stems.

# April 30

## Baby Red Tails

In her book *Red Tails in Love*, Marie Winn tells the story of a faithful crowd in New York City's Central Park that is taken with a young red-tailed hawk they name Pale Male. They watch him as he woos a mate, and eventually, Pale Male and his mate build a nest on a Fifth Avenue building near the apartments of at least two prominent celebrities. They raise a family there, all under the watchful eyes of a rapt human audience.

This is the time of year when red-tailed hawk eggs are hatching, or about to hatch, after a month of both parents incubating the eggs. The babies fledge after about seven weeks, but their parents will feed them for months to come.

I have usually seen and heard red-tailed hawks from afar. Their piercing cry often comes from atop neighborhood conifers. Once, though, Tom and I came upon one hanging out in a Tarrytown, New York, cemetery. It wasn't clear why this hawk was hanging out near a tombstone, and we were concerned for his or her welfare. He or she seemed unflustered by our presence, and we marveled at the pronounced red tail feathers, which I hadn't fully appreciated through binoculars. We also marveled at the sheer size of the hawk. Later, I read that even the largest females of the species weigh in at only three pounds. Hollow bones serve these expert flyers well.

Soon the hawk was off to whatever was next on its agenda, flying off into a local spruce and then taking wing from there, going even higher. I still think back to that day with fondness.

## May 1

### Mud, Grass, and New Neighbors

Keep an eye out for clumps of mud interspersed with grass atop porch columns. At first it looks like the result of some random mudslinging. But if you are lucky, each time you look the mass will have grown and taken shape into a recognizable nest. Then you will spot eastern phoebes coming and going. The females are the builders, and nests can take up to two weeks to complete.

These birds can be stealthy if they know you are around. Try to make yourself scarce and to act uninterested when you can't help making your presence known. Listen for the raspy song, which does sound a bit like someone calling out, "Phoebe!"

We were sad to find remnants of a broken egg on the porch below the phoebe nest. We moaned with sadness and I wondered—had the egg fallen? Could it have been pushed? Did a predator drop its stolen goods? I learned with horror that house wrens will destroy the eggs and young of other species. We had hope that some would survive, since each clutch has up to six eggs.

Nests are said to symbolize good luck. There is something about the mud and grass dwellings just outside the front door that make it feel like our house has been blessed.

## May 2

### Vultures at Bedtime

I know they have the distasteful job of eating mostly carrion, and their faces are lumpy on disproportionately small heads, but when I walk the easy road up to Laurel Hill Cemetery, I admire how black vultures glide on the thermals. Last evening's walk was just before sunset, and the undersides of their ragged wings were lit by the last of the light. In that moment the phrase "gorgeous vultures" was far from an oxymoron.

When I got to the cemetery, there were two groups—one in a pretty, budding tree and the other in an older, dead-looking tree. I watched them soar majestically and then come in for clumsy landings. The only noise I heard was the clatter on branches as they landed, popped over to another tree limb, or took off again for yet another glide. The primary reason for gliding may be hunting, but it looks like a lot of fun too.

There must have been twenty of them. I thought about how other birds make bedtime calls to each other but not the black vultures—at least not in my presence! I wondered what thoughts or impulses dictated their gathering together like this.

A piece by Jack Connor at All About Birds told me a lot. There's a popular theory about birds gathering for security—strength in numbers. But vultures don't have predators to worry about, except for those who will find their ground nests. Black vultures roost as a means of sharing information. They might want to know where to get good food. The young follow their elders from the roost in the morning, and mates follow each other to the best sources too.

Black vultures also use turkey vultures as scouts. Turkey vultures are better fliers, with a better sense of smell. I have spotted turkey vultures roosting among the black ones; it's the least the black vultures can do— welcome them to rest in their tree for a while.

## May 3

### Double-Crested Cormorant: Pet Rock and Corpse Collector

He or she—males and females look similar—was perched on the end of a piece of driftwood in Pratt Cove, looking sedate, even meditative. Often, we see them with their wings spread; they don't have as much feather oil as other water birds and don't dry off as easily, so they stand with their wings spread out. Then again, that trait may help with underwater speed when hunting fish.

I decided I was seeing a double-crested cormorant, although there is also the great cormorant to consider. The greats are burlier, and they also tend to favor larger bodies of water. Since I had no birds to compare side by side and the Cove is a relatively narrow affair, I went with the smaller option.

I mused about how cormorants don't seem to get as much attention as other, more eye-catching local water birds, like swans or great blue herons. But I didn't have to go far to learn fascinating, quirky cormorant facts.

Here's the first bit that caught my eye at All About Birds: "It frequently picks up junk, such as rope, deflated balloons, fishnet, and plastic debris to incorporate into the nest. Parts of dead birds are commonly used too." Whaaaat? Then, "Large pebbles are occasionally found in cormorant nests, and the cormorants treat them as eggs."[65] Well, that's kind of endearing—pet rocks.

They have orange-yellow skin on their face and throat—I got glimpses of that through my binoculars. But they also have some pretty features, only seen up close, that I couldn't have guessed—aquamarine-colored eyes and mouths that are bright blue inside! The blue mouth color emerges during breeding season.

The bird's name derives from the Latin for "sea raven." Way back when, people used to call gluttonous people cormorants since the birds are known to gobble quite a lot of food.

## May 4

### Pill Bugs Outgrowing Their Clothes

How often as a child did I come across a pill bug, sometimes called a roly poly? This tiny gray, armored creature is ubiquitous in the garden row.

They help the soil by feeding on decomposing plants. Kids tend to love them since they curl into a ball at the slightest provocation.

They sure molt a lot. They start by molting a day after leaving their mother, and the first molt allows them to gain a body segment. Two weeks later, the next molt allows the seventh pair of legs to grow in. Over the next eighteen weeks, these creatures molt every one or two weeks, first shedding their posterior "skin" and then the skin up front.

The pill bug isn't an insect, but, rather, a terrestrial crustacean. They carry their young like marsupial mammals do—in a pouch. Scientists were surprised to learn recently that, in addition to old vegetation, they also eat stink bug eggs.

## *May 5*

## Dewy Decor: A Nonsticky Situation

My friend Janice and I independently took nearly the same photo one morning: a closeup of a bejeweled-looking funnel weaver spider web woven across a shrub. These webs are everywhere, but the morning dew demands we notice them.

There are about one hundred species of this type of spider in North America, and twelve hundred worldwide. Australia's got a scarily venomous version, but around here they are not something to worry about. In fact, some people call them money spiders, as they are rumored to bring good luck.

I must have riches rolling in soon because a moist morning recently had me finding the webs at every turn. The spiders themselves are not so easy to spot. After all, the spout shape below the flat surface is designed for stealth; this is where the creature sits in wait, ready to ambush the next hapless insect that wanders onto its lair. The fibers are not sticky but can trip the victim up as its predator runs easily across the web and injects some numbing bites before dragging its meal away below deck.

Mating will occur later this summer or in the fall. If you find a disc-shaped sac covered in silk mesh on the underside of a rock or some loose bark, you may have found a future generation of about fifty that the mother produced before she died. She's often found still clinging to it.

# May 6

## Apples for Animals

My office has an apple tree in full bloom outside. I'm not sure any humans eat the apples, although it's possible someone using the building snags one from time to time. Come to think of it, are they crabapples? My memory fails me on this score. I just know the pink and white blossoms are stunning right now.

I wondered aloud to Tom what nearby Scott's Orchard looks like in bloom. We've only gone in the fall and can't spot the trees when we drive by. Searching Internet images for "apple orchard in bloom" quickly convinces me we need to drive through several orchards this time of year. There's a long strip along an upstate New York highway that is flush with orchards; it must light up the otherwise dull drive this time of year.

House finches and cedar waxwings eat apple blossoms. I am not sure how many types of insects eat the blossoms themselves, but plenty like the leaves and even more, of course, relish the fruit, not to mention branches, trunks, and roots. How do orchardists sleep at night?

One of the first things that came up on my apple blossom search was an article by the state Department of Energy and Environmental Protection on rejuvenating apple trees to help local wildlife. There are a host of trees that were likely once regularly harvested and have now fallen to neglect, finding themselves in newer growth forests. And wild apple trees can take root in clearings.

With some care to prune and let light in, these "resurrected" trees can help quite a few creatures. White-tailed deer, ruffed grouse, snowshoe hares, cottontail rabbits, gray squirrels, fox, fishers, porcupines, bobcats, and red squirrels all partake of apple tree nutrition. The trees also provide a good habitat for woodcocks, bluebirds, flycatchers, robins, and orioles.

How do you like them apples?

# May 7

## Fiddlehead Fern Fronds Unfurling

Have you ever eaten a fiddlehead? There's much to know about them if you are seeking to find, cook, and nibble on these young plant parts before they unfurl into their full glory as ferns. Not every fiddlehead—a term for how the fern looks at this stage— is edible! It depends on the type of fern. Ostrich ferns are the best-known source of edible fiddleheads.

Whether or not you are on a mission to hunt and eat fiddleheads, it can still be fun to look. Wild fiddleheads sprout up along waterways and off the beaten path, so it's likely you'll find some pretty scenery as you go.

I haven't yet harvested my own, but I agree with Dave Hurteau's assessment of the flavor in *Field & Stream*: "sort of between asparagus and green beans."[66] I might enjoy the aesthetic of these young plants even more than the taste —their vivid green spiral designs like small flags signaling spring. When they grow into full-fledged ostrich ferns, they are lush, graceful looking, and quite tall—up to six feet high! These plants often go dormant in the heat of summer, so we here in the North can relish the lives of these bright coils now, soon to morph into fanning decor across our landscape.

## May 8

### Snakes in Alaska?

Leaf litter in the garden wriggled. Looking closer, I saw a common garter snake, about a foot and a half long. A month or two ago, it emerged from its winter den ahead of many other snake varieties. Besides burrows in the ground, mud banks, and stumps or logs, garter snakes sometimes move in with muskrats or crayfish for the winter. During brumation—similar to hibernation—and also when they bed down for the night in warmer months, they congregate with many other snakes to keep warm. Their cold-bloodedness means their body temperatures drop rapidly once evening comes.

About 70 percent of snakes lay eggs, but garter snakes fall into the 30 percent that give live birth like us humans. Between July and October, the female will birth as many as forty young. I watched a few videos of garter snakes giving birth, and it's wild. It's as if new snakes are materializing by the minute, although perhaps the female doesn't view it quite as breezily.

Garter snakes eat a lot of other creatures, and a lot of other creatures eat them. They eat mostly frogs, toads, and salamanders, but also worms, slugs, snails, crayfish, mice, and even nesting birds. Many birds—owls, hawks, turkeys, crows, robins—eat them, and so do many mammals—raccoons, skunks, otters, foxes—along with frogs, large fish, and other snakes.

These snakes are true survivors that make it even in extreme environmental conditions. In fact, several sources say that common garter snakes are the only type of snake found in Alaska! It's thought they are not native there but have been introduced by humans, or in some cases by flooding.

## May 9

### A Case for Unwashed Windows

My friend Cecilia took me on a tour of the University of Rhode Island campus, which boasted impressive plantings. It was a good day to walk, and we snapped pictures of many blooms.

Walking along the edge of a gleaming newer building, we saw a spot of yellow on the pavement. A dead bird—a yellow warbler, I think. He or she had hit the enormous clear pane hard, and that was the end. Toward the other end of the same building, we found another, but we saw this one was breathing hard and fast. He or she roused when Cecilia cupped her hands around it, to bring it to a safer place.

At first, the bird spun on the cement like a dervish, clearly dizzied by the hit and freaked out by human touch. Then it calmed and looked a bit steadier. We placed the bird in a dark cove under a shrub, hoping it could recover quickly there and wake up in soft surroundings, not too badly concussed to function normally again.

The Tufts Wildlife Clinic says a hundred million birds are killed by collisions with windows each year. They think they are flying into more landscape instead of its reflection. The Clinic site lists suggestions that involve breaking up the visual field—window decals, planting shade trees nearby, soaping parts of the window or spraying parts with canned "Christmas snow." Attaching dead branches to the exterior is a novel idea, with the thought that the birds will slow as they prepare to land there.

When I got to the bottom of the list, I realized I am ahead of the game here at home. The last bullet says, simply, "Don't wash your windows."

## May 10

### Chipmunk Stripes: A New Perspective

I've been leaving sunflower seeds by Chippy's doorway near our stoop. She or he is quick to come get them, although not when I am watching. Tom has seen her dive back into her hole. We've been living alongside chipmunk families for years, generation after generation, although they usually stick to the stone wall near the basement door. This one by the landing has ventured out, claiming a new neighborhood.

I'm taken with the fact that newborns are about the size of a bumblebee. Breeding happens twice a year and the last bout would have been February through April—gestation takes about a month. So, there could well be some tiny chip-bumblebees down that hole. If they are down there, it's the mom popping up to get the seeds. Males and females come together only to mate, then the females become single moms.

Gavin gave me an old novel to read by a writer known for his nature observations. Hal Borland's *When the Legends Die* is about Thomas, a man with Ute ancestry who endures many hardships in his life. Without giving too much away, there is also truth and beauty in the book. Toward the end, Thomas recalls what his mother told him about the chipmunk: the stripes are the path from its eyes, with which it sees now and tomorrow. Its tail is always behind it, and a part of yesterday. She went on to comment that, although we humans don't have tails, we, too, have our pasts following behind us.

I don't know from where Borland derived this fable, or if he made it up. But there are actual Native stories on the chipmunk and its iconic stripes. One tale on Oneida Indian Nation is about how a dispute between a chipmunk and an angry bear led to the "claw" marks on the rodent's back.

## May 11

### Paradise in Parking Lots

Joni Mitchell paired the phrases "paradise" and "parking lot" in her song "Big Yellow Taxi," lamenting paved-over nature. Gavin is home from a permaculture course at Rancho Mastatal Sustainable Eco Lodge in Costa Rica, and I thought of that song when I heard his story.

On Gavin's last full day, when he was biding pre-flight time at a high-way-side airport hotel, he climbed a tree alongside the parking lot and marveled at leafcutter ants marching there. I wonder: if you grow up where leafcutter ants abound, do you take for granted their organized, industri-ous performance and their practice of farming by feeding the leaves they cut to a fungus back home, which in turn becomes their only foodsource?

Maybe it's easier to find fascinating things in a hotel parking lot when you are in an unfamiliar locale. But it's good to be reminded of all the fascinat-ing flora and fauna that survive and even thrive in the margins alongside the asphalt.

I recall hearing a barred owl calling from the thin strip of woods next to one hotel where we slept. I remember how the Oakland Trail in Manches-ter, once I got past a strip marred by graffiti, beer bottles, and the rumble of passing trucks, led me toward a deep, lush, gorge tucked away in a resi-dential neighborhood. I remember looking at rows of spindly, bare trees in a superstore parking lot and noticing a spate of hummingbird nests from the prior spring.

Let's stop paving paradise, but let's also notice what's right in reach of what seem to be everyday, humdrum places. The world is thrumming around us.

## May 12

### Quaker Ladies, Venus's Pride, and Bluets that Fly

Linda, my sister in Vermont, was envious when I told her there are bluets everywhere in Connecticut right now. A wildflowers database tells me we in Connecticut have two kinds: *Houstonia caerulia* and *Houstonia purpurea*. The former is known as Quaker ladies, the latter Venus's pride. There are other nicknames too—azure bluet, summer bluet, purple bluet. The kind I see most, the *caerulia*, are also called common bluets, and that makes sense. They are everywhere, popping up in little conferences on unmown lawns, gracing the spaces just inside the curbs I walk past on the way to town. They stand in small seas of fragile-looking, blue loveliness.

There are several threatened or "special concern" bluets in the state, but only one of them is a plant. The word bluet is simply a derivative of the word blue, so it's been applied to damselflies as well as our ubiquitous tiny spring plants. Sadly, there are five types of damselflies on the latest state list of endangered, threatened, and "special concern" species—bluets of the scarlet, pine barrens, Atlantic, little, and attenuated varieties. The loss of wetland habitat is a major culprit, as are pollution and pesticides. The threatened bluet of the plant variety is called a longleaf.

It's comforting to know there are good people out there who pay attention to species in danger. In the United Kingdom, they opened a Dragonfly Centre ten years ago, and it boasts twenty-two species. And the Xerces Society works to conserve invertebrates and their habitats. Besides supporting groups like these, one straightforward way to help dragonflies and damselflies is to build a backyard pond.

## May 13

### Flying Vegetarians: The Color Tells a Story

I had the treat of watching a male American goldfinch land in clear sight yesterday—no hiding behind foliage, a common move by the birds I am trying to watch! Yes, it is a common bird in these parts, but that doesn't make seeing its gold plumage any less uplifting. It's hard to have low spirits when focusing on such a bright being.

The yellow feathers come from eating carotenoids, found in plants. This makes sense; in fact, American goldfinches are among the strictest vegetarian bird species. The theory goes that the male's yellow color helps the female gauge his fitness and health; the brighter the better, because that could indicate excellent food-gathering skills.

The birds' vegetarian diet may help protect them from cowbirds, who like to lay eggs in their nests. The unfortunate cowbird offspring, should they hatch, won't be able to survive on the seed-only diet.

The European goldfinch is an introduced species in America, seen comparatively rarely. It seems that American and European goldfinches are closely related in name only, and the American variety is a much brighter sight. But the European variety has been a star in a plethora of renaissance paintings, said to symbolize the soul or redemption, or alternately, sacrifice and death. Ornithologist Herbert Friedmann counted 486 devotional pieces containing the European goldfinch, including works by da Vinci and Raphael.

## May 14

### Unzipped Dragonflies and Cecil B. DeMille

Dragonfly larvae (nymphs) are aquatic and not very noticeable or attractive. The creatures spend most of their lives as drab, gray-to-brown beings whose main hint at a future full-fledged dragonfly is the bulging eyes. I've pulled some up in nets, and they blend in with the decayed leaf litter and muck from the pond.

When it's time to transform, a nymph will crawl from the water and hang onto a rock or some vegetation. Then, it "unzips" the skin along its back, vigorously pumping its body to fill it with air and get fluid going into the wings. Voila! In a short time, the wings pop up. Once the body and wings have had a chance to dry, the dragonfly can take off.

Famed film director Cecil B. DeMille told an affecting dragonfly story. Alone in a lazily drifting canoe, DeMille watched a dragonfly nymph crawl up on the boat and appear to die. When DeMille looked up from his book a bit later, he watched the creature's back zip open and the dragonfly emerge. He talked about how the newly minted dragonfly hovered over the water's surface just inches from where other nymphs were swimming below. He shared, "They did not know it was there." I'm not so sure about the part where he recounts flicking the now-discarded nymph shell back into the water and watching the other nymphs back away from it. Could he really see all that?

But I get his point; there are transformations we cannot know about. We are sometimes in a fog in life, unable to see the big picture at all. DeMille remarked, "If God does that for a water beetle, don't you believe He will do it for me?"[67] Whatever your beliefs (or lack of them) in an afterlife, transformations like these are worth pondering.

## May 15

### Do Birds Ever Sleep In?

Have you ever wondered why birds have a sing-along as the sun rises? Scientists have wondered too. Of course, there are theories, and each may carry a grain of truth. Some say it's a good time of day to sing, since it's too dim to do much else. Others say the dawn chorus is how birds broadcast their health and vitality, attract mates, and define their territories. It's thought that the height at which a bird typically forages, as well as eye size, determine how early the bird will sing, since these factors affect light perception.

One August my Master Naturalist project was about the dawn chorus. I got outside to a lawn chair under our Norway spruce by about 4:45 a few mornings in a row. Always, one lone bird started the chorus, like the first oboe starting the orchestra in its tune-up. Some mornings I heard some random bird starting ridiculously early, about 3:30 or so. No one joined in. It's as if the rest of them were rolling their eyes at this overly perky early riser.

The weather has been dreary for May, but still I hear the swell of birdsong early in the day. I remember a paper that said birds start their chorus later on cloudy or wet days. I haven't verified the theory with my observations, but there are fewer birds singing when it rains. So maybe some of them want to sleep in when the day is gray, just like we do.

## May 16

### Light in Our Hands: The Wonders (and Worry) of Mica

Tom handed me a slice of mica he found among the driveway gravel. The layers separated in my hand and I moved it side to side, admiring the glimmer.

Mica is a good "gateway" substance into the world of minerals, easy to love at first glance. There are thirty-seven types, also known as sheet silicas. The mineral's name comes from the Latin *micare* ("to shine"), and other things in nature share that root. The *Philodendron micans* plant is known for its iridescent shimmer. There is an African leafhopper bug called *Recilia mica*. To me, the bug looks like a shimmering, elaborate Egyptian sarcophagus.

Many sources, such as University of North Carolina's Research Laboratories of Archaeology, report that several Native cultures used mica in trade as well as in crafts. A 2015 *Citizen Times* column on the topic by George Ellison covers a range of history; for example, large mica sheets were once popularly used as windows, called isinglass. Ellison says ancient Hindus believed mica was preserved lightning flashes, and they used it in medicine, for glazing windows, and as a surface for paintings.

When I Googled "collecting mica," I expected to find similar fans discussing their happy finds. I was shocked to find news coverage of child labor in African and Indian mica mines. What they collect ends up in many products we use—electronics, trains, even makeup. The contrast between the pleasure of this glimmering find and the exploitation of children to collect it evokes deep sadness. I found opportunities online to sign a petition in protest, and UNICEF is working to help address the issue.

## May 17

### Hard to Spot, Impossible to Ignore

When I was small, I fell asleep picturing unseen yet vocal exotic birds among the leaves of our tall trees. Later, I learned these "birds" were gray treefrogs.

It is mating season for gray treefrogs now. The reproductive act happens in the water, with marshy, shrubby areas the preferred locale. The female attaches the egg masses to plants, up to forty eggs at a time and totaling about eighteen hundred over the season. Outside of breeding, the frogs stick to trees and live mostly solitary lives.

It's the males we hear singing, and there's no mistaking their unique, insistent, high-pitched call. This is what gets the mating season going; the female chooses the male whose song appeals to her.

These frogs can change color—gray, green, or brown—based on the environment they are in and/or the time of day. A fact sheet by the Smithsonian's National Zoo says their skin becomes much lighter at night and darker during the day. When they hold still, they do an excellent job resembling lichens or bark. Gray treefrogs only reveal their bright yellow or orange thighs as they leap away; this flash of color is thought to warn off predators.

## May 18

### Tiny, Dotted Lives

Rutgers University runs a yearly Personal Bioblitz effort, hosted on iNaturalist. Folks posted more than 69,000 observations of 8,903 species in 2021. Impressive, in that only 115 people logged finds. These were some very busy people!

I love the democracy of every species being counted and relish the variety represented. The most commonly observed species were American beeches, American robins, red maples, eastern gray squirrels, and garlic mustard.

Scrolling through the observations, my eye fell on maple bladdergall mite galls, so named because they look like microscopic bladders. Each holds eggs laid by adult mites, and the fascinating thing about galls is how the plant develops them in response to another creature's activity. In this case, mite feeding causes the leaves to develop tons of pouches that will protect the tiny mites within. The galls start out green, then turn red, and finally drop. Over the winter, the new crop of adults waits for the following spring under tree bark or in bark callouses. Then, it all begins again.

For the trees, these galls are usually just a cosmetic issue. For those of us walking by, galls can be a source of fascination.

I found a slide show on birds in urban environments and was amused by presenter David Leatherman's description of galls as "arthropod piñatas." Birds and squirrels eat galls, and some can be especially nutritious. And other tiny insects can parasitize galls. I guess that could make for a double-decker treat for some bird.

While variety is unceasing year-round, if we know where to look, the rush of abundance in a northeastern spring is truly magical. As I wrote from my porch today, I spotted my first hummingbird of the season, and gray treefrogs and catbirds were calling. We've been finding broken eggshells on the lawn. New life abounds.

## May 19
### Noisy Neighbors (Starling Condo)

I've been taking part in a weekend retreat at Mercy by the Sea, a stunning swath of land on the Long Island Sound. Beloved author Robin Wall Kimmerer is the star of this gratifying show, sharing her wisdom and some hope for our beleaguered earth. It's been a gift, and if you enjoy reading about nature and how we connect with it, I recommend her book *Braiding Sweetgrass*. Robin is an enrolled member of the Citizen Band Potawatomi Nation and brings the Native American perspective on the land and its creatures into the conversation.

After a learning session, we were all sent off to spend time on our own in nature. We were supposed to be writing, but mostly, I was distracted by the noises that rose and fell from a series of rectangular holes along the edge of the building. It didn't take long to figure out that birds were nesting within. It sounded like scores of new lives squawking, rising to fever pitch as parents approached with food. The parents moved fast, zooming in and out of the holes with worms, and I thought these were European starling families. They had yellow beaks, and starlings often nest in holes in buildings. The babies made a raspy, trilling sound.

I was amused to learn that males build the nests, but the females oversee the final arrangements and may discard some of the males' decor. They also add fresh green plants into the mix throughout the nesting and incubation period. I had guessed their speckled look might have given starlings their name, alluding to the stars across a black sky. But it turns out that, with their short, pointed wings, their silhouettes in flight look like four-pointed stars from below.

# May 20

## Old Man of the Spring

In the book *Uncommon Beauty*, author Neil L. Jennings writes that the genus name for fleabanes, *Erigeron*, means "spring" (*eri*) and "old man" (*geron*), and probably refers to the overall hairiness of these types of plants. The common name of fleabane comes from the ancient practice of using bundles of these blooms to drive away fleas. It doesn't sound like its anti-pest properties were too impressive, but at least the remedy looked pretty.

It takes some studying up to tell the fleabanes apart. I think the yellow and white bloom I found today is eastern daisy fleabane, but at the moment, I'm not prepared for a botanical identification exercise. I am simply appreciating the bunches I find all over the place these days, whatever their names.

Bill Hilton, Jr.'s blog at Hilton Pond Center in South Carolina does a fantastic job describing "A Day in the Life of Daisy Fleabane," and I think this could turn into a great children's book. The plant is visited by several tiny pollinators and plays host to leaf-miner fly larvae, katydids, caterpillars, aphids, juice-sucking true bugs, and several spiders. I think the photos were taken over the course of a week, but that's forgivable. Most forgive Thoreau for condensing his twenty-six months at Walden Pond into a year in his master work.

Art takes time, and I hope these lovely blooms give us something good to look at while busily serving a vital purpose for so many creatures.

## May 21
### Veery Lane

There's a lush, green corridor that travels along the house side of the pond at Trail Wood in Hampton, Connecticut. The Teales, who donated that former farm property to Connecticut Audubon, named it Veery Lane.

Veeries are common enough in these parts during breeding season, according to All About Birds, and they are a species of low concern on the conservation spectrum, despite a gradual decline noted over the last century. They like damp areas near beaver wetlands, which makes great sense at Trail Wood where the beavers have a dam not far from the lane.

Veeries are medium-sized thrushes, and the first part of their scientific name, *Catharus*, comes from the Greek word for "pure," likely referring to their song quality. All About Birds describes their song as "ethereal" and "reedy," a common sound at both dusk and dawn in summer. The "veery" song, described as "a series of variations on veer," is how males defend their territory, pitch descending slightly and sounding as if it's whirling around in a metal pipe.[68]

These birds would have come back from Brazil around April and from now into June is the typical nesting time. They station their cup-like nests on the ground, or close to the base of a shrub. They mostly eat insects, but late in the summer into early fall—approaching migration time—they especially enjoy spicebush berries.

## May 22
### Roadside Cucumbers (Well, Sort of . . . )

On several neighborhood strolls, I have noticed the strong, distinct smell of cucumbers wafting from a leafy border, with no gardens in sight.

I think I'm smelling salad burnet from within some green tangles, and my new mission is to dig in and hunt for it. This perennial can be planted, but it often grows wild in warm weather, staying low to the ground and sporting a rosette with leaves that look a bit fern-like. The leaves can be added to beverages or cream cheese, or used as a salad component—as the name implies—and there's an old Italian saying that "salad is neither good nor pretty without burnet."

In Spain it's called *hierba del cuchillo*, and its fresh leaves (best when young) are added to cold drinks. It was also used as a medicine centuries ago, and Sharon Brown at Dave's Garden recounts soldiers in the American Revolution drinking burnet tea the night before battle to keep them from bleeding to death.

The pretty, if a bit alien-looking, red and purple flowers bloom in spring, and the bees enjoy them.

## *May 23*

### Squat, Graceful, Fragile, Creeping: Pondering the Creek Snail

Yesterday I beat the rain by getting out early to Chatfield Hollow State Park. In a favorite spot by a lively creek, I noticed what I call a periwinkle, a small, conical snail all by its lonesome in the bed of the waterway. I also call this kind of snail a periwinkle when I find it in salt water. But is it really the same creature? Salt and fresh waters are vastly different, beyond the salt or lack thereof—different temperature ranges, inhabitants, predators, prey, etc.

Tennessee state forester Steve Roark shows a picture in his blog of what looks like my find and explains that, at least in his area, these freshwater snails are known as periwinkles. They are gilled snails that can breathe underwater, which isn't true for every aquatic snail. They have a "trap door" they close when predators come calling.

Roark's got an interesting theory as to the name periwinkle; he says the original spelling was pinewincle—"wincle" a nickname for a snail and "pine" referring to the pin folks would use to get at the meat. More official etymology seems to differ, but I like his story.

When I click into Connecticut on the American Fisheries Society's map of freshwater snails of the US and Canada, I count about forty. Among their many common names are the squat duskysnail, the graceful fossaria, the fragile ancylid, and the creeping ancylid. My favorite name is the banded mysterysnail, so named in 1834. The Minnesota Department of Natural Resources says they are so named because "females give birth to young, fully developed snails that suddenly and 'mysteriously' appear."[69]

I still don't know which periwinkle I found—maybe a henscomb hydrobe? I'd need an expert to help me sort it out. In the meantime, periwinkle will do.

# May 24

## First Fireflies

What a thrill to spot the year's first fireflies! At first, they almost seem like an hallucination, just some small, far off, flashing lights here and then gone. They are so very emblematic of summer. Could it be that the year's longest, warmest days are just around the corner?

Most firefly beetle larvae live underground or in rotting logs over the winter, although they can also reside in deeper spaces between tree bark. The larvae look worm-like but have also been likened to armadillos as they have protective, overlapping plates on their backs. Interestingly, all the larvae across firefly species are bioluminescent, but some adult fireflies lose their ability to glow. The Xerces Society says that of the glowing adults, some are glow-worm females that produce a long-lasting glow, while others emit their glow in a flashing pattern.

On several late spring and summer walks in East Haddam, my companions and I have been treated to a glorious, enchanting light display of the flashing variety. It's impossible to imagine tiring of this show.

# May 25

## Moose Spit and Related Musings

My time outside has been limited as I recover from a knee replacement. I have dreams of this new knee taking me down many trails. (And if I can get that second new knee, too, that will really be something!)

The silver lining of being confined is the opportunity to catch up on good reads. I was delighted to find two reads by prolific writer David G. Haskell in the *Emergence Magazine* that came with me to the hospital and back. One of the pieces is "Eleven Ways of Smelling a Tree,"[70] and he does a good job conveying science as well as the personal perspective on how we relate to our tall, leafy friends and their particular scents.

In the part about white oaks, whose tannins contribute to scents like dark tea and cloves, Haskell riffs on the specificity of animal saliva to work on tannins in plant matter. Moose saliva, for example, subdues the tannins in aspen and birch. Haskell explains that hungry moose likely benefit from low-dose tannins and other plant chemicals to combat fungi and bacteria, and chemical oxidation. If animals have upset stomachs, they will seek out tannins as this can purge intestinal parasites.

Also, spit is specialized. Beaver saliva works well with willows; mouse saliva fits perfectly with acorns. We humans can handle tannins well with our saliva, and we are set apart from other animals in that we can manage this all year and across many plants. Often, saliva readiness is seasonal for other creatures. Black bear spit can also manage a good array of tannins.

I like to contemplate how we mammals have so much in common and yet are also highly tailored, each to meet our own species' particular needs. The old Biblical expression, "fearfully and wonderfully made," (Psalm 139:14) captures this for me. "Fearfully" rings odd to the modern ear, but it's an old use of the word meant to convey awe and reverence.

## May 26

### Kin Are a Leash, a Skulk, an Earth

I only spotted kin once, but I look every time I walk by. An old barn nearby has been host to a fox family. A group of foxes is referred to as a leash, a skulk, or an earth. Earth also refers to the home of the fox.

One of the three fox pups that peeked out from under the barn was braver than the others, driven by curiosity about me. Ki would take a few cautious, yet delightfully bouncy steps and then head back toward its den.

The only red foxes found in Connecticut are hybrids of red foxes introduced from Europe plus red foxes native to our continent. We also have gray foxes, but they are more reclusive. The pups I saw were gray, but to make matters more confusing, sometimes red foxes aren't red!

Did you notice I wrote "ki" instead of "he," "she," or "it," and "kin" instead of "them"? Robin Wall Kimmerer, author of *Braiding Sweetgrass*, explains this much more eloquently, but here's my try: How we talk about creatures reflects and influences how we view and treat them, and the fact that we often refer to animals and plants as "it" doesn't jibe well with viewing them as our equals, in that they, like us, are dependent on the earth and the connectedness of all things. In the Potawatomi Nation's language, per Kimmerer, there is no way to call a creature an "it."

Kimmerer's suggested new pronouns for living beings that are not human: "Ki" instead of "it" derives from the sound at the end of an Anishinaabe word meaning "a living being of the earth." And the plural of "ki" can be "kin." So, with the foxes, kin are under the barn. I like the warm sound of it, and how it highlights the many brothers, sisters, and cousins we have.

## May 27

### Spring Loaded: Mountain Laurels Gearing Up to Bloom (and Pounce!)

My friend has a mountain laurel party every year. What better way to celebrate spring?

Earlier this spring, I came across rows of mountain laurels in the woods and thought ahead in anticipation; how lovely it will be to walk this path when they are in bloom! I haven't seen this happen in my area yet, but maybe it's time to climb into the state forest and investigate. Will I find the burgeoning buds?

The unopened blossoms have little, funny-looking knobs. These end up, when the flowers open, to be little pockets that hold the anthers where the pollen is stored. The weight of a pollinator, such as a native bumblebee, will trigger the constricted anther to spring and dust the bee with a nice dose of pollen. Clever, huh?

I wondered about the color of the blooms, which I recall as being both white and pink. A 1978 article in the *New York Times* by Joan Lee Faust talks about studies that took place back then: "For those who thought mountain laurel has only white flowers, the research collection at the station's Lockwood Farm near Hamden is a revelation. Some have deep red buds that open to pink flowers, giving the laurel a calico effect. Others have almost pure white flowers. One named Goodrich has what is described as a banded flower — a deep red band on the edge of the petal is lined with a pencil-thin white trim. Other flowers are pure pink, some almost red."[71]

What variations will we find this spring?

# May 28

## Confined and Comforted

For three days running since my knee replacement, I have made it out to the porch. Seemingly tiny excursions are surprisingly exhausting, but porch trips are well worth it.

One of my post-op reads is *Man's Search for Meaning* by Viktor R. Frankl. In it the Holocaust survivor recounts his experience as a concentration camp prisoner, but it is much more than a memoir; Frankl writes about what gives life meaning.

While out on the porch, it struck me how even the most transient encounters—a tiny spider descending a long strand from our bedroom light fixture, the briefest sighting of a hummingbird buzzing by the begonias, a handsome house finch pair flitting nearby—have given me such a lift.

So I shouldn't have been entirely surprised to see Frankl treasuring the same types of things right alongside unspeakable scenarios in the camps. One time, a fellow prisoner called the others outside to witness the astounding colors of that evening's sunset. Another, Frankl recalled when a bird landed on a nearby heap of soil and watched him steadily, right when he had been thinking about his wife. I was moved by his conversation with a dying young woman who was talking to a blossoming chestnut branch outside her window. She reported, with surprising cheerfulness, that the tree talked back, telling her "I am here" and "I am eternal life."

Exposure to natural scenes, even if "secondhand" in the form of murals or videos, can have a calming effect for prisoners. In the book *Nature, Love, Medicine: Essays on Wildness and Wellness,* essayist Nalini Nadkarni recounts the Moss-in-Prisons project at minimum and medium security prisons. The inmates observed and recorded data on moss growth over eighteen months. One inmate watched the moss avidly, observing: "though it's been shut up in a dark place for so long, it's still alive and growing this morning . . . like me."

## May 29
### Foot of the Shagbark: A Place for Patience

Alongside our garage is a shagbark hickory, a tree easy to identify in any setting given its namesake telltale bark. I have wondered why I never find any nuts near its base. An agricultural extension website tells me these trees do not produce nuts for about two decades, and relatively few are made until about the four-decade mark. Optimum nut production comes between sixty and two hundred years.

The shagbark has both male and female flowers; male flowers are in bundles called catkins, and female flowers are in clusters known as petallets. I didn't look closely enough to see them earlier this spring and will have to go out with binoculars to see what I can spot toward the top.

Chef Odessa Piper's article at the Art of Eating says shagbark nuts have "more flavor . . . more snap, more tooth feel than either pecans or walnuts."[72] Will our family be at this house long enough to sample some of the tree's output? I hear shelling these long-awaited treats is a bear, but I also read that Native Americans developed an ingenious process for it—a tidbit to hang on to for some future harvest, if I'm here long enough!

## May 30
### Not Suitable for Nesting: Tell It to the Robins

The American Rhododendron Society says rhododendrons and azaleas (both of the *Rhododendron* genus) are found everywhere, from the Arctic to the tropics. Here in New England, rhododendrons are ubiquitous, gracing many yards with their purple flowers this time of year.

We have seen robins flying in and out of these shrubs pretty predictably over the years. We can't always spot their nests clearly, and they are shy and watchful of our presence. Robin mothers can be so fearful of predators that they will avoid approaching the nest if they think they are being watched. So we resist the temptation to snoop.

This year our rhododendron robins built their nest below our hall window. We can press our faces against the glass and look right down at the mom incubating her clutch, and we marvel at the four bright blue eggs when she flies off. If a squirrel, snake, crow, or blue jay doesn't interfere, we may get to watch the babies hatch and fledge.

I looked up "rhododendrons and nests" today and was amused to read that rhododendrons do not make a suitable nest spot because their branches don't make three-pronged forks. Apparently, no one has told the many generations of robins who have started families just adjacent to our house, unfailingly in rhododendrons.

## May 31

## Weeping, with Joy: Trees to Climb Inside

I fondly remember the twin weeping mulberry trees on my grandparents' front lawn in Freeport, New York. Not only could we pick the berries, but we could disappear through the long, leafy strand branches and stand alongside the trunk, looking at the world through leaf-colored lenses. I wish I could go back there now, climb inside and inhale the scent, enjoy being hidden and shaded, and sense a "hug" from the tree.

As I researched more trees that beckon us into their depths, I realized that these are often trees that "weep." Bayard Cutting Arboretum on New York's Long Island has had to fence off its iconic, 130-year-old weeping European beech, but whenever I visit, I long to climb into the inner sanctum and recline along a large, rangy limb. Yale University also boasts such a tree and Yale Nature Walk has the perfect description: "In the late spring, summer and into autumn, the canopy creates an umbrella-shaped room, almost fully enclosed on all sides, dark green leaves creating the roof and walls."[73]

Our rhododendrons don't weep, and they aren't big enough for an adult to climb into, but I have a treasured memory of Gavin climbing into the bush below our kitchen window when he was small:

> Crouched below
> the green and purple show,
> his cave boasts pressed mud floor,
> curving shelves, a secret door.

> He sinks softly into welcoming loam,
> gazes through leaves to dazzling sun,
> inspects the nest beyond his climb,
> hums a tune to pass the time.

At dusk, he crawls from the arms of the boughs,
out from his spell, back into the house

Drifting to sleep, his mind again seeks
his cave below blossoms,
his treasure beneath.

## June 1

## The Camper's Soundtrack

Last night Gavin slept in the yard in his well-appointed camping hammock, complete with mesh tent and rain fly. Maybe "slept" is a generous
term. He considers the evening a trial run that will allow him to sleep
better next time, when he will take a sleeping bag into the hammock to
keep all parts evenly warm. His insomnia-tainted report was mostly about
sounds; sleeping outdoors really tunes us in to creature neighbors we take
little notice of during the day. The star of the night show? A cacophony of
gray treefrogs. They seem much more plentiful around here lately. We owe
that to our neighbor's new man-made pond.

I haven't had much luck spotting these frogs; they blend in remarkably
well with tree bark and change color in response to their surroundings.
And, of course, they are active at night, making a search for them harder.
The best chance for spotting them is when they are mating in the water.
The male grasps the female with his front legs as the female deposits up
to two thousand eggs that get externally fertilized. Small egg clusters are
attached to structures via a transparent, outer mucous layer.

I've been generalizing a bit here, as there is more than one type of gray
treefrog. In New England, we have the northern gray treefrog as well as
Cope's gray treefrog, and they look identical! It's the calls that distinguish
them. Cope's calls are much faster.

There's a bird-voiced treefrog down south, common in the Florida Panhan-
dle. They look similar to the Cope's variety but their songs sound more like
those of exotic birds than of their cousins' songs in the North.

As Gavin finally drifted into a good sleep, the dawn chorus—my favorite
sound in nature—woke him at 4 a.m. He made a recording. Maybe his
backyard audio adventure was worth some missed sleep.

## June 2

### Gold and Green, With Sweat to Thank

Saturday found me at Zen Mountain Monastery in Mount Tremper, New York. As I sat by a small, peaceful pond, I noticed how much more life resides there than might initially meet the eye. The pond itself boasts minnows, salamanders, tadpoles, dragon- or damsel-flies ovipositing, and green frogs. And that was just the obvious stuff! I wished I could walk into the muddy muck and see what else I might find! The earth around me crawled with ants and crickets, and an occasional yellow butterfly flitted past.

I sat on a log and leaned toward the water, my hands hanging lazily off my knees. Soon a diminutive insect landed on one pale hand, straddling my blue vein. Its iridescence had me mesmerized. Mostly it was a glimmering green, but its wings were a handsome amber, laden with sparkle to rival any jewel.

A sweat bee had found me. As their name suggests, these tiny bees are drawn to human perspiration, and I had plenty of that, having just climbed a big hill on a warm day. Some make their home in rotting wood, which was all around me. Others nest in the ground. Unlike other common bee types, many sweat bee species are solitary creatures. They are important pollinators of quite a few plants.

Maybe this one got a bit of nutrition from me. I enjoyed watching it wander on my hand for quite some time; he or she only flitted away when I created a shadow with my phone during several failed attempts to photograph it. I didn't resist the urge to capture this insect's beauty in a permanent image, but I wish I had. Time slowed to a wondrous crawl during its visit, and it was, although tiny, a blessing that felt expansive.

## June 3

### While You Were Sleeping: Stealth Pollinators

I released a gray and white moth from my front hallway into the wilds of my porch yesterday, hoping he or she might still have substantial time left to enjoy the spring nights, meet a mate, maybe do some pollinating. On average, moths have an adult life of two to four months. My find looked like it would blend beautifully with tree bark, slipping into the picture undetected.

I know that moths are pollinators but was delighted to read about new research that elevates that role much higher than we first thought. A study in *Biology Letters* found, as summarized by Science Daily, that "moths transport pollen from a high number of plants also visited by bees, butterflies and hoverflies, but also interacted with plants not commonly visited by these insects."[74] The lead author noted that moths' nocturnal roles have been overlooked; they do a thorough job complementing the work of daytime pollinators while at the same time feeding birds and bats. Studies have focused on their marvelous, unfurling "tongues" (proboscises), but it turns out their fuzzy bodies do a great job picking up pollen as they sit in flowers. (Note: many adult moths do not eat. They got over that when they left caterpillar-hood behind. But these noneating varieties can certainly pollinate by virtue of where they might land!)

When Gavin was young, we'd go on the porch at dawn and see what moths had settled on the wall. It was wonderful to watch his eyes widen in discovery! Spending some time looking at an outer wall—or if your house is like mine, even the front hallway—can be a fun entomological journey and further proof that, as my friend Lynn says, nature finds us—no complicated expeditions required.

## *June 4*

## Inside the Spring "Snow Globe"

Having a cottonwood tree means that about this time of year, there is a swirling "storm" of white fluff on a breezy day.

I wondered how far a cottonwood seed could travel. One tree can disperse up to twenty-five million seeds, each embedded in a fuzzy mass of fibers. Few will germinate; they need to land in a sunny, moist spot, and they only remain viable for a week or two. Those that hit the right spot under the right conditions sprout within a day.

One clever study released mock seeds attached to tiny yarn fragments painted with fluorescent paint. Scientists used black lights to help collect the glowing "seeds" at night. The farthest seed was found one thousand feet away. Most fell within thirty-three feet of where they started.

Wind, water, animals, explosions, and fire: these are the many ways seeds can travel. Water wins the prize for facilitating the biggest drift range—how far a seed can travel. A tropical member of the morning glory family produces something called "Mary's bean." It's been found to travel from southern Mexico and Central America, via ocean waterways, all the way to Norway, fifteen thousand miles away.

The "explosion" means of dispersal is, of course, a micro-explosion, but if you are there when some seedpods burst open, you can hear the popping noises! Wisteria and violets are some plants that "explode." As for fire, certain types of pinecones require heat from a fire to open.

Seeds transported by animals can be excreted or carried (e.g., burrs). How far can these travel? A University of Cape Town study suggests African savanna elephants win the prize for land animal seed carrying distance— up to sixty-five kilometers. Their digestive systems can hang onto a seed for up to ninety-six hours.

This entry started with local cottonwood fluff and ended with African elephant dung. It mirrors seed dispersal; you never know where something might end up!

## June 5

### Beach Birds at the Farm

It was a Chinese food takeout kind of evening, and I wandered idly along the edge of the parking lot behind the little mall, impressed with the vast variety of plant and insect life in such an "unremarkable" strip. I found a gall posing as a pine cone, spittle bug nymphs disguising themselves, and unusual-looking black ants who seemed quite taken with the garlic mustard.

Immersed in the "grassroots jungle" as I was (thank you, Edwin Way Teale, for the term), I almost forgot there were cows to see beyond the fence. Then I had another surprise—killdeer running around among the cows! They pranced rapidly through the grass with the same gait as plovers on the beach.

I've only had a handful of close-up killdeer encounters, but each time their presence surprises me since they look like they should be on the shore. Last week, Gavin spotted a pair in an enormous, abandoned parking lot. Yesterday, I watched them coexist with the cows and their menacing hooves, running around like they owned the place. I guessed that the tasty insect life was particularly rich there. Were they nesting right there in the pasture?

I learned that they are known to nest on or near dried-out cow manure! Also, besides the "broken wing" act that ground nesting birds typically use to lure predators away from their nests, around cattle the killdeer will puff up, raise their tails, and charge at the unwitting bovines. There are reports of cattle being struck on the muzzle, then the return of peaceful coexistence once the nest is no longer threatened.

## June 6

### Butterflies and Punctuation

I took a video of an eastern black swallowtail fanning its wings on my driveway gravel. It wasn't easy to get the footage—I give butterfly photographers a lot of credit!

I've seen yellow swallowtails lately, too, and all these colors flying by have made me wonder what other butterflies I might spot. An oversized National Geographic book by my bed, *Birds, Bees & Butterflies: Bringing Nature into Your Yard and Garden*, reminded me that maybe this summer I will identify an eastern comma or a question mark.

It wasn't hard to find out why these spotted orange butterflies are so named. The eastern comma has a small, central white or silver comma-shaped marking on its more dull-colored underwing. The question mark butterfly has a question mark in a similar location, although to me it's more like a comma with a period to its left. There's also a satyr comma found out West. These flying punctuations like fruit, sap, and dung in particular, but they'll indulge in nectar as well.

You'd need fast and excellent eyes (or a patient and precise lens) to ID these markings, and I wonder if I'll ever succeed at that. In the meantime, I learned that Johann Christian Fabricus named the question mark in 1798. This Danish zoologist managed to name almost ten thousand animal species. The comma was named later, in 1842; this makes me think that its namer, Thaddeus William Harris, found what he thought was a question mark and then noticed the missing dot. This guy managed to be both a Harvard librarian and an accomplished naturalist. Oh, and he was a physician too. (I am starting to feel like an underachiever.)

Whoever named them, and whether or not you can find the punctuation markings, these butterflies are among the prettiest of flying spectacles that grace this time of year. Period.

# June 7

## Pond Flags

I assumed some irises are called "flags" because someone thought they looked like flags. Makes sense, right? But Adirondacks Forever Wild says "flag" comes from the Middle English "flagge," which meant "rush" or "reed." Not all irises are referred to as flags. There are about 280 types of irises worldwide, and about twenty-eight species are native to the United States, says the US Forest Service.

Mary H. Dyer at Gardening Know How says "flag iris" typically refers to a wild variety, such as the blue flag or the yellow flag, the latter from Europe, but now found worldwide in temperate climates. Both of these types enjoy watery areas.

Research on iris evolution in *Frontiers in Plant Science* suggests that over eons they have shifted back and forth—spots or no spots, common purple versus common yellow flowers, insect pollination shifting to bird pollination and back again. Scientists say that pollinators probably affected how the flowers shaped up and how species in this genus continue to diversify and diverge.[75]

# June 8

## Anting: Not Just for Crows, Not Just for Ants Either

NPR featured Bill Chappell's piece on how a photographer captured an odd-looking crow behavior. The crow was anting: spreading ants on its feathers and wings. The main theory is that this helps crows keep clean because natural substances excreted by ants help kill or stave off mites, fungi, other insects, diseases, etc.

This isn't a crow-specific thing. According to Eldon Greij at BirdWatching Daily, more than two hundred bird species have been observed anting. Something the ants emit may soothe bird skin during molting, since this behavior mostly coincides with late summer and early fall molts. And then there's the theory that rubbing ants rids them of their formic acid, making them much tastier.

Birds perform this behavior with other insects, too, like millipedes and beetles. Not only that, but birds have been observed rubbing moth balls on themselves, as well as lemon and lime rinds and, sadly, cigarette butts. It's not clear why, but may have to do with combating insects or parasites.

It's funny to think about all the birds I have watched, and yet I've never seen this happen. I *have* seen birds taking dust baths, which keep feathers conditioned. What else is going on in the bird world that we humans are unaware of or cannot quite understand?

## *June 9*

## Caterpillar Construction

In nature I enjoy the game of "one of these things is not like the other," which anyone who watched *Sesame Street* will remember with a sing-song lilt. I have gotten better at noticing when a plant looks different in some way, when some other creature has built a home within the leaves. I refrain from opening the door of that home, as curious as I am to see what's inside. I know I can look it up later.

I found evidence of a leaftier and a leafroller living in the same plant neighborhood. (These are not "official" names of caterpillars, just of their behaviors). A quick search brings up advice for gardeners on how to get rid of these creatures, which I understand. But it also makes me sad since they are just doing what comes naturally. At the very least, can't we admire the ingenuity of these soon-to-be butterflies and moths? At least seventeen families in the *Lepidoptera* category build shelters with leaves. A paper in the *Journal of Insect Behavior* says the silk and the caterpillar behaviors co-evolved to allow this clever construction to take place.[76]

I would love to have watched the caterpillar building the leaf "dome" that I found, spinning its silk, and pulling the leaves in one by one. I wonder how long it took? The simpler rolled single leaf I found seems less of a feat, but I was still intrigued to see how carefully its resident had sealed the leaf closed.

These shelters don't serve only the caterpillar. Hundreds of other insect types (crickets, beetles, spiders, etc.) can move in (well, not all at the same time!) when the caterpillars move out. A study showed that these "tenant" changes take place in the Brazilian rainforest, which has a dry season, and many tiny creatures find protection from ultraviolet rays in the caterpillars' creations.

## June 10

### To the Manor Born: The Copper Beech's Fortunate Mutation

The copper beech stands out. Purple leaves in spring, copper in autumn, and it reaches an impressive height and girth. It's said these trees were planted in front of prominent homes as a sign of statesmanship, and that they are trees for the rich because they are challenging, and thus expensive, to maintain. It may be thought of as a tree for the rich, but all of us can enjoy the sight of it, and if we are lucky, can find one in a public park to give us a generous helping of shade.

The purple leaves are a spontaneous mutation, and sometimes a mature beech can put out just a single branch with these leaves, according to Emilie Bonnevay at UK's Woodland Trust.

Towns love their copper beeches. Pittsford, New York, had to say goodbye to its iconic, but badly diseased, town copper beech several years ago. But they collected healthy cuttings from it and prepped them for plantings around town. Ivoryton, the town next to mine, also lost its famed, three-hundred-year-old copper beech tree in front of the inn named after it. A couple years back, someone donated a mature tree to replace it, carted all the way from New Hampshire.

## June 11

### A Book of Sedges

What is a sedge?

I didn't pay them a lot of mind before, but during my Master Naturalist class, I learned that there are entire books dedicated to these plants, like *Sedges of the Northern Forest* by Jerry Jenkins or *Sedges of Maine* by Matt Arsenault and colleagues.

In simple terms, you might say a sedge is like a grass, but they are in entirely separate families. Grasses in the *Poaceae* family typically have hollow cylindrical stems and alternately arranged leaves. But sedges, in the *Cyperaceae* family, have solid triangular stems and leaves arranged in a spiral.

Sedges are usually perennial, and they like damp environs. They tend to fly under the radar since they favor muckier spots and don't boast attractive flowers. But a blog by Edmonton Master Naturalists points out, "While sedge may not have a typical flower, an up-close look at the plant reveals its beauty; the flowers of sedge have been reduced to scales or bristles that can be quite intricate in form."[77]

They provide food and shelter and also can stabilize an area against soil erosion. What eats sedges or their seeds? Ducks, grouse, wild turkeys, sandpipers, sparrows, caterpillars, and small mammals. What shelters in them? One famous but worrying example is the sedge wren, known to build ball-like woven nests in sedges or rushes. The worrying part is that habitat decline is putting them at risk for extinction.

All those laws about wetland protection and conservation serve not just this special wren but myriad creatures in the web of wetland life.

## June 12

## The Better to (Not) See You With

My neighbor Susan sent a snapshot from her garden. A big-eyed elater was hugging the stem of her forsythia.

Neither of us knew the name for this beetle before looking it up, but it immediately made sense! (Well, at least the "big-eyed" part!) It would be hard not to notice those oversized, unblinking "eyes."

It is a click beetle, and this made me think of Eric Carle's classic and endearing kids' book, *The Very Clumsy Click Beetle*. Like the click beetle in the story, the big-eyed elater can jump, clicking as it does so.

False eyes, or eyespots, can deter predators. Experiments have shown that birds avoid caterpillars with eyespots in the correct place—correct in that it most closely mimics a snake's appearance. In the case of "eyes" on butterflies, these markings are more about conspicuous and disorienting patterns that can throw predators off. Eyespots can also attract mates, or redirect predators to a less vulnerable body part.

## June 13

### Glossy Ibis on Eagle Day

Today is a momentous day in the life of a Boy Scout. Gavin will officially have the rank of Eagle bestowed. The project he chose was grueling at times in the midst of high school demands. But the outcome? Thrilling. His gracious contact at the Stewart B. McKinney National Wildlife Refuge sent him some photos with a note: "Yesterday I was in the wildlife observation blind you folks built, and I got a few nice photos of glossy ibis. These birds nest on the Westbrook islands every summer (these could even have been born here), and they frequent the marsh to feed. Your blind will certainly help people better connect with wildlife while at the same time not disturbing them."

Glossy ibis are a treat for the eyes. From a distance, they simply look dark, sometimes mistaken for cormorants at a glance. But on closer inspection, if the light hits them right, you are treated to a mostly maroon bird with metallic green, bronze, and violet on the wings.

These birds forage by both sight and touch. They can visually pick out insects or tasty grains when foraging on dry land. But from the blind, we may get to see them probing the marsh mud for eats or even swinging their bills like a scythe. In breeding season, we may see the birds bow to each other, rattle their bills together, and preen one another.

Happily, this species has been thriving. While human disturbance, pesticides, oil spills, etc., can put them at risk, glossy ibis are listed as a species of low concern.

## June 14

### Nothing Boring about This Borer

Walking toward Simsbury's Flower Bridge yesterday, I spotted an elderberry borer along the path. He or she was about the size of a quarter (not counting the long horns). Its body was a highly sparkly indigo.

I learned that my find is in the flower longhorn family of beetles. This insect specializes in the elderberry plant and is also sometimes called the cloaked knotty-horn beetle.

According to the Blue Ridge Discovery Center in Virginia, beetle parents of this type lay eggs at the base of the elderberry's stem. The hatched larvae then burrow into the stem and down into the root system. After feeding, they form a pupal cell in the stem tissue, and it takes a full two years for the insect to mature and emerge.

When the adults greet the world, they quickly move on to snacking on elderberry pollen. Their gorgeous, not-at-all shy coloring warns predators away. The BugLady's writeup at the University of Wisconsin-Milwaukee adds that the elderberry plant can discourage grazers by making "a sneaky glycoside that produces cyanide within its consumers as they metabolize it," also pointing out that the elder flowers and ripe berries are edible, fine for human consumption. The insect's toxic appearance plus the cyanide-producing properties of the plant amount to a very cavalier existence.[78] This beetle had no need to blend into the background!

## June 15

## Cecropia Envy

I've come across a spate of photo posts from people spotting cecropia moths. Along with these, I've found photos of luna moths too. I've come across a luna moth once or twice; once at a McDonald's rest stop along I-95, resting on a shrub along a well-traveled walkway. More and more travelers stopped to peer down at the lime green being who seemed to emit a gentle glow. It only lives up to ten days in this winged state, the final stage in the life cycle, reserved for reproducing. Most of their lives are lived as caterpillars.

Cecropia moths belong to the same family and subfamily—*Saturniidae, Saturniid*—as luna moths. But they win the prize for size, being the biggest North American moth. Cecropia wing spreads measure five to seven inches, versus the luna moth's four-inch average! Cecropias are spectacular in the caterpillar stage, too, some boasting spiky yellow, blue, and red decorations along a long, pillowy body. Luna moth caterpillars are much more prominently green and have a more segmented look.

So how can I go about finding a cecropia? Well, at the caterpillar stage they especially like cherry, plum, apple, elderberry, box elder, maple, birch, and willow. Eventually, in the fall, the caterpillars will spin their three-inch cocoons for overwintering. So it seems a good idea to start with these plants. This is where the mature moths will lay their eggs.

Then again, Ric Bessin at University of Kentucky's page on the species says, "They are often found at lighted windows at night."[79] Another good excuse to linger on the porch well into evening.

## June 16

### Do Birds Speak with Us?

My friend Alison, ninety-nine, has told several tales of connecting with birds. She swears that birds appeared at certain times in her life and were messengers of deeper truths. She felt they were embodying departed loved ones, coming back to check in and reassure her. Alison is not alone—this experience crosses cultures around the globe.

You might or might not accept this belief, but science tells us that at least one type of wild bird does in fact regularly communicate with humans. The honeyguide uses a special chattering call to lead humans in Mozambique to hidden beehives; then the birds get to benefit from the human harvest. No one has trained these birds, and this win-win relationship has been going on for at least five hundred years.

I've just read *Bird Cottage* by Eva Meijer, a fictionalized account of Len Howard's life. Howard was a British naturalist who, after a career as a musician, turned her attention to cohabiting with and studying birds in Ditchling, in the UK. She argued for bird intelligence, not just instinct, and wrote *Birds as Individuals* and *Living with Birds*. Meijer seems to have done her homework, poring over Howard's archives, and if the novel stays true to the research, Howard believed that birds communicated with her, not so much vocally but by very pointed and repeated actions.

Howard became reclusive, and it seems this choice was motivated chiefly by a desire to let the birds live undisturbed, including in nest boxes in her home.

Do birds have similar conversations about us, wondering if we communicate with them?

## June 17

### Nothing to See Here: Just a Green Heron Fishing with Bait Again

Last evening, I watched the Wading Birds webinar hosted by our local Connecticut Audubon branch. Expert Joe Attwater did a great job covering all twenty-eight types seen in Connecticut, including various egrets, herons, bitterns, ibises, cranes, and rails. The best fact I learned is that the green heron is known to fish using bait! Sure enough, there are myriad videos online of these birds using bread to entice their prey. All About Birds adds that green herons have also been known to use twigs, feathers, or insects to bait fish.

Not long ago, a praying mantis was "caught" fishing for the first time, watching the water closely before reaching in and grabbing its prey (although I don't believe there was any bait involved). This makes me wonder what else nonhuman creatures may be doing when we are not watching. Their experiences and perceptions remain so unknown to us, so often. Carl Sagan said, "Our difficulties in understanding or effectuating communication with other animals may arise from our reluctance to grasp unfamiliar ways of dealing with the world."[80]

What a joy to watch and learn, with the delightful possibility of being truly surprised!

## June 18

### Bright Jewels in the Canopy: Follow the Straight Trunk

I followed a Master Naturalist on a winter walk where we identified trees by shape, bark texture, and patterns. I still find this difficult—no foliage, flowers, nuts, or berries on the trees to clue me in. One hint my tour guide gave was about tulip trees—they are known for their straight trunks!

Of course, we are at the cusp of summer, so our recent family walk at Stewart B. McKinney National Wildlife Refuge's Salt Meadow Unit was graced with a bounty of foliage and flower clues. My sister found the first clue to a tulip tree: a pale but bright green petal sporting a generous orange tinge. Once we saw one petal, we saw them all along the trail. Sure enough, we found the tall straight trunk of a tulip tree, also known as a tulip poplar, near the trailhead.

Every so often, when I happen on tulip tree petals, I am lucky enough to find a full flower that has fallen. Each petal's yellowish pale rim gives way to a deeper green, and then the orange at the base. The petals overlap to make a pleasing form that fits right in my palm. The center is reminiscent of a crown—spiky projections fanning out from what looks a bit like a pineapple—a cone from which seeds arise.

The full flowers thrive high in the tree's canopy and seeing them in their "natural habitat" often requires some neck strain. Even in winter, you can see a beige-y, dried-out-looking "flower" that retains the basic architecture of the colorful spring version.

Birds and squirrels, of course, have no trouble getting up close with the living flowers, and they relish the seeds from the blooms' inner sanctums. The trees also host tiger swallowtail and tulip tree silk moth caterpillars. Pollinators include hummingbirds and bees—and I hear tulip tree honey is pretty tasty.

## June 19

## Ninety Long Days—Will They Make It?

I thought I saw a humongous turtle from a distance as Tom and I emerged from the car. Probably wishful thinking, I thought. I am always conjuring owls from jagged tree limbs, rabbits from rocks.

This time, however, I *was* seeing a turtle—a snapping turtle in all her egg-laying glory! We gave her space but couldn't resist peeking. She had dug a hole and was dropping ping-pong ball-sized eggs into it, and they sounded like ping-pong balls too! After our twenty-minute walk, we came back, and she was still at it. I learned that this process takes several hours. Does it hurt?

We had to get to work, as much as we longed to see more. Had we been able to stay, we might have seen the turtle lay up to forty eggs in her shallow, bowl-shaped nest before covering them up and returning to the bottom of the river, where she lays in wait to clamp down on prey. Up to 90 percent of these nests are destroyed by predators, and if the young turtles are lucky enough to survive the nest, they must still make it to the water without being eaten.

I worry about these eggs, left alone. Another Deep River Landing visitor worried too, and he was contemplating erecting some kind of surround to give these new lives a better chance. I'll be visiting the spot this summer with hopes for the best.

These babies need to make it through about ninety days. Come to think of it, they'll start their trek to the water right around my birthday—with any luck! If these multitudinous siblings make it that far, they will graduate from being a group of hatchlings to being a bale of freshly hatched turtles.

# SUMMER

# June 20

## Mayflowers, Pilgrims, and Native Peoples

Those of us who attended school in the US no doubt instantly associate the word "mayflower" with the ship that transported the Pilgrims to the new world. That ship was named after what was often called "mayflower" in England, also known as the hawthorn. It's believed that the stern of the ship sported a carving of the bloom.

Here in the states, mayflower is another name for trailing arbitus and is believed to have been around since the last glacier period. This time of year, its fruits are maturing; flowering is typically in April or May. Fruits are fleshy and white, and often hard to spot.

As the name denotes, this plant trails, or "creeps." Ants have the important job of carting its seeds away, as they are attracted to the seeds' fleshy coating. This helps the plant disperse.

It's said that this plant was the first spring-blooming plant Pilgrims saw after the arduous first winter here in America. The North American Ethnobotany Database says the mayflower's blooms are the sacred tribal flower of the Forest Potawatomi people, and it is believed to have come directly from a divine source.

These plants are now considered rare, with many state laws protecting their removal. Once plucked, trailing arbutus will likely never grace that area again.

# June 21

## Budding Mountain Mint

It's a bit early for mountain mint flowers, which typically bloom from July to October. But buds on the narrow-leafed mountain mint have taken shape. Edwin Way Teale wrote about his wife, Nellie, checking on this silvery-green, foot-plus high plant in Starfield Meadow about this time of year, finding rounded masses of buds on top.

Nellie was likely motivated by her knowledge of the realms of pollinators that visit the plant when it is in full flower. I have experienced this on my block—the delight of watching scores of bees, flies, butterflies, and wasps dipping in and out of the blooms.

The genus name for mountain mint, *Pycnanthemum*, means "densely flowered," and there are more than twenty native mountain mint species in the US.

In the *News Tribune*, Nadia Navarrete-Tindall writes that, ironically, you won't find many mountain mints in the mountains![81] In this area, they like woodlands and river margins. Elsewhere, their territories include prairies and savannas. They can persist even at roadsides and other mowed or disturbed sites—as long as no one is using an herbicide there. It's said, at least for the narrow-leafed type, that rubbing the leaves on skin repels mosquitoes.

## June 22

## Foxes Starting Out: One Event-Filled Year

Today I put Buddy in the car and drove to Fountain Hill Cemetery to see what was happening at the pond.

The peak moment happened before I even parked. A slight, sleek, young fox high-stepped across the church lawn, carrying his black-feathered breakfast. I rolled down the window to get a better look and couldn't resist making some sound so I could watch him turn toward me. He (or she) seemed to have that unvarnished curiosity of youth and stared for a few moments, then went about his business around the bend.

Nicole Cosgrove at PetKeen says, "A fox's growth stages are all compressed into one event-filled year."[82] They go from being helpless cubs to adults ready to start families. The fox I saw was still quite young but likely at least twelve weeks old. At that point they begin to forage on their own.

Ecologist J. David Henry found that foxes only manage to snag birds about 2 percent of the time.[83] It surprised me a bit to learn that insects are on their menu, caught 82 percent of the time. They have a 23 percent success rate with snagging mammals.

Foxes are known for their expert pouncing strategies. They approach their prey slowly, and a successful pounce has their front feet landing smack dab on their prey. Rodents tend to get swallowed whole, but they take the time to defeather birds. And, like cats, they may play with their still-live meal before they dispatch it.

## June 23

### Summer Prizes, Berry Abundant

I've been given a list of ripenings to watch for while Gavin is away on his long-distance hike—wineberries, raspberries, blackberries, blueberries. He's attached to the ritual of berry harvest and would be crestfallen if the birds beat him to it, but I don't think these fruits will peak until well after his return. Still, I promised to watch, just in case.

Wineberries are also referred to as wild raspberries, so it gets a little confusing. A column by Mike at Gardens Alive reminds me that cultivated raspberry canes start with flowers, followed by "little hard button-shaped things that gradually develop color."[84] Wineberry flowers, however, progress to little pods, then the pods open to show their berries. Both berries pull away from the plant easily when ripe, the inedible core left behind. The resulting fruits looks pretty much the same to me.

I mirror Mike's ambivalence about wineberries, which are deemed invasive. He writes, "The topic of plants deemed to be invasive is as thorny as the canes of these berries. Are they really displacing other plants by virtue of their success? Almost certainly. Has the history of plants always been one of displacement and succession? Almost certainly. Nature is never static, and the rules of Darwin guarantee a constant changing of the guard."[85]

Josh Fecteau's New England Wild Edibles Monthly Guide tells me that both wild northern blackberries (also known as dewberries) and blueberries (high and low bush) will come out in July. The dewberries grow low to the ground, so they can be harder to spot among summer's leafy tangles. Chipmunks and mice appreciate the plants' proximity to their realm.

How rewarding to poke and pick, even with thorns demanding a careful approach. I love to watch the colored prizes pile up in my bowl, and with wineberries I get the extra satisfaction of making a dent in this invader's ever-spreading empire.

## June 24

### Something There Is that Loves (on) a Wall

At Gillette Castle State Park, Tom and I walked through the dark, dank railroad tunnel and wondered what creatures might favor its walls. A mossy, abandoned bird's nest occupied one corner, but the large slug we spotted—maybe four inches long—stole the show. I think it was a leopard slug, *Limax maximus*. When I looked it up after getting home, I learned some amazing facts.

I learned from Robert Nordsieck's The Living World of Molluscs that I could have examined the coloring on the sole of its foot to be sure it wasn't *Limax cinereoniger*. But maybe the fact that I missed this opportunity means our slug got to complete its mission to mate. Mating leopard slugs crawl to an overhanging part of a wall or branch and then climb down a long slime thread and intertwine their male organs—these and many other slugs are hermaphrodites. The sperm they exchange will later fertilize their eggs. The formation made at the end of their intertwined bodies is referred to as a "flower." The deed done, one slug climbs back up the slime, eating some on the way; the other drops to the ground. Up to two hundred offspring come from each pairing.

Slugs in this family, keelback slugs, have a rudimentary shell hidden underneath their mantles—what I think of as the "neck" area. This is vestigial; slugs evolved from shelled snails! They traded the protection of the shell for the protection of a unique and slippery slime. Also, when slugs are attacked, they contract their bodies, making it difficult for other creatures to eat them.

There is certainly much more to the leopard slug than its spots and impressive length. So many creatures have wild tales to tell—even the most sluggish of them.

## June 25

## Basic Palette, Colorful Life: Catbirds Have Stories to Sing

We must be at the height of gray catbird season in my neck of the woods. Sometimes I swear they are following me as I walk the forest path. These ubiquitous avians won't win any special recognition for their largely gray and black coloring, but they make up for that with points for originality in song. Besides their namesake meowing, which even an amateur birder can recognize, they copy songs of many other birds and patchwork them into a melody, sometimes as long as ten minutes.

Gray catbirds winter in the tropics. They come north to the same habitat year in and year out. Banding has confirmed this. If a catbird is feeling drab compared with our cardinals, jays, finches, and warblers, how must they feel when roosting in the vicinity of toucans down in the jungle?

Joe Smith, in his blog, Cool Green Science, at the Nature Conservancy, notes that time in the tropics may help explain the catbirds' taste for fruit—soaked raisins, orange slices, and even grape jelly. Their predilection has made it into Mary Oliver's poem "Catbird," one I recommend! I look forward to offering some raisins, as Oliver did, and watching the catbird's delight unfold.

## June 26

### Starting Life above the Water

A host of aquatic insects oviposit, or deposit their eggs, on vegetation in or above the water. Edwin Way Teale recounted seeing a thatched-looking elderberry leaf above Hampton Brook that contained hundreds of brownish, slanted, elongated eggs. Each egg had a small projection, which Teale recognized as characteristic of the Neuroptera order—the net-winged insects. Teale watched in fascination as minuscule, lizard-like larvae wriggled free of the eggs and plunged into the brook. There they would swim or creep around, perhaps burying themselves in mud or clinging to stones, feeding on other aquatic larvae.

In about a year, the larvae come out of the water and pupate, eventually becoming flying insects that start the whole life cycle over again. Fly tyers imitate the shapes of the adults, knowing they will tempt fish!

## June 27

### The Fisher King

At our family getaway in the Catskills, I kept glimpsing a fairly large, blue-gray and white bird in the front yard trees and eventually put the loud, mechanical rattling sound together with the bird—a belted kingfisher. He looked exotic to me—All About Birds says they are robin-sized, but he looked bigger, maybe because of the crest on his head or his out-sized bill.

How is it that these birds are, according to The Connecticut Audubon Society, "found throughout Connecticut year-round," and yet I never see one? Maybe when I am near the water I get distracted by the herons and egrets.

Their rattling vocalizations are distinctive, and I suppose to their prey—mostly fish, but less often, shellfish, insects, berries, reptiles, amphibians, and even young birds—their call is a death rattle. All About Birds describes how a kingfisher hunts, and they are clearly skilled in this regard: "When it spots a fish or crayfish near the surface, it takes flight, dives with closed eyes, and grabs the prey in its bill with a pincer motion. Returning with its prize, it pounds the prey against the perch before swallowing it head first."[86]

Belted kingfishers make burrows in bare earthen banks, typically close to water, but sometimes in a ditch, gravel pit, sand pit, etc.—not necessarily waterside. Males do most of the digging. The burrow has a macabre decor scheme, often lined with a chop shop of fish bones and scales and other leavings from crustaceans or insects.

This is one of the few bird species where the female is more colorful than her spouse. The females sport a rusty red color band around their bellies.

## June 28

## Orchestrated Maneuvers in the Dark: The Firefly Species with Rhythm

My friend Cecilia and I took a nighttime stroll this week in East Haddam and were greeted by massive numbers of fireflies putting on a show above boggy areas. I've never seen so many in one place.

They weren't in sync, and the random timing and location of the flashes were part of the treat. We tried in vain to capture it with phone camera stills and videos—no snapshot did it justice! But it was so entrancing that Cecilia brought her husband back the next night.

She was right to hurry back, since mating season lasts just two weeks during the two-month adult life span. The lights help males and females find each other. Males fly high, and those who flash brightest and fastest may stand out to the females. Females stay low, resting on the ground or the grass. When they spot a male firefly whose flash pattern speaks to them, they flash back to signal interest.

You may have heard that fireflies flash in sync, but this is only true for one American species. According to a synchronous firefly page hosted by the Great Smoky Mountains National Park in North Carolina and Tennessee, of the nineteen species of fireflies that live in those mountains, only one species is synchronous—*Photinus carolinus*. In the park, the naturally occurring synchronous firefly event is so popular that people must enter a lottery to try for a parking permit. This is surely an outing for the bucket list.

## June 29

### Glorious for Horseflies and Deerflies Too

I took Buddy, quite early, to Fountain Hill Cemetery, a lovely, lush place for summer walks. We circumnavigated the pond. A great blue heron flew off when it saw us across the water. I saw the early, bristly starts of wineberries. I watched for snakes in the lily pad-laden water. But mostly, I was consumed with swatting deerflies. Their black forms hovered, landed, and injected me with sharp little bites. They seemed to especially like my hands, and my cup of coffee.

Yes, mosquitoes, ticks, deerflies, and horseflies are part of the "nature experience" too. And, though vastly unpopular, they play specific roles in the ecosystem. For example, ticks feed many creatures. A trail cam captured an opossum eating ticks off a deer's face. To me, the deer looked grateful!

One of my first finds when I researched deerflies was an article in the *New York Times* by my writer friend Christine Woodside. It had a great title that I riffed on for today's entry: "July Is a Glorious Month to Horseflies, Too." I learned there is quite a throng of biting flies in Connecticut. The females need blood to support egg laying, and they are drawn to our breath and our sweat. They use sharp mandibles to get at our blood, hence the "ouch" factor.[87]

It's going to be another vexingly hot day, and I will be mostly at my desk for work, thus avoiding things that bite. I know one thing, though. I won't stop circumnavigating the pond. By early August most of these pests will subside, just in time for a final wineberry harvest.

## June 30

### A Twiggy Tale

Northern walkingsticks are quite abundant and found in most US states. Yet I've only had a couple close encounters with them in a natural setting.

Someone found one lingering outside the front door of my workplace and, knowing my love for most crawling things, brought it to me. It walked slowly up my arm, and we marveled at how closely the insect mirrored a gnarly twig. These nocturnal creatures extend their legs straight above and below their bodies and stay mostly still during daylight hours. Despite this clever stick mimicry, birds, mantises, and rodents are onto them. Walkingsticks end up on many creatures' dinner plates.

Walkingsticks live in the canopy and especially favor fresh oak and hazelnut leaves in their diet, so they rarely come down to where we are likely to encounter them. Plus, they feed at night. During the summer, females drop one egg at a time from high up in the canopy, each producing about five hundred eggs in her lifetime. The seed-like eggs overwinter in the leaf litter before hatching bright green nymphs who will climb up the nearest tree to feed—and later, breed.

The BugLady of University of Wisconsin-Milwaukee did a great job delicately writing up what she calls "adult content" concerning these creatures' one-year lives: "Some male walkingsticks are known to, ah, remain 'in the embrace' of a female long after sharing bodily fluids with her, becoming what Waldbauer calls 'living chastity belts' [and from which convenient position, males will also fight off rival males]. In fact, the, um, endurance record for copulation for the insect world seems to be held by walkingsticks."[88]

Unseen amorous adventures, tiny new lives tumbling from the sky—I love to think of these elusive twiggy wonders when I lean back to look at the green treetops.

## July 1

## Tiny Alligators or Bristle Brushes? Ladybug Childhoods

Maybe I missed that day in grade school when we learned about the life cycle of a ladybug. To me it's as amazing as the butterfly metamorphosis story, but I didn't learn what ladybug larvae looked like until I was an adult!

I describe them as tiny black and orange bristle brushes—I guess their spikes call out to me most. But others liken them to tiny alligators, which, weirdly, makes sense, too, when you look up close at their long, armored backs. In any case, they sure don't look like what they will eventually become—the universally recognized ladybug.

Between the "bristle brush" stage and the iconic ladybug treasured by many children, these larvae will pupate, attaching themselves to leaves and remaining still for seven to fifteen days. The metamorphosis is like that of a butterfly in that the insect's composition is basically broken down and remodeled. The finished product is smaller, shinier, and prettier (in my opinion).

Here's a new, cost-free hobby for me and other nature nerds: checking leaves for attached golden ladybug eggs and their pupating older siblings or cousins. Bonus points for watching an adult ladybug enter the world!

## July 2

### New Bunnies

I still remember how, one summer morning, Buddy proudly emerged from beneath a rhododendron with three very new bunnies in his mouth. He held them gingerly and luckily heeded Tom's command to put them down.

Chances are these were eastern cottontail bunnies, which look a lot like our native New England cottontails. The New England type are, unfortunately, at risk due to loss of habitat. Eastern cottontails mate between February and September and, while litters contain up to nine babies, only about half survive. Rabbits, of course, are known for prolific breeding. In the case of eastern cottontails, the mother can mate again hours after giving birth. They can have up to four litters each year.

Mostly, rabbits are quite solitary, and the new bunnies will leave the nest after just seven weeks, ready to mate within the month or so that follows. Eastern cottontails are mostly nocturnal, so I guess when I see them around dawn on so many local lawns, they are getting close to bedtime. I like to watch them re-emerge at dusk, quietly nibbling, occasionally standing on their hind legs to check their surroundings. Walking Buddy, a hound, during these times can end up being quite an adventure as his nose steers us frantically and determinedly toward every bunny scent in the vicinity.

## July 3

### Talented (and Macabre) Mud Daubers

I got outside early today and before long was snapping photos of impressive "condo complexes" built by mud dauber wasps on the bricks above the town library's door. Mud dauber wasps are much less aggressive in defending their homes than are other wasps, like yellow jackets, and they tend to be much more solitary too. On the other hand, if they are provoked to sting, they can sting repeatedly without dying! When you see the work that goes into building their homes, you'd think they'd be more motivated to defend them vigorously.

Female dauber wasps make their nests by gathering balls of mud and then shaping them with their heads and mandibles, using saliva as a smoothing agent. The macabre part? The female systematically gathers spiders, made so much more cooperative after she paralyzes them, to insert into the nest—about a dozen per chamber. Then she lays her egg, one per chamber, and seals the opening. When the larvae hatch, they feast on the still-alive spiders, growing and molting over time until they chew their way outside, leaving a trail of carcasses. If you are curious, search images of "spiders in mud dauber nests." Fascinating, but horrifying, especially if you are a spider.

## July 4

## High Bush, Low Bush

Gavin's been checking wild blueberry bush progress at the top of a ledge in the woods. I admit to years of ignorance about wild blueberries, and I'm still learning. I'm sure I've walked by countless blueberry plants on countless walks, oblivious to their presence. They'd never been pointed out to me when I was younger, and the plants, especially before the blooms and then berries show up, look rather . . . unremarkable to me. As with many botanicals, I am training my eyes to spot them.

If you live in my region, Maine takes the cake—more appropriately, pie—for blueberry fame. These sweet summer treats aren't limited to Maine, but the state has a reputation for blueberry goodness and blueberry passion. A blog post by Van Drunen Farms says some Mainers, as well as Canadians in the region, take time off work to help harvest wild blueberries. While the berries are often found in the wild, folks also set aside fields for letting them grow. The introduction of bees for pollination helps maximize output.

"Low bush" means you must kneel or stoop to get to the berries, while "high bush" shrubs can grow up to twelve feet. It seems worth the stoop, as the low bush berries are sweeter and more intensely flavored.

I was impressed to read that, on a good day, a black bear might eat 30,000 berries. Birds often come to mind when I think of creatures that facilitate seed distribution, but I was reminded that bears are important seed dispersers too. Seeds leave their digestive tracts whole, promising a new generation, randomly planted. A video at bear.org shows bears eating a series of berries, one berry type at a time.[89] I noticed the bear eating blueberries wasn't picky about ripe versus unripe specimens.

I went to Maine's *Bangor Daily News* to learn more, discovering a symbiosis made in heaven—or in Maine, which to some people is the same thing. Bob Duchesne writes: "Blueberries figured out how to beat the infertility of glacial soil, forming a symbiotic relationship with a particular fungus. The fungus is capable of extracting nutrients from sand, making them available to the blueberry. In return, the blueberry produces a sugar from the nutrients that it shares with the fungus. Both live happily ever after."[90]

## July 5
### Dizzying Speeds, Admirable Acrobatics: Watching the Swallows (or Swifts?)

I watch birds doing loop the loops over a marshy area. If only they would slow down, I could figure out if they are swifts or swallows!

The National Audubon Society had some answers in an article by Martha Harbison. To distinguish what Harbison calls the "feathered fighter jets"[91] that are swifts and swallows going after insects at breakneck speed, you can consider a few factors. But first, a fact that surprised me: these birds are not related, although they are often talked about at the same time. They've just developed similar traits over the years.

The best clue that I was seeing swallows was that they flew low; swifts tend to pursue their prey higher up. But I didn't notice flashes of blue, green, orange, or iridescence, which would have been another vote for swallows. Were the wings long, skinny, and fluttering (swift), or thicker near the body and then tapering (swallow)? Not a clue. They were too fast. Some swifts have been clocked at seventy miles per hour. If I could follow them to their nests, I might have some definitive proof. Swift nests are stick-based, attached to a vertical surface. Swallow nests, on the other hand, can be made of mud or are inside a tree cavity.

Putting together the clues is part of the fun of birding, and I admire the patience and tenacity of committed birders. But I am more drawn to the way writer Jonathan Franzen describes his initiation into birding in the documentary called *Birders: The Central Park Effect.* "It was like the trees were hung with ornaments . . . It was one of those rare times in an adult's life where the world suddenly seems more magical rather than less."

Whatever you call that fast bird you see dipping, plunging, and soaring to catch its meal, it's a win when you can appreciate the enchantment of that moment.

## July 6

## Too Windy for Windflowers?

Last evening our family was on the porch, watching a powerful storm. Before the thunder and lightning, before the rain, trees were swaying in the wind, framed dramatically against the uncharacteristically dark sky. Watching the power of the wind led me to wonder—a bit tangentially— about windflowers. The word "windflower" has a soothing sound, and I was sure I had looked it up before. But what were they, exactly, again?

Many gardeners know this flower by another common name—anemone. They are small, delicate, poppy-like flowers that come in a host of colors. They fit into the *Ranunculaceae* family—buttercups! And even if you know nothing about the windflower type, it's easy to guess how they got their moniker—they move with even the lightest breeze.

White Flower Farm says once windflowers are established by the gardener, they will move to fill any available space, adding they are "far too charming to be called invasive." The farm's casual use of "invasive" may be misleading as the word is typically used for plants that have been introduced from other regions and spread like wildfire in their new habitats. This differs from plants, like the windflower, that more accurately are called "aggressive." There are nine windflower species native to North America.

Narrowing the search, only one comes up as native to Connecticut— *Anemone canadensis*, or Canadian anemone. (It is a threatened species here in Connecticut.) I have spotted this sweet, white bloom with a yellow center on many woodland walks and along some roadsides, and now I will be able to name it.

## July 7

### Handsome, Fertile, Sneaky

Maybe they've been in our area quite a while, and I've just started to notice them more. Our state's Department of Energy and Environmental Protection says brown-headed cowbirds used to be prairie birds, but they've extended their range as more land has been cleared over time.

I find male cowbirds so handsome, their brown heads standing out from their shimmery black bodies. I'm not sure I would immediately ID a female if I saw her; her subdued coloring is very sparrow-like to me. Size would be a clue. All About Birds says these birds are bigger than sparrows but smaller than robins—slightly smaller than a red-winged blackbird if you want to get specific! Cowbirds are, indeed, in the blackbird family, and in the wrong light you might miss the brown head.

Brown-headed cowbirds don't build nests. Rather, they keep watch for other birds building nests, or they may race through green growth in a campaign to flush birds from their nests. Then the female hastily lays an egg in another bird's nest, having eaten or killed one of the resident eggs. Sometimes they can lay more than thirty-six eggs in one summer, and reportedly, the nests of up to two hundred bird species are parasitized by cowbirds. It appears each female favors one particular type of nest for egg deposit, and apparently, nest tastes really vary!

Why the word "cowbird"? They used to follow bison to take advantage of the insects kicked up by the bovines' heavy steps. They've also been called lazy birds, cow buntings, and buffalo birds.

## July 8

### Earwigs in the Mailbox (Again)

I admit it—I don't feel all soft and compassionate when I see an earwig. Could it be the name and its creepy association? There is a persistent myth that they like to burrow into people's ears and sometimes adventure even farther, into the crevices of the brain. It could be because they tend to creep around at night and can smell waxy, but the consensus is they can do little harm to humans, other than the occasional and not very ominous pincer squeeze in self-defense.

If you are leaning in to try to smell that waxy earwig smell, take note of the pincers and see what gender you've found. Males have curvier pincers. Also, earwigs can fly for short bursts, but I have never witnessed this!

Like every creature, they fill a specific niche in the ecological hierarchy. They clean up dead and decaying plants and insects and make a nutritious meal (or at least part of one) for birds, frogs, centipedes, spiders, and more. Does this make them more lovable?

Jason Bittel, at the *Week*, wrote, "How I Learned to Love the Evil-Looking Earwig."[92] What convinced him? The females are doting mothers who protect their eggs and then fetch food for their babies for several weeks after they hatch. It's almost enough to make you forget that the nymphs eat each other's poop (and sometimes each other).

I am going to work on a spirit of benevolence next time I get ready to open the mailbox.

## July 9

### Beware the Vicious Swallow!

Ah, swallows, so pretty to watch! But sometimes you might be innocently walking along when—wham!—a swallow aggressively dives toward your head. It's nothing personal. This is a defensive behavior to protect the nest. Swallows aren't the only birds who do this. In fact, mockingbirds are best known for this behavior. Robins also dive bomb, as do raptors, which sounds the scariest—their talons are sharp!

The universal advice is to simply avoid the nest area if you can and consider carrying an umbrella if you must be near the spot! This will allow the new babies to hatch and fledge. And, of course, keep pets away! The birds aren't likely to hurt them, but your pets could potentially harm the parents or fledglings.

## July 10

### Tents in the Trees

If you've spent any time outside here in Connecticut this past month, you've seen them—large, silk "tents" in the forks of trees, teeming with tiny (at first!) eastern tent caterpillars. I walk by some of these tents regularly and am impressed with how fast the residents grow and move out. By this time, most tents have been vacated. The host tree and surrounding foliage fed them well, and their mass exodus from their tree "nursery" means it's cocoon time. In three weeks, the moths emerge.

No one seems impressed with these caterpillars, often described as unsightly and credited with defoliating trees (some say they don't typically wreak wide-scale havoc). No one seems to pay much attention to the reddish brown moths, either. But I like what Dr. Sarah Treanor Bois of the Linda Loring Nature Foundation has to say in an issue of *Yesterday's Island, Today's Nantucket*. Eastern tent caterpillars work together to build those tents, piling layer upon layer in a feat of engineering. They lay silken threads that other caterpillars can follow for food, biting the thread when the leaves in that area have all been harvested.

Also, they are studied as indicators of climate change, according to Dr. Bois. Food for thought, and also, food for the birds. More than sixty bird species eat these creatures, so I am sure they appreciate the tent caterpillars' presence! I have a soft spot for these often unwanted "creepy crawlies" and for the soft, fuzzy-mantled moths into which they mature, living such short lives.

## July 11
### The Beaver Meadow

Doing a search on beaver meadows, I saw quickly that so many things are named after them—a golf course, a school in New Hampshire, an apartment complex, even a brand of butter! The beavers did such a remarkable job that human places and products memorialize their tireless work.

In his piece "Get Busy at Beaver Meadow Audubon Center," Scott Adamson makes his point about how beavers change their environs right at the top: "It is not some random glacial leftover. Rather, the pond is the product of a thinking force."[93] That's right—these creatures' smart and busy engineering is dramatically altering the landscape. And it is only when they move on from their work at each pond that the landscape then becomes a beaver meadow.

Tim Stanley, a forester and director at the Fresh Air Fund, explains in his blog titled the *Native Beeology* that the disturbance caused by beavers sets back succession (the filling in of an area with trees), allowing a bevy of

plants to take root in the cleared area now better lit by sunlight. When abandoned dams decompose, they provide fertile, well-drained soil for plants like
boneset and Joe-Pye weed. This, in turn, makes pollinators happy!

The US Fish and Wildlife Service describes beaver meadows as "islands"
of wetland plant communities very different from surrounding areas. The
snags created by beavers girdling trees and flooding the area makes many
birds happy too. There's something about happening upon one of these
distinct, snaggy patches that makes me happy along with the meadow's
more direct beneficiaries. It is a pocket of wilder existence, often tucked in
among our own industrious engineering.

Simon Worrall's *National Geographic* article framing beavers' return from
near-extinction as a conservation success notes that these energetic mammals can help combat climate change by keeping rivers and streams wet all
year, compensating for less snowpack and glacial melt. He cautions, "We
just need to stay out of their way."[94]

## July 12

### It's a Bird, It's a Plane, It's . . . a Water Strider?

The most asked question about water striders (also known as water skimmers, pond skaters, and Jesus bugs) concerns how they walk on water.
They take advantage of a delicate membrane that forms on the surface of
the water and are aided by minute hairs that repel water and capture air. If
you look at a close-up video, they look much like accomplished ice skaters,
gliding with ease across a slick surface.

As if walking on water wasn't miraculous enough, there's the whole thing
about their wings. Matthew L. Miller at Cool Green Science explains that
the presence and length of their wings is dictated by habitat. Wings are
shorter for water striders that live in fast-moving waters; this way they are
less prone to damage.

Also, wings can skip generations. If the habitat is threatened, wings are
needed to find a new place. But if the striders find themselves in a plentiful habitat, the young will not need wings because they won't provide a significant benefit, and they require more energy. Some water strider types
(there are 1,700 species) live in the ocean—no wings needed there! It is
thought that ocean varieties feed on dead, floating animals, while their
freshwater cousins sup on fallen dragonflies or mosquito larvae.

I've never seen a water strider fly, but maybe I will now that I am scanning the sky for them, having just tuned into their flying lives. It would help if I was creating a garden pond. Miller marvels at how, when a new body of water appears, such as a garden pond or when a canal is filled, the striders often arrive within minutes.

## July 13

### Forest Oranges

It's no surprise that autumn walks in New England woods are suffused with orange, owing to chlorophyll breaking down in the leaves of countless trees. But I have found that orange "pops" more in summer; it's generally low to the ground and more scattered.

Forest oranges had been on my mind since Gavin found some choice chanterelle mushrooms in the Cockaponset State Forest. The foraging experience isn't just blissful gathering and savory meals. Poisonous jack-o'-lantern mushrooms can be mistaken for chanterelles, as can false chanterelles. So, careful ID is key! One small trick: real chanterelles smell like dried apricots. That said, it's easy to convince yourself that this is what you are smelling because you want your chanterelle to be the real thing! There are many other factors that must be checked for safety.

Fun factoid: jack-o'-lantern mushrooms glow in the dark! The glowing compound is the same one that makes fireflies glow. Darrell Cox and Andrew Miller at the Illinois Natural History Survey site say, "people in the far north are reported to have marked forest trails with pieces of rotten, glowing wood to enable them to find their way back at night."[95]

A casual check makes me think the mushrooms I found today might be orange peel mushrooms, described by Wikipedia as, "edible, though not necessarily choice."[96] And another orange find today—a tiger lily. These are edible, but, as with mushrooms, you must be sure what you've got! For example, if you eat an Asiatic lily, you will suffer dire consequences.

Reflecting on all the cautions and caveats regarding oranges forest finds and whether they are edible, I am content to feast with my eyes.

## July 14

### A Whiter Shade of Pale: The Indian Pipe

When Gavin and his friend Sara were very young, they came across Indian pipe in the woods and quickly decided it was an alien creature, here to take over, something to run away from while giggling and exclaiming!

There is something otherworldly about the Indian pipe's ghostly white, droopy blooms. Some of its other names—ghost pipe and corpse plant—speak to this effect. I learned today that it's also been called ice plant, not only because of its looks but because it "melts" when handled. Its scientific name, *Monotropa uniflora*, means "one turn, one flower," the one turn referring to the droop. That droop is gradually corrected once an insect pollinates the plant.

Unlike most plants, the Indian pipe doesn't use photosynthesis. It gets its nutrients from mushrooms, which act as middlemen between tree roots and the ghostly growth.

The US Forest Service notes that Emily Dickinson was a fan. In a letter, she wrote, "I still cherish the clutch with which I bore it from the ground when a wondering child, an unearthly booty, and maturity only enhances the mystery, never decreases it."[97]

What do you remember being intrigued by as a wondering child? Have you held on to that awe, that sense of mystery, as Emily did?

## July 15

### Yucca and the Baader-Meinhof Phenomenon

I doubt there's been a mad rash of people planting yucca everywhere, but it sure seems that way! One day I noticed these white "belled" plants as the star of a particular parking lot's median landscaping, and my friend Susan had to tell me what they were. In the weeks since, I have seen yucca all around me. Suddenly noticing something everywhere is referred to as the Baader-Meinhof phenomenon.

Mr. Smarty Plants, the advice columnist at Lady Bird Johnson Wildflower Center in Texas, was surprised to learn yucca plants grow in Connecticut. Yuccas are most often thought of as desert succulents that survive arid conditions. There are twenty-eight native North American types, and exactly one is native to Connecticut. *Yucca filamentosa* (Adam's needle) is anthropogenic, meaning it likes man-made or disturbed habitats—plenty of those in Connecticut. The USDA reports that its roots were used by the Cherokee, Catawba, Nanticoke, and other Native peoples to stun fishes. The roots were also used as a soap component because they contain saponins, which make foam when shaken with water.

Wimberg Landscaping's gardening blog declares yuccas "thuggish," saying, "If you want to change your mind about having a yucca, or just want to move it, it will leave its calling card behind and you will likely find more yuccas popping up in short order."[98]

Maybe this "vice" of spreading "thuggishly" is a virtue in cemeteries. I saw masses of yuccas on my recent cemetery walk. They have been called eternity plants as they can live for hundreds of years and have been used as grave markers when a headstone was unaffordable. Historical reports reflect yucca use in old African American cemeteries, which may also connect with Haitian beliefs in the living spirit, never ended by physical death.

Now that I have brought yuccas to your attention, maybe you'll start seeing them everywhere too!

## July 16
### Harvestmen in the Thousands

I was astounded to learn there are more than six thousand species of arachnids known for their especially long, thin legs and compact bodies. Harvestman is a common moniker, as is daddy longlegs. These are not true spiders since their bodies aren't divided into two distinct segments.

Many of these arachnids feed on both creatures and plant matter. Why the "harvestman" nickname? They are often seen in fields at harvest time.

Master Gardener Candice Hawkinson writes that it was once believed that these creatures could find lost cattle. If you picked one up by seven of its eight legs, the free leg would point in the right direction.

Unlike true spiders, harvestmen have only two eyes and they don't weave webs. Their legs are seven-jointed, with the unique advantage of easily detaching and sometimes continuing to twitch, so these creatures can scurry away from a predator.

## July 17

## Sweet Music for Hummingbirds

Trumpet vines are in full force by the library parking lot. To us humans and other mammals, the leaves and flowers can cause skin redness and swelling, and ingestion is not a good idea—the USDA says the plant is slightly toxic. UConn's plant database describes this gorgeous bloomer as having "invasive tendencies" as it can "escape" from cultivated areas. It seems to be more of a problem in the Southeast, where the plant has nicknames like hellvine and devil's shoestring. Experts advise cautious admiration and careful babysitting to be sure it doesn't get out of control.

The lingo around plants amuses me. We have "escapees," but I've also heard random plants that pop up in the garden called "volunteers." I guess some plants hunger to break OUT of the garden perimeter, while others are eager to get IN!

Whatever humans think of this plant, trumpet vines are music to the taste buds of hungry hummingbirds. The shape of the blooms is a perfect fit for their long tongues. The high nectar content doesn't hurt, and the brilliant color is like a beacon. Hummingbirds are trumpet vines' primary pollinator, according to Matt Candeias at the In Defense of Plants blog.

## July 18

## Flying Blue and White Fluff

I see them here and there, but today I finally caught one—what looks like a bit of fluff from milkweed or some other such plant but, on closer observation, is a flying, blue insect, much smaller than my pinky nail and trailing an impressive white train.

The blue part? The insect's body. The white part? What seems an impossible amount of "fluff" in proportion to its body size. The "fluff" is more accurately described as "white, waxy filaments," per Charley Eiseman, a freelance naturalist and writer. A grandmother commenting on Bryan Pfeiffer's blog about these same creatures, woolly aphids, shares, "I tell my grandson that these are faeries," and I can see why. They look ethereal. The one I caught today seemed so fragile; I was worried that, despite my gentle handling, I might have done some damage.

Despite their wispy and frail appearance, these insects have a few peculiar strengths. Their reproductive capabilities in springtime require no males, and the wingless females born from this male-free form of reproduction perform live births (versus lay eggs)—quite unusual in the insect world. Later in the year, there is egg laying as a result of more typical mating between genders.

At a wingless stage, these tiny creatures coat a plant in white "fluff," convening en masse as they suck liquids from it.

The Connecticut Agricultural Experiment Station says these aphids are more likely to present a serious problem for plants when they are protected from their natural enemies (like in a greenhouse) or when insecticides have destroyed their natural enemies. They have lots of natural enemies: ladybeetles, lacewings, syrphid fly larvae, pirate bugs, and parasitic wasps.

## July 19

### Chanterelle Enchantment: Under the Foraging Spell

"Empires come and go. Chanterelles are timeless." So says Sylvain de Ville-Amois in her book, *The Chanterelle Chronicles: A Myth*.

Last night we shared chanterelles cooked in butter and garlic over angel hair pasta. I am 95 percent sure these were true (not false) chanterelles (both are edible) and absolutely sure they were not toxic jack-o'-lantern mushrooms—also orange and sometimes mistaken for the real deal. Gavin was thrilled to harvest them. On his first attempt, he was crestfallen when he realized he'd brought home jack-o'-lanterns—the stems in that case were orange through and through.

There is something enchanting about picking dinner in the woods, but the name "chanterelle" implies "cup" and has nothing to do with the word "enchanted." I think we might have had the smooth chanterelle variety, *Cantharellus lateritius* (translates to "bricklike cup"—the "brick" referring to a specific anatomical feature), but there are others that might pass for it. *Cantharellus cibarius* means "cup of food," and I like the ring of that name better.

I'm not sure I'll ever graduate to expert forager, but the little steps along the way, with puffball mushrooms, old man of the woods, chicken of the woods, hen of the woods, and jelly roll mushrooms before this, have been a blast. It's fun to expand the repertoire. Whether or not you choose to go down this tasty but ever-vigilant path, I hope that you find something to feast on in nature today, if only with your eyes, ears, or spirit.

## July 20

### After the Fires

Fireweed first caught my eye while watching an episode of the survival show *Alone*, the Arctic season. A clever survivalist was gathering all the fireweed he could because the plant packs a lot of nutrition and medicinal qualities, invaluable once winter reaches its peak.

Then I listened to a WERU (Maine) podcast by Rob McCall. Fireweed, a member of the evening primrose family, was on the topic menu! McCall explained the name: this plant is one of the first to float in on fluffy fibers, like milkweed, and take root after an area has been burned clean of plant life. He noted that it's been called "bombweed" in the UK because of its appearance in bombed out areas during WWII.[99]

Most of the US states, except about twelve in the south, and all of Canada host this plant, according to a USDA map. It's the official emblem for Canada's Yukon Territory and some Alaskans have argued it should be their state flower, instead of the forget-me-not.

When the plant is in its "fluffy" state—gone to seed—it has a spindly look and rhubarb-ish color. But in warm weather, it's entirely different. It's described by the USDA as a "tall, showy wildflower" (up to nine feet!) that likes meadows, streams, roadsides, and forest borders. Sometimes it can fill whole meadows with brilliant pink flowers. The promise of its showy purple or pink blooms is not lost on bees and butterflies, and humming-birds like the nectar too.

How many times have I walked by fireweed, *Chamerion angustifolium*, having no idea what it was? I think of the increasing wildfires out West and fireweed's potential role in the aftermath. I find it comforting that something that looks so pretty and even frail proves so pioneering and tenacious.

## July 21

### Amateur Lepidopterist

My neighbor Susan sent snapshots of a moth clinging to her outer basement wall, and my best guess was that it is a blinded sphinx moth. Why blinded? Its eye spots during the caterpillar stage don't have the typical "pupil."

Why is this moth family named sphinx? BugGuide shares an 1858 quote, showing they are so named because of the "the fancied resemblance of the larva, when in repose, to the Egyptian Sphinx." That seems quite a stretch to me, as to me the caterpillars look kind of. . . goofy, all big heads and "eyes."

Most of the fun, for me, is in the watching and wondering and learning, rather than the naming. The caterpillars eat the leaves of deciduous trees, and we've sure got a lot of those here. I found a YouTube video with footage of blinded sphinx moths mating.[100] The effect is a bit kaleidoscopic—repeating curves and angles, intertwined.

## July 22

### Fern Balls Everywhere!

Yesterday allowed time for only an abbreviated walk, and Winthrop Cemetery was a great place to stretch my legs, muse about history, and see what was growing and thriving. This cemetery was once known for its rare, wild orchids, and I'm not sure if they still pop up here. The most eye-grabbing "décor" came in the form of multiple ferns with their leaves balled into orbs—it was easy to see that these orbs had been pulled together with silk webbing.

Who made these enclosures, how, and why? Joe Boggs at Ohio State University's Extension site writes about at least three moth species known to be fern leaftiers during the caterpillar stage. During their development, the caterpillars "sew" multiple balls, so they are sometimes seen in close clusters. It's not clear if in some cases the caterpillars and their orbs are exclusive to one type of fern or the other, and one leaftier species was only identified in 2011, so there is still much to learn. But one theory is that these constructions help protect the caterpillars from parasites. From what I've read, this process is generally not harmful to the ferns—not on a significant scale, anyway.

Leaftiers have "cousins" that are leafrollers, and last week I found a "cigar" made of leaves on a beech. A time lapse video of a leaftier at work shows quite a lot of frass (poop), and it seems frass is used to help conceal their presence.[101]

## July 23

### Green Frogs and Their Tadpoles

At first I think there are no frogs among the lily pads and muck of Fountain Hill's shallow pond, but then I spot one bug-eyed, brownish-green head sticking up. Before long, I see another, and another. I hear a little squeal as a frog on the grass detects me and plunges back into the water.

*Lithobates clamitans* is the scientific name for the green frog. The first word is Greek, and I understand it means "a stone" (*litho*) and "one that walks or haunts" (*bates*). *Clamitans* is Latin and means "loud calling." So a hauntingly ambulatory stone that makes a lot of noise?

When the green frog is still, it is still as a stone. And then, of course, we detect it when it moves or cries out. I'm not sure about the "haunts" implied by the name, but that can fit, too, in the sense that it keeps reminding us of its presence during the dark of night.

The Virginia Herpetological Society helped with these translations and other facts too. According to their write-up, by this point the breeding period has finished in my area. Eggs nestle among aquatic vegetation within a foamy layer. Stooping down and peering into the pond reveals tadpoles, linked to a happy memory of Gavin's day care center taking all the kids, boots donned, to the pond with buckets and nets, pulling up and releasing frogs and their young.

The rubber band quality of the green frog song is up there with cricket vocalizations as a song of summer. Now that I know the meaning of the scientific name, I am reminded of a Bible verse in which Christ talks about how the stones would cry out if the humans were to fall quiet.

## July 24

### Sumac, that Cool, Refreshing Drink

I harvested some sumac with Gavin. We were careful to follow the principle of the Honorable Harvest, which we read about in Robin Wall Kimmerer's *Braiding Sweetgrass*. We made sure to leave some so other creatures can benefit and the plant can continue to propagate.

A misconception that all sumac is poisonous continues. Ronald Halwell at the Edible East End does a great job explaining the differences among sumac varieties. It would be hard to confuse edible sumac and poison sumac. The edible type, staghorn sumac, is common in my area and boasts large, red cones, while the poisonous plant has small white berries in clusters.

I was an adult before I was aware of the tasty sumac that's so abundant. Once you start looking, you see it everywhere. A leader on a nature hike encouraged his charges, me included, to lick the staghorn. Lemony! Recipes for sumac-ade are easy and abundant. They basically involve crushing the sumac in cold water, straining the concoction, and adding sweetener.

Sumac plays an important role in birds' lives, especially when fall comes and many other foods, like the summer berries, have come and gone. Birds chomping on the cones may be getting some extra protein in the form of insects that nestle within the clusters.

## July 25

### Monarch or Viceroy?

To untrained observers, monarch and viceroy butterflies look alike. Plus, butterflies have the vexing habit of refusing to hold still so they can be identified! If I am lucky enough to watch one who has stopped for a bit (and maybe snap a photo so I can look even more closely afterwards), I can see whether the butterfly in question has a black line across the hindwing. That would indicate a viceroy.

I learned from Journey North that monarch flight is more "floaty" and less erratic or quick than viceroy flight—and monarchs have a characteristic, "flap, flap, glide" pattern. It doesn't help much to know that viceroys are smaller, because I'm not sure how often I will see the two types together. But it's almost a full inch difference in wingspan range—monarchs wings are about 2 1/2 to 3 3/8 inches. Determining this measure is a case of "guestimation" as the butterfly alights and quickly moves on.

Timing is another differentiator. Around here, monarchs don't usually return from Mexico until mid to late June, but adult viceroys (who do not migrate) typically emerge from their cocoons by late May.

Since they are now on the endangered species list, I find the presence of monarchs especially heartening. It seems viceroys are better off, overall, in terms of survival—maybe the lack of a long migration journey helps them? They are a species of "least concern."

The look of black "leading" between the illuminated orange swaths on both these butterflies reminds me of stained glass. I can't imagine any scenario in which my heart doesn't lift, if only just a little, when spotting these airborne works of bright and beckoning art.

## July 26
## Nine Acres of Fluff

You wouldn't believe the number of rabbits at Hammonasset Beach State Park. Walking Buddy down the roadway there was akin to water skiing. I was pulled at a rapid, jerky, and unrelenting pace from rabbit to rabbit, treated to the music of baying when the scent's effect was too much for Buddy to contain.

Connecticut only has one native rabbit—the New England cottontail—and they are vulnerable. They need thick brush to thrive, and there has been less of that kind of habitat over time, thanks largely to human development. The brush they need is the kind you and I have trouble walking through.

The good news is that the New England species used to be considered threatened or endangered. A concerted effort by foresters, farmers, bird-watchers, biologists, hunters, and other conservationists meant that, by 2015, these rabbits' numbers had bounced back to a healthier level. Given the human propensity to clear land—along with some other factors—we need to remain watchful of this species.

Eastern cottontails came to Connecticut in the early 1900s and are much more abundant and widespread than New England cottontails. They can get by with thinner brush and smaller areas of it.

How do you tell your cottontails apart? Very carefully! They look almost identical. Connecticut's Department of Energy and Environmental Protection (DEEP) reports that about half the eastern population shows a white, star-like shape on the forehead (not seen in the New England variety). The most reliable ways are comparing skull characteristics or analyzing DNA, so if you don't find that telltale star, you will be left guessing. Whatever variety you are seeing, the DEEP estimates that they typically cover a range of nine acres.

## July 27
### Dog Days

The term "dog days of summer" goes all the way back to the Roman Empire. Nature writer Hal Borland, who lived in Connecticut and wrote columns for the *New York Times* for years, explained in *Twelve Moons of the Year* that, while the term refers to a stagnant season, it is derived from the dog star, also known as Sirius, rising at this time. It's the brightest star in our sky.

Dog days are in July and August, and Borland wrote that snakes often shed their skins around this time and are "briefly blind and sometimes truculent during the molt." No one wants to run into a truculent snake. But even if they weren't molting and experiencing a transient loss of sight, isn't it possible that the dripping wet heat around here makes them cranky? Mosquitoes are said to bite more during this time too. Not sure if they are cranky, but I sure get that way after several consecutive bites on a hot day.

Early morning can be the best time to be out during this time of year. It's still a bit cool then, and perhaps the snakes and mosquitoes are still sleeping.

## July 28
### Tiny, Brilliant, Jumpy: Notes on a Short Life

In April I wrote about spittlebugs, who take refuge in clumps of what looks like saliva. If my research isn't failing me, the tiny creature I found today, sporting a vivid green body with commanding orange stripes, is a rhododendron leafhopper. Leafhoppers are similar to spittlebugs but don't share that clever mechanism for hiding their young; they simply lay eggs. Not surprisingly, rhododendron leafhoppers lay their eggs in rhododendron leaves.

I was astounded to read on a Maine government site that "there are more leafhopper species worldwide than all species of birds, mammals, reptiles, and amphibians combined."[102] What? I had never stumbled on this creature until the other day, despite tons of rhododendrons in my yard. Given the sheer number of leafhopper types, I would be foolish to promise my find was a rhododendron leafhopper—and, true confession, it wasn't hanging out on a rhododendron. Whatever it was, I found it beautiful.

I learned that these insects also like azaleas and mountain laurel, and was again reminded to pay more attention. I didn't note what kind of leaf I found my new friend on, which might have helped with identification. As always, I vacillate between getting caught up in identifying and just plain appreciating, whatever the name!

Eggs for the next generation will be laid starting in mid-September with new lives hatching in the spring; adults will be long gone by then.

## July 29

## Hotspot of Biodiversity, Hotspot of Turtle Danger

Today featured an unexpected mission: driving an eastern painted turtle with a fishhook in its eye to a local expert. This cringe-worthy adventure left me wondering how many turtles get hooked like this.

The US is what the Connecticut Department of Energy and Environmental Protection calls "a turtle biodiversity hotspot." But I was dismayed to learn that nine of Connecticut's twelve native turtle species, including sea turtles, are on the state's List of Endangered, Threatened and Special Concern Species. These unfavorable odds aren't unique to Connecticut; nearly half the world's species are at risk.

The eastern painted turtle is the most widespread North American turtle. We see them sunning on logs at the pond. At night, they sleep below water. While they can live more than thirty years, females are at risk when they leave the water to find a nesting site. This is when they are run over and why there are fewer females than males. Painted turtles are not on the at-risk list for Connecticut, but the last list was updated in 2015—something to watch.

What can we do to help turtles? Experts advise never keeping turtles as pets, as this prevents reproduction. If you do have a pet turtle, though, it shouldn't be returned to the wild, as it can introduce disease. If you want to move a turtle from the road, guard your own safety and move her to a safe spot in the direction she was already headed; she is on a mission to lay eggs and may be headed to her home range.

You can make your yard a more turtle-friendly place by avoiding pesticides and fertilizers, and letting leaves and brush piles linger to serve as shelters. Should you find a turtle that's been harmed (or any injured creature), check with your state for rehabilitators. This helped me find the expert for today's rescue run.

## July 30

### Tern, Tern, Tern

My friend Cecilia watched a tern hunt the other day, admiring its precise plunge to grab its slippery, silvery meal. All About Birds says common terns subsist mostly on smaller fish, sometimes grabbing them from close to the surface and sometimes with a quick plunge to just below the water. They also steal fish from other terns, and from gulls.

Cecilia might have seen a common tern. Nearly all Connecticut common terns nest on Falkner Island, part of the Stewart B. McKinney National Wildlife Refuge. The island is best known for the fact that roseate terns love the place. Both common and roseate terns have nested there since at least the 1960s.

Roseate terns are endangered in the Northeast, and the only way to save them is to fiercely protect the nesting sites that are left. That means the island can have no visitors—other than during one carefully orchestrated open house in September.

The island boasts Connecticut's second-oldest lighthouse, now used as a prime place to spot roseate tern predators, such as black-crowned night herons and peregrine falcons. A research crew spends time on the island each May through August, monitoring reproduction and studying the best ways to maintain the population.

It can be difficult to tell a roseate tern from a common tern, but during breeding season the roseates are more pale than other terns, with most plumage turning silver-gray above and creamy white below a rosy-pink chest and a black cap. All About Birds says you can best see the pink coloring on an overcast day; otherwise it can be hard to spot. They also grow long white tail-streamers for breeding season.

Roseate terns will migrate fairly soon—late August to early September—to a tropical locale like Trinidad or Brazil.

## July 31

### Seeps and Their Dancers

I see flying jewels everywhere these days. Sometimes they hold still long enough for me to lean in toward their gossamer wings. One or two have even posed for a quick picture. And then they are off again, swooping and flitting.

Today one amber dragonfly had me catching my breath—an eastern amberwing perhaps? I saw another, a stunning turquoise, and was perplexed by its name. A seepage dancer? It turns out that these types of damselflies like nonmoving water, unlike many other species that prefer slow-moving water.

Reading on, I realized I'd never come across the term "seep" when reading about nature. Seeps form puddles in the middle of meadows and grasslands—they are places of low elevation where underground water surfaces.

If you get a few moments, go out in the sun, especially near some water, and look for your own flying jewels. When you get too hot, go online and admire all the dragonfly and damselfly photos and names. Insect Identification shows forty in the Connecticut database. Widow skimmers, red saddlebags, orange meadowhawks, blue-fronted dancers, common sand dragons—the list goes on and on. So many new kinds to meet!

These were once drab-looking larvae in the water who one day "cracked open" and released a stunning aerialist.

## August 1

### A Beak, but No Bird

It took a while, but I eventually identified my picture of a green, fuzzy "lollipop" on a shrub as a beaked hazelnut. At the time I snapped the photo, I had no idea that each of the lollipops (the best word I have for their shape) contains up to six nuts.

My field guide says the nuts can be roasted, ground into flour, or candied. The husk must turn brown before they can be harvested. But beware the stinky, staining liquid oozing from the casing! Even if you get past that, these are, quite literally, tough nuts to crack.

A 2019 interview on New England Public Media claims that the eastern filbert blight keeps us from having a robust hazelnut industry in the Northeast. The destructive fungus gets under hazelnut (filbert) shrub bark. An industrious biologist, Tom Molnar, was able to breed a hazelnut that resists such a blight. Is there hope for some promising hazelnut crops? In the interview, host Ailsa Chang joked, "More than seventy percent of the world's hazelnuts come from one place—Turkey. And that, of course, leaves Nutella lovers everywhere very vulnerable."[103]

But seriously, filberts were a New England staple for an impressive span of time. A 1680 book on the "commodities and discommodities" of New England counts filberts among other bounties, including "Mulberies, Plums, Raspberies, Corrance, Chesnuts . . . Walnuts, Smalnuts, Hurtleberies and Hawes of Whitethorne [near] as good as our Cherries in England."[104]

The USDA says Native Americans (specific tribes not named) ate the nuts either fresh or roasted. They also used nut milk for a variety of medicinal purposes, and the wood was used in making arrows, fishing traps, and spoons, with the shoots used to make rope. An admirable example of using every part of the plant.

# August 2

## Snakes in Basements

"Can snakes climb stairs?" The answer is yes, at least in the case of the biggest snakes. However, it's unlikely to happen with a typical basement snake in my area.

Tom, who as a home inspector has found a good number of shed snakeskins on basement walls, spooked a long and fat black snake into our basement yesterday as he mowed the lawn. Is it still there? I may find out when I do the laundry. But I know that there are only two poisonous snakes in the state, and this is not one of them. Both the northern copperhead and the timber rattlesnake are quite distinctive looking.

I am guessing Tom spooked an eastern ratsnake. These black snakes are the largest in Connecticut. I had thought of them as all black, but if you look closely, they have white chins and bellies, and little flecks of white on their backs sometimes. They like forests and forest-adjacent meadows, so that means our basement visitor has likely slipped back outside through the gap, returning to his favored territory. Maybe he got a mouse before he left.

My friend George rescued two northern ring-necked snakes from his home. The Connecticut DEEP site describes them as "small, secretive and distinctly marked." Yes, the yellow ring around the neck is easy to spot, as is the yellow belly! Sometimes their bellies are spotted. They spend most of their days hiding, moving about more freely at night. They often use stone walls for cover.

My research tells me this type would be unlikely to climb the basement stairs, but how did one end up in George's foyer? I am glad it ran into someone who is compassionate and not driven by that age-old fear of our legless friends that slithers about in many human hearts.

## August 3

### Wild Hydrangeas

I have the pleasure of seeing blooming hydrangeas everywhere this time of year—along Main Street in Essex, at the entrance to Mount Saint John in Deep River, and in great abundance in our own yard. There were three fat and happy hydrangeas in our Long Island front yard when I was young. My grandparents contributed a plant for each child born.

Over the years I have learned about some of the cultivars. I find bluebird hydrangeas especially pretty. And I learned that another is called twist-n-shout! There are five or six main types in North America, but if you try to count cultivars, which result from selective breeding, the list seems endless.

Since nearly all hydrangeas I have noticed have been in gardens, I never thought much about wild hydrangeas. But they are out there, native to eastern woodlands. They are also sometimes called smooth hydrangeas, sevenbark, or tree hydrangeas, according to the Morton Arboretum in Lisle, Illinois. According to Tony, a citizen of the Cherokee Nation blogging at *My Cherokee Garden*, "sevenbark" is an allusion to the fact that the bark tends to peel off in layers, with color variations.

The US Forest Service says common ornamental shrubs in the wild hydrangea family include sweet mock orange (*Philadelphus coronarius*) and panicle hydrangea (*H. paniculate*). They like mesic forests, which have a well-balanced degree of moisture. So, the "hydra" in their name makes good sense. Wild hydrangeas are largely white, and they attract eastern bumblebees as well as hairstreak and azure butterflies.

There are featured on a host of home and craft websites with advice on how to dry and preserve hydrangeas, but I have noticed that even in cold weather they retain a pretty architecture. We don't need to help them along in that endeavor!

## August 4

### Snail or Beetle?

I thought I found a bunch of little snails the other day. They were sitting placidly on some leaves in the brush, glistening in the early morning light. I admired their rows of spots and their miniature existence—about the size of my pinky nail! I hadn't seen them before.

It turned out these were not snails. I felt a bit foolish when I learned they were the larvae of the false potato beetle. The larvae are known to fall off the leaf when approached closely and disappear into dense vegetation in self-defense. I was lucky—these sleepy specimens didn't seem to mind my gentle touch. Once they grow up, they will be much snazzier looking, with handsome yellow and brown stripes.

These larvae especially love to eat Carolina horsenettle, so if I spot them again, it may help me ID the plant. I also learned that another budding naturalist thought the larvae were snails at first, which makes me feel better. As I researched, I stopped counting local snail types at fifty, but my learning journey from snail to beetle taught me that there are quite a few land snails in Connecticut, and at least twice as many beetles!

A 1959 paper by G. E. Hutchinson in the *American Naturalist* has a delightful footnote: "There is a story, possibly apocryphal, of the distinguished British biologist, J .B .S. Haldane, who found himself in the company of a group of theologians. On being asked what one could conclude as to the nature of the Creator from a study of his creation, Haldane is said to have answered, 'An inordinate fondness for beetles.'"[105]

## August 5

### Fluttering by the Bergamot: Blurry Double Take

I was pleased to see a hummingbird by the wild bergamot on the first day of my writing residency. I never tire of watching these tiny, sped-up wonders.

Something made me look again, though, and I realized I was seeing a hummingbird clearwing moth. The US Forest Service says there are four of these moth types in North America, this one and the snowberry clearwing moth being the most familiar. Besides the rapid wing flutter, they have long, unfurling tongues and make a humming noise, just like the birds they mimic. Or is it the other way around?

Who is imitating whom? There are many cases of convergent evolution among creatures. Certain species evolved in a similar way because it provided an advantage, like being more difficult to track and catch.

There's a whole other genus like these clearwing moths in Europe. Eric R. Olson at the PBS Nature site says they lead to many false hummingbird reports—unquestionably false because Europe has no wild hummingbirds!

## August 6
### Katydids: A Telltale Summer Metronome

Compared with many other tree insects, katydids are late to the summer singing game. I've always liked their shade of green—bright like a new leaf—and their substantive forms.

The New England Wildlife Center confirms that it is more than folklore—this insect's namesake evening call becomes more and more spaced out (a longer pause between "katy" and "did") as summer draws to a close. Folklore says frost will arrive three months after the first katydid is heard, and some sources quote a shorter time frame.

On a warm summer night, it's hard to imagine that frost could ever come, and I don't want to think about that yet. I instead choose to pay attention to the "romantic" action going on here. Males sing together, generally, but apparently, they are competing to be the first to chime in. Research shows that females prefer males who get an early start—by milliseconds—on the song.

## August 7
### Intense Stare, Insect in Prayer (and It Fishes!)

In April I wrote about my first-ever sighting of a Chinese praying mantis egg case, striking for its resemblance to a toasted marshmallow.

I was reminded again of mantises by my friend Camilla, who spotted a large one recently in North Carolina. I can't be sure, but it looks like hers was probably the European variety. Both Chinese and European mantises can be either brown or green, but the Chinese variety has a striped face.

I learned that the European praying mantis is Connecticut's state insect. The Nutmeg State's official web page about its chosen six-legged symbol notes that while this creature is an import, it eats pests and is therefore of benefit to farmers.

Even the least insect-attuned among us can quickly see how the mantis' approximation of folded hands gives it its common name. In Latin, the European variety's name is *Mantis religiosa*. But I have always been more compelled by the swivel of its head combined with its prominent eyes, giving me the feeling that I am being watched quite closely.

These insects have recently been found to see in full 3D; they are the only invertebrates known to do this. Also, insect lovers were thrilled to learn recently that mantises were observed fishing for guppies. This behavior hadn't been observed before. Jake Buehler at *National Geographic* wrote: "The mantis would step out into the middle of the pond using floating water lily and water cabbage leaves as fishing platforms. There, it would wait patiently for a guppy to stray too close to the surface, plunging its deadly legs into the water at the critical moment to snare its piscean prize."[106]

## August 8
### More Doppelgangers in Nature (or Who Counted the Teeth?)

Susan snapped a photo of a four-toothed mason wasp, one of many frequenting her garden. I wrote recently about monarch versus viceroy butterflies, and this is another case of one insect often being mistaken for another. Mason wasps are black and white and can look quite like bald-faced hornets. Karen G. Blaettler at Sciencing explains that four-toothed wasps are black with a wide white band at the upper end of their abdomens, while bald-faced hornets, also black, have white stripes at the stinger end of the abdomen.

I came over to see for myself, and the four-toothed mason wasps were loving Susan's mint plants, as were a good number of sweat bees and some other flying orange-tinted creatures we couldn't ID.

Why "four-toothed"? Tony DiTerlizzi at BugGuide explains that the Latin name, *Monobia quadridens*, coined by Linnaeus in 1763, derives from the words for "four, square" and "tooth." But this apparently refers to the four "teeth" on the abdominal band. I find this misleading and am a bit disappointed to learn that there are no tiny wasp choppers to be counted.

I learned from wasp expert Eric R. Eaton's blog, *Bug Eric*, that solitary female four-toothed wasps typically nest in abandoned tunnels left by other creatures, such as carpenter bees. They paralyze small caterpillars and then deposit them in the nest. They also leave some empty tunnels, presumably to fool predators. When the eggs hatch, the larvae eat the doomed caterpillars. Within about twenty-one days, they emerge as adult wasps—although some might overwinter before that process can happen.

Eaton points out that these creatures can capture leaf-rolling caterpillars even when chemical applications can't fully eradicate them. He adds, "It just goes to show that nature has its checks and balances, and sometimes we should just let them operate on their own schedule."[107]

## August 9

## Muck into Gold: Dragonfly Alchemy

Racing glimmer everywhere. I sidle over to where the nearest dragonfly is perched, craving a closer look. Sometimes they hold still, sometimes we have eye to eye contact, and other times I watch the creature from behind, drinking in its delicate design and popping color. Either way, this proximity can feel like a sacred visitation. More often, the dragonfly (or damselfly, the type that folds its wings behind it) flits away, and I've only gotten a teasing glimpse.

Dragonfly eggs hatch in the water, and most of the dragonfly's life is spent as a nymph, a dull brown, sort of beetle-ish creature. Wings eventually grow from what starts as a hump, and the nymph stage can take up to four years.

When the time is right, the nymph will crawl out of the water and shed its skin. In short order it is a wholly different being—the adult dragonfly, the wandering glider, orange meadowhawk, or azure bluet we know and love. This phase of life is short—about two months—and I like to imagine the newly sun-bathed dragonflies as reveling in their high, bright flights.

We experience them in full color, and I have learned that the dragonflies themselves see the world in what NewScientist calls ultra multicolor. Some dragonflies have up to thirty different light-sensitive proteins, called opsins. We humans have just three.

Mating is done on the fly—literally; it's an aerial feat. Then the female leaves her eggs on a plant stem or sometimes in the water, starting a return to the mucky part of the life cycle.

## August 10

### In Praise of Mallows, and Specialized Bees

Gavin and I took the ferry to Outer Island, part of the Stewart B. McKinney National Wildlife Refuge. The island is small, with one half closed to the public. But we delighted in the open half, peering into tidal pools and the pollinator garden with its monarchs, and out at the gulls and cormorants.

I've written about marsh mallows before—yes, this is the plant from which the original marshmallow confection derived. And I see that the large, floppy purple-pink flower I found on the island today can be called marsh mallow, swamp rose mallow, crimsoneyed rose mallow, etc. I see why some folks insist on using scientific names—less confusion! The Latin name for what I saw today is *Hibiscus moscheutos*.

These blooms require salt or brackish marshes by the coast. Only a limited set of flowers have this locale on their wish list. Also, they draw a specialized hibiscus bee for pollination. This type of bee is often mistaken for a bumblebee. UC Berkeley Urban Bee Lab explains, "Some specialist bees forage for pollen that can only be found on one plant species. These specialist bees emerge from their nests at the same time their host plant begins to flower. The host flower sometimes depends on pollination from one specific bee species and the bee depends on pollen from their specific flower species. This mutualistic relationship can be found all over the world."[108]

There are generalist bees too. It sounds like their lives are a bit easier since they don't have to be as "picky" and well-timed as their specialist counterparts. Kim Eireman at Ecobeneficial says generalists are in the vast majority.

Why are specialists needed? Research suggests they provide a greater effect per visit to the flower. So I guess, in short, they are more efficient at getting their specific jobs done.

## We See (and Sure Hear!) the Smallest Snippets of Their Lives

I saw the outgrown and abandoned exoskeleton of a cicada nymph the other morning, clinging to a rock and looking very much like a live insect at first. An hour later Buddy was "wrestling" with a buzzing cicada. I was able to rescue this creature cloaked in several shades of green and set him on a tree trunk.

It is the males who sing, to attract the females. Only certain types are periodical cicadas, who spend most of their lives underground in thirteen- or seventeen-year cycles and emerge for a brief period to mate. Cicada Mania has a "brood chart" for these types, in which you can see when these emergences are expected. Dan Mozgai, Cicada Mania's founder, gives advice on how to manage the big brood year emergences without pesticides and with maximum compassion for the creatures. He even supplies a Cicada Wedding Planner for those outdoor weddings in danger of being overtaken. Birds will take care of at least some of the population; cicadas are part of the pre-fall migration diet.

Periodical cicadas get all the press, but there are also annual cicadas, and since it's not a brood year in Connecticut as I write this, I think the one I found falls into that bunch. There are over 190 types in North America, but my best guess is that I found a dog-day cicada. Whatever the type and whether a cicada is annual or periodical, they only live for five or six weeks above ground. Most of their lives are spent out of sight and out of earshot. They are quite active down there, tunneling and eating sap.

I was happy to help my find get back on track to his moment in the sun, and I hope he got up to the canopy and was able to broadcast his song, assuming he was, in fact, a male.

*August 12*

## Begonia B & B

I'm a bit worried about the baby Carolina wrens in our hanging begonia. The noises they make are so faint. Are they too young to have much of a voice yet, or is there something wrong?

I'm sure the worry I feel is nothing compared to that felt by the parents. I've been scolded loudly for the offense of sitting on the porch. Then again, I think the parents are getting used to me. I've seen both of them bring bugs to the begonia and, as I write this, I'm watching a baby crane its neck up to get breakfast. I've noticed that, once the meal is given, the parent hops to the power line nearby and starts to sing. I've also noticed they can call (or scold!) quite well while holding food.

My neighbor Susan has been watching another wren family in one of the many ceramic birdhouses she has made nestled in the shade of her rhododendron. She's kept the cat away and even put some brush down to help make the fledging experience a little bit softer. Her efforts were rewarded yesterday as she watched all the babies launch from the nest, the last one seeming to need extra courage before jumping down. I hope I get to see this with our little porch family. They have a cushy yew hedge awaiting their landing.

This isn't our first begonia bird family. One of the pleasures of Carolina wrens is their affinity to put nests in often human-made nooks and crannies. *Pittsburgh Post-Gazette* columnist Scott Shalaway has found nests in mailboxes, cans of nails, old boots, a clothes pin bag, and a one-gallon bucket. In one case, a family reported a nest in their bathroom. The family put up with the parents' protective dive bombing in support of the chicks.[109]

## *August 13*

## Hail the Squash Blossom

There is something so summery about seeing the generous yellow squash blossoms in gardens this time of year. Last time I grew them, I was so taken with the blooms that I barely registered the actual squash at first!

New Mexico has an official State Necklace, the Squash Blossom Necklace. Said to symbolize wealth, it was originated by the Navajo tribe and traditionally worn by both men and women,

People tend to be more familiar with eating squash than their blossoms, but stuffed, battered, and fried blossoms are a summer favorite for many. They can also be eaten raw, perhaps in a salad, or sauteed.

Lots of animals, including squirrels, racoons, and skunks, enjoy them too!

## August 14

### Toothpaste-Stealing Architects

Fifty or so of what seem to be the small, common type of ant I see on our stoop suddenly commandeered the bathroom counter. They climbed to the pinnacle of the Listerine bottle and were enamored of the toothpaste.

I wondered how far they had traveled to get to our bathroom. Writing for Harvard Forest, Ariel da Cruz Reis says the jury is still out on this question. Some claim they can travel the distance of up to three football fields. Maybe these ants basically climbed the equivalent of Everest to pillage our dental hygiene stash.

All this pondering reminded me how much I admire ant hills, how I have wondered if species vary in their design preferences, and if they have any mind for decor. I have seen some hills with rims around the edge, others with larger holes. In Roberta Gibson's *Wild About Ants* blog, I read that harvester ants collect a variety of objects and deposit them around their nest entrances. They favor pebbles, but folks have also found charcoal, snail shells, and tiny fossils, seemingly collected with purpose. A scientist found that the ants replaced the charcoal if it was taken and theorized that it might deter other species.

Most people seem more interested in the inside architecture of an ant colony than how the "front door" looks, and it's worth it to spend a few minutes looking at stunning photos online of indoor ant architecture. My brief foray into the world of ants, which led to more questions than answers, makes me even more of an admirer of E. O. Wilson, who studied them closely for many decades. We lost him at the end of 2021 at the age of 92. He was as intrepid as the creatures he studied.

## August 15

### Clever Amplifiers

Sometimes the buzzing from the trees, a "soundtrack" of outdoor summer life, can come to sound mono-melodic. But if you stop to listen closely, you can pick the buzzing chorus apart—some parts higher pitched, others droning on longer, etc.

I listened online, at Songs of Insects, for the sound of the two-spotted tree cricket. It was instantly familiar, although I don't think I've ever seen this cricket. It's the adult females that have two large, dark spots on their backs. They are less than an inch long.

Songs of Insects explains that two-spotted tree crickets are tricky to observe since they don't spend much time on the ground. But they sure make their presence known. Patrick Coin at BugGuide says males "chew holes into leaves which they then place their wings up against while singing. The leaf becomes an extension of their wings—to amplify their sound."[110]

There are sixteen tree cricket types in the US, and David H. Funk, in *Scientific American*, talks about how the male's singing is a prelude to a "fascinating array of reproductive strategies."[111] After copulation, females store the sperm package, or spermatophore, within their bodies. It will release as they lay their eggs. The females also eat a secretion that the males make, which many describe as a "nuptial gift." Matt Pelikan, with the *Martha's Vineyard Times*, is more straightforward: "His succulent back secretions . . . distract the female from dining on the spermatophore."[112]

So, in essence, he offers her song and something to eat to increase the chances of a successful reproductive outcome. Their "date" involves a concert and then a bite to eat, insect style.

## August 16

### Wistful for the Long Shore: Mermaid Purses, Seaweed Popping, and Scallops

We practically lived at Jones Beach every summer when I was a kid. I looked east and west and saw the Long Island land stretch into the distance, the "never-ending" coast hugging the Atlantic.

Like most kids, I assumed my experience was everyone else's. Didn't everyone look for bubbling in the sand when the waves receded, which might lead to a tiny, white crab burrowed below? Didn't everyone absently pick up mermaid's purses (skate egg cases) and palm them around? I later learned these were likely clearnose skate egg cases; they are often found in New York ocean waters. The strange-looking, leathery pouches protect young skates until they can swim and be on their own. The black type I found so often was super lightweight and most likely long discarded, churned up from the sea floor. Some sharks produce similar cases. The

UK-based Shark Trust is conducting The Great Eggcase Hunt, a citizen science project for tracking shark and skate presence and diversity.

And then there was the never-ending joy from popping the firm "bubbles" in some seaweeds. I didn't know they held the promise of the next generation. These satisfying deflations blasted open receptacles for seaweed eggs and sperm meant for the ocean.

Finally, the search for shells—how rare the unbroken shell, especially the larger specimens. Ribbed and fan-like scallop shells could be especially pretty. When I sought to learn more about scallops, what came up mostly was craft projects and recipes. But have you ever seen a diagram of a living scallop, eyes all along the periphery, pale blue arteries, and the two-chambered heart, the strong "foot" that some scallops use to cling to rocks, while others may run along the ocean floor? Imagine their wild lives before the chef's or beachcomber's harvest.

## *August 17*

### Look Closer: Black Trumpets!

Our family followed The 3 Foragers around a nature center trail. This local family has written a book and travels the state educating others on the ins and outs of foraging.

I remember the gleam in their eyes when our group stumbled on a trove of black trumpet mushrooms. They said that people often walk right past them, as they blend in so well with the forest floor.

Black trumpets like hardwood forests and damp, dark areas. They grow in patches, so once you spot one, you may suddenly realize you have a whole bunch! Iso Rabins at the ForageSF page says these are perfect for beginning foragers—easy to ID. They are related to the beloved chanterelles.

They don't have gills, and unlike some other mushrooms, they don't fruit on wood. They don't have poisonous lookalikes. That said, sometimes an eager, amateur forager can convince themselves they have an edible, so it's always important to check with experts!

Black trumpet mushrooms are "generalists": rich in enzymes that can break down a wide array of organic compounds. They do a great job busily returning vital nutrients to the soil by reducing them into usable units.

Alan Bergo at the Forager/Chef site says, "Black trumpets have one of the most potent flavors of all wild mushrooms, especially fresh. They may be fragile or small, but they pack a punch."[113]

Gavin dehydrated the small bunch he gathered, and they have an intense, truffle-like scent. In fact, Regina Schrambling from the *New York Times* calls them "training wheels for black truffles,"[114] which can be an acquired taste. They are sometimes referred to as the "trumpet of death"—I think because of the funereal color? On the flip side, they are also known as "horn of plenty" mushrooms. Go figure.

## August 18
### Mudbugs, Yabbies, and Astacologists

Gavin emerged from the Esopus Creek in the Catskills—our home away from home—cupping a crayfish. His find looked like a miniature lobster, and they are, in fact, quite closely related. Lobsters, though, are salt-water dwellers, crayfish are freshwater dwellers. They are sometimes called "freshwater lobsters," or by the nicknames "mudbugs" and "yabbies." Most people know the more common ones—"crawfish" and "crawdads."

I flashed back to my very first nature blog years ago, inspired by another creek not far from Esopus. I quoted Edwin Way Teale then, and I'll quote him now, from his book *Journey into Summer*: "To the lost man, to the pioneer penetrating new country, to the naturalist who wishes to see the wild land at its wildest, the advice is always the same—follow a stream. The river is the original forest highway. It is nature's own Wilderness Road."[115]

Gavin plans to do just that—follow the waterway as far as he can, and I'm sure he will find more crayfish.

I was surprised to learn there is a whole subfield of biologists who specialize in these crustaceans. There are 640 types of crayfish in the world, so that should keep the astacologists busy.

Crayfish are not picky eaters. They like plants, fish, insects, and even leaf litter and, rarely, other crayfish! These animals live for about two years. They are hardy in some ways and super vulnerable in others. They can tolerate quite a range of temperatures and even waterways going dry; when that happens, they burrow and estivate (go into dormancy), or they migrate. But they can't take pollution or other contamination by humans well at all. So if you have a healthy crayfish population, you likely have a relatively unpolluted body of water.

## August 19

### They Get Around: Eastern Swallowtail Adventures

I think the photo I snapped is of an eastern swallowtail butterfly. There are other swallowtails that look like it, but the two-tailed and Canadian tiger varieties seem to have fancier and more colorful tail ends.

Not too long ago this beauty was a fat, green, goofy-looking caterpillar with false eye spots. I was amused to read Tony Gomez's description at Monarch Butterfly Life: "when the [eastern swallowtail] caterpillar coloration starts to resemble a UPS truck, you'll know the next phase of caterpillar transformation is about to begin."[116] Gomez is precisely right; UPS brown foretells the chrysalis phase. After several weeks, or even after a whole winter, the full-fledged butterfly emerges.

Eastern swallowtails' wing spans are up to five inches wide, which makes them hard to ignore! And they do get around. It gave me joy to read *New York Times* writer Dave Taft recounting his many sightings around the city, although not all were picturesque: "I can recall thinking as I watched one flit past a traffic jam on the Bruckner Expressway that crossing the Bronx is not nearly as challenging on pretty yellow wings. I have also been inches away from another sipping nectar from a flower growing from the brickwork of the interminable Gowanus Expressway. On a whale watch, one fluttered past over the open Atlantic; still another lapped up something leaching from behind a portable toilet in eastern Queens."[117]

Look for eastern swallowtails puddling—they drink salt and other minerals from mud puddles. While they puddle, look for dark varieties. Males are always yellow, but females can either look like males or be dark, with just the suggestion of stripes. The females may also have a bit of blue in the tail.

I'd like to live like their caterpillars for a little while, resting on silken mats between feedings.

## August 20

### Fanciful Mushrooms

One of the joys of noticing mushrooms is trying to figure out what you've found and what fanciful name it may have. This time of year, you might see chicken of the woods, oysters, chanterelles, or giant puffballs.

Nature writer Mary Holland writes about seeing tiny velvety fairy fans this time of year. Her photo of these mushrooms shows a prominent brown stalk surrounded by white. Maybe the fact that they are less than an inch high explains why I've never spotted them. The order they belong to also includes earth tongues and jelly drops.

My favorite mushroom finds are bird's nest fungi (yes, they look just like tiny birds' nests!), wood ears, and dead man's fingers, which look like a buried hand reaching up through the dirt!

I'm still not sure I can tell a turkey tail from a false turkey tail, but I love the wavy, swirly lines of earth-toned color they sport.

## August 21

### Jagged, Stealthy, and a True Bug

Those many plastic insect-viewing containers my mom bought when I was a child made their mark. I have trouble walking past greenery without leaning down to see what I can find nestled within or hovering about. I don't capture my finds anymore—except with a camera.

Yesterday, near Esopus Creek, I peered at an oddly shaped, tiny creature perched on a yellow bloom. Its lower half was wide and green, but there was an overlay of dark coloring across this half and its narrower upper body, including a wide band crossing its tail end. Someone on iNaturalist helped me determine that I had found a jagged ambush bug.

It is a true bug. While many of us call all insects "bugs," only creatures belonging to the *Hemiptera* order are true bugs. They typically have tough forewings and no teeth—their mouths are basically straws—the better to suck juices from their preferred meal.

Master Gardener Betty Gray's paper on these bugs says they are helpful to gardeners. They hide on flower heads and, as their name implies, ambush unsuspecting prey. Their forelimb design is much like that of the praying mantis, so they are good at grabbing! Hornets, wasps, and bees are favorite meals; goldenrods and wild carrots are favorite habitats. But they also eat moths, flies, and fellow true bugs.

The more I read about entomology, the more I'm reminded that it can be a violent and macabre world. These bugs stab their victims with those mouth-straws (aka styluses), thereby injecting poison and liquefying the contents of the prey—easier to slurp them.

Between this rather horrifying "hell's kitchen" methodology, its pattern of colors, and odd shape, I think this bug's name will stick in my memory.

## *August 22*

### After the Storms: Monsoon and Fire Silver Linings

Here in Colorado, where we are getting Gavin settled into college, locals say it's been a good, much-needed monsoon season after way too long a dry spell.

Chris Spears at CBS Denver explains that the monsoon is a seasonal shift in wind pattern with a direct connection to the tropics. The season runs July into August, and it seems fairly dry here now, although we crossed several bubbling, healthy-looking rivers as we drove from Denver to Durango.

While this weather pattern seems exotic to me, it is serious business. The damage from the now all-too-frequent wildfires worsens the threat from monsoons. A major highway here was closed due to mudslides earlier this month. Flash flood warnings abound during this season.

The aftermath of all this moisture means that the San Juan Mountains are full of bolete, chanterelle, and *Agaricus* mushrooms. Herbalist and microbiologist Anna Marija Helt recounts finding such an abundance on just a short walk. Mushroom foragers in an Outdoors Inspired video[118] say this has been the "greenest" mushroom season in Colorado since 2016, sharing their enthused search for black morels, which they hungrily describe as smelling like "wood and loveliness."

North Spore says that morels, especially, inspire fervor among foragers, perhaps because they are so elusive. They blend in with so much on the ground, like darker pinecones, burnt nubs in areas that have suffered from fires, and rocks that are darkened by fire. The nubs and dark rocks can be quite prevalent in post-forest-fire zones. There is a lot of passion among foragers when it comes to seeking "burn morels."

It's not just mushrooms that can blossom because of monsoons. Rainwater, beyond simple hydration, brings a host of life-giving nutrients. The sulfur in rain, picked up as condensation forms, is an important constituent of plant amino acids.

## August 23

### Learning the Oaks: In Search of the Chinkapin

Today I walked an arc of Reservoir 6 in West Hartford. The spot beckons wildlife. Even the well-worn, sandy path to a favored bench was hopping with Carolina locusts, and I watched a goldfinch zoom out from the water-side brush and into a tree. Swallows dipped and soared. Cicadas resumed their buzzing with vigor as the day warmed.

I looked up into the leaves of an oak and saw how ruffled they were, how much they differed from oak leaves with sharper edges I had collected as a child. I think my childhood oaks were mostly eastern black oaks and northern red oaks, although I didn't give much thought as to which was what, back then. Today's ruffled leaves looked like they were *Quercus alba*, northern white oak.

A *Connecticut Explored* article by Dale Carson, of Abenaki descent, talks about how Natives shared acorn flour, along with amaranth and cattail flours, with the colonists, helping them survive the first winter and accli-mate to their new environs. I often hear that acorns are bitter, that to be eaten they must be put through a laborious process to get rid of the excess tannins. But today I read that the chinkapin's acorns are sweet and palat-able—even when raw (although roasting is recommended). It might take a lot of these smaller nuts to make a meal or even a decent snack, but they are something new to seek out and taste!

## August 24

### Tigers Everywhere

If you're from the East Coast and you find yourself in Colorado, you spend a lot of time looking up at the vast mountain ranges in many hues, including the red shades reflected in the state 's name—Spanish for "colored red."

I didn't have to crane my neck far, though, to keep spotting diminutive black and white moths, flying fast enough to be a bit of a blur. What were they? I'd never seen any back home. Finally, one hungry moth landed and was too busy sipping nectar to mind being photographed. The colloquial name for this moth from the tiger moth family is "police car moth," named after the once-ubiquitous color scheme of police cruisers. Most moths feed at night, but this type feeds during the day, so they are often mistaken for butterflies. They are a western species.

When we're back in Connecticut, I'll be looking for local tiger moths, like the harnessed tiger moth or the parthenice tiger moth; these two also have quite striking designs. They feed at night, so they will be much harder to spot!

The scientific name for this subfamily, which also includes lichen moths, is *Arctiinae*, from the Greek word for bear! Not what I expected, but the name derives from the hairy appearance of the caterpillars. Lichen moths, by the way, are named for what they eat during the caterpillar stage, not for their appearance. There are other caterpillars that eat leaf litter or moss.

## August 25

### It Stretches Coffee, Tells Time Too!

I know it's everywhere, and some states list it as a noxious weed. But I never tire of looking at chicory's soft blue-purple blooms brightening our roadsides.

The "tells time" part of the title is, admittedly, a stretch in the context of our modern-day precision devices, but I was intrigued to learn that Linnaeus—the eighteenth-century biologist who founded our naming system for organisms—included it in his flower-driven "clock" because it marks time with the opening and closing of flower petals. Chicory opens at daybreak and folds when it is first hit with heat or direct sunlight.

Tom and I have great memories of the renowned Café Du Monde coffee from New Orleans and for years ordered cans of it at Christmastime. Chicory is what makes it special; when its roots are roasted, they taste similar to coffee, and it's stretched the coffee supply during lean times, like the Civil War and the Great Depression.

On Naturally Curious, Mary Holland reports seeing no less than nine species of pollinators visiting chicory, most of them bees. She notes that, come winter, American goldfinches and other birds will be grateful for the plant's widely available seeds.

## August 26

### It's the Pits: The Curious (and Vicious!) Antlion

Earlier this week our local wildlife refuge posted a mystery for their readers. What insect makes conical pits in sand or dirt? I see these small depressions all the time and have absently wondered what makes them. It turns out it's the work of antlions, creatures I have never seen up close and in person.

At first it seemed curious that I spent so many childhood hours watching ants and never happened upon an antlion. But then again, I generally watched the ants' hills and immediate "yards" for their busy comings and goings into and out of the mound's doorway. Was an ant somewhere inside noticing that a few less were returning home each day, some having slid into the antlion's violent pit?

It's the larvae who dig the pits—shallow to us but treacherously steep for insects. Also, antlion is a family, not a species. There are about sixty-five types. They use their abdomens as plows and bury themselves with just their jaws protruding at the bottom of the pit. Unlucky bugs who fall into the lair promptly get their juices sucked out, their carcasses hurled back to the surface. My warning to ants is like that we make to luckless humans in horror movies, who never listen and fall prey to the lurking evil: If you see a pit surrounded by desiccated corpses, do NOT approach!

Our family has been calling leaf-footed bugs "doodlebugs" for years. No special reason, we just thought they were cute and deserved a pet name. But I learned that "doodlebug" is commonly used to describe the antlion. Why? Wikipedia says it makes "odd winding, spiraling trails while relocating." Another clue to look for in the dirt and sand.

## August 27

### Crow Cousins and Bird Funerals

We don't have magpies back East, so I was mesmerized by the ones I saw in Colorado. These large, black and white birds with long tails draw the eye. They are in the same family as crows and jays (*Corvidae*). Like their glossy, black crow cousins—ubiquitous where I live in Connecticut—magpies eat carrion along with fruit, grain, and insects. Like crows, magpies raid other birds' nests for eggs.

In *Popular Science*, Nicholas Lund asks why birds in the corvid family are "such jerks," citing behaviors like mobbing other birds to drive them away and pulling mammals' tails to distract them from food, along with nest raiding. But Lund explains that a lot of these behaviors reflect how smart these birds are, and the scientist interviewed for the piece defends corvids.[119] They are not the only birds with these behaviors, but folks can be quick to give them a bad rap. Maybe their rather harsh-sounding vocalizations don't help their PR.

Magpies and crows share a behavior that has given many observers pause. Animal behavior expert Dr. Marc Bekoff, in the *Daily Mail*, says magpies lay "wreaths" of grass next to roadside magpie corpses. In Nature News at the Bay Nature site, Anne Marshall-Chalmers describes what happens when a crow spots another crow that has died: "Sometimes it's only a handful, other times up to 60 or 70 birds settle onto branches or whatever aerial perch allows good viewing of the corpse and the surrounding scene. For a short time, the birds remain quiet and still, only to break into a chorus of shrill calls. Back and forth, silence and aggravation for about 15 to 20 minutes until nearly all at once the ink-black birds launch and disperse, leaving branches to quiver."[120]

## August 28

### Tracker, Driller, Mesmerizer, Mom

On our Catskills trip, I watched a huge insect with fascination. She had a huge, orange, well . . . horn on her tail end (for lack of a better word) and was rocking back and forth on the tree bark where she sat, pumping this appendage up and down. At first, I wasn't sure what I was seeing. Were there two wasps there, arched in the rhythm of mating? This thing was big! The "horn" alone was at least three inches long.

No, just one bug there, and I needed help from my Master Naturalist friends to help me ID it. I had found a giant ichneumon wasp. I was watching her oviposit (lay her eggs).

Ichneumon means "tracker," and the moniker is fitting. The female searches the surface of tree bark until she finds horntail wasp grubs. Then she uses her enormous ovipositor to drill into the wood. There, on the horntails that this determined mom has located, her parasitic babies will hatch and feed. (The "drill" appears so big because it's housed by a protective sheath).

It's a gruesome business, and nature photographer Ian Adams wrote, "Charles Darwin had difficulty accepting this process, and wrote to Asa Gray in 1860: 'I cannot persuade myself that a beneficent and omnipotent God would have designedly created the *Ichneumonidae* with the express intention of their feeding within the living bodies of Caterpillars.'"[121] I get it, Charles. Nature is both lovely and brutal.

It can take an hour to complete the drilling and egg laying, during which time the female is quite vulnerable to predators; I'm sure the size of this insect makes her quite a prize for birds. Apparently, chipmunks like them too.

People often fear this wasp, thinking the big ovipositor is a stinger. But only the horntail wasp grubs need worry.

## August 29

### Knowing the Thistles: A Spiny Issue

When I think of thistles, I think of leggy plants that grab my eye. They have spiky purple "crowns" atop a bulbous, green section a bit reminiscent of a tiny pineapple.

But there is way more to thistles than the tall thistle, this local icon from the thistle family. In a study reported on by the *Journal of Applied Ecology*, about a quarter of all bumblebee visits were to thistle flowers. Another study showed visits by thirty types of butterflies. The Xerces Society published an entire book about native thistles alone, of which there are about sixty-two species in North America.

"Thistle" is used to describe a lot of plants with spines, some of which are not true thistles. And it turns out that what I think is a tall thistle could be a field thistle, the main difference being the field thistle's deeply divided leaves.

The Xerces Society's book advocates for conserving and restoring native thistles, which have been in decline. While distinguishing between thistle types may not matter much on summer walks, knowing which are native versus nonnative does matter if you are gardening, clearing land, or farming. The highly invasive Canada thistle, for example, invades row crops and small grains, also threatening fruit crops and pastureland. Biocontrol programs released thistle-eating insects that ended up devouring both invasives and noninvasives. And sometimes well-meaning people weed out helpful native thistles, confused about natives versus invasives. It can be so tricky!

Edible thistle is a staple food of the Salish people of the Pacific Northwest. Swamp thistle is a caterpillar host plant for the endangered swamp metalmark butterfly. More than two hundred species of pollinators visit native thistles, with at least one bee specializing in a particular thistle's pollen— reminders of the ripple effect from each creature.

## August 30
### Wild Cats: What Kind Have You Seen?

Tom watched a wild cat cross the road with her three kittens, and he likely made a mistake many Nutmeggers make; he decided he had seen a mountain lion family. In retrospect, he remembered seeing short (or bobbed) tails—a clue that he had seen bobcats. Size is another distinguisher, with mountain lions being much bigger, but that's hard to gauge when a sighting is a fleeting surprise and you have no way to do a size comparison.

Erik Ofgang wrote a *Connecticut Magazine* piece titled, "There Are no Mountain Lions in Connecticut, so Why Do We Keep Seeing Them?" The official word is that mountain lions are extinct in our state, and bobcats are the only wild cats here and are in fact surging.

Then again, there was what seems to have been a bona fide mountain lion sighting here in 2011, complete with paw prints and a blurry photo. It is believed that same mountain lion was the one killed by an SUV the next week. It was confirmed to have come all the way from South Dakota.

An expert interviewed for the article admitted there could be outlier mountain lions wandering about, but was quick to point out how people tend to grossly overestimate wild cat size. Also, bobcats' rear legs in motion can mimic a long tail. But I agree with Ofgang: "There is also something appealing about the idea that there is an animal out there so cunning that it has escaped our notice and the eyes of our cameras."[122] Then again, mountain lion attacks are a real thing, if rare. California Fish & Wildlife reports seventeen attacks since 1986, including an attack on a six-year-old girl recently; her injuries were minor thanks to a quick-thinking adult with a good punch.

Whatever state you are in, there may well be an official mechanism for reporting big cat sightings.

## August 31
### Pewee in the Neighborhood

I haven't seen him, but his call is giving him away. Somewhere, high in the treetops, we have an eastern wood pewee. Using "pee-a-wee" to describe his call doesn't do the trick. The call is a bit reminiscent of the three-note whistle humans use to get someone's attention. All About Birds is right, though—it sounds slurred.

There are western wood pewees as well, and All About Birds says the call is the best way to distinguish the two types. The site says the western bird's call is much burrier and nasal than that of the eastern wood pewees. What does "burrier" mean? Notes that are "burry" or "buzzy" have a pitch that rises and falls rapidly, with burry versions being comparatively more musical.

Our eastern wood pewees are more often heard than seen, and they do a great job camouflaging their nests, encrusting them with lichens and sticking them on heavily lichened tree limbs. They use spider silk to help them stick to branches.

Pewees belong to the flycatcher family, so they are rarely at bird feeders. They excel at catching insects in flight, but they also pick them off leaves or off the ground. They tend to find their food higher in the canopy.

Eastern wood pewees travel far at migration time—down to South America or even across the Caribbean. They are one of the last birds to return from warmer climes in the spring.

## September 1

### Imported Earthworms and Pill Bugs

One of my earliest memories is of exploring the earthworms and pill bugs who lived in our garden soil on Long Island. The pill bugs (also called roly polys or wood lice) made themselves into perfect tiny balls when I poked them. The earthworms wriggled vigorously, as if ticklish.

Neither of these creatures are native to the Northeast. Ice age glaciers pushed our native worms south. European settlers brought our current worm species here, mixed in with ships' ballast and plant root balls. I was surprised to hear that, while good for garden soil, these worms are a threat to our forests. Matt Candeias at the In Defense of Plants blog explains: "Worms break through the duff [humus] and distribute it deeper into the soil where tree and forb species can no longer access it. Worms also pull down and speed up the decomposition of leaves and other plant materials that normally build up and slowly create this rich organic soil. Finally, earthworm castings or poop actually speed up run-off and soil erosion."[123]

About the pill bugs—it seems they got here later than the earthworms, likely via the lumber trade in the 1800s. They are crustaceans (think lobsters, crabs, shrimp)—the only ones who have adapted to living full-time on land. But they need to be around lots of moisture. Their Latin name is *Armadillidium vulgare*, and Mandy Howe at BugGuide.net notes the translation to be "vulgar little armadillo." Well, that sounds insulting! I get the armadillo part, but what have they ever done to us? Despite their "wood lice" moniker, they only eat decaying plant matter and, unlike their earthworm friends, they have not been accused of wanting to take over the woodlands.

## September 2

### Lingering Summer: Not All Has Ripened

Today I walked a "road less traveled." Actually, it's a well-traveled road (Route 80), but less traveled by me because it's not as scenic and peaceful as my other choices when I step out the door. This key Deep River artery is not without merit; there's Roger's Pond, where I have spotted muskrats, and a low stream that runs near the Route 9 exit ramp. People who never foot this path might not realize the stream is there.

As usual, Buddy yanked on his leash, eager to sniff out life in the brush. As usual, I mused about where exactly my house had once resided along the route; it was moved in the sixties to make room for the new Route 9. And then, even though I memorialized this annual happening in *The Book of Noticing*, I was surprised by the aroma of grapes that suddenly demanded my attention. Ten feet or so on, I found the vine. I seem to lose track each summer of exactly when they are expected to fruit, but I prefer the surprise that comes each September.

I call the lovely, tart blue grapes with slip skins "fox grapes," but they could be wild summer grapes as well. The fox variety is bigger, so I think that's what I found. They are not ripe yet, and the anticipation of returning to harvest them soon is sweet.

In *Northern Woodlands*, Robbie Meyers wrote a great column about harvesting wild grapes. It was there that I learned Robert Frost wrote a poem titled "Wild Grapes."[124] Here's a small piece:

> What are you doing up there in those grapes?
> Don't be afraid. A few of them won't hurt you.
> I mean, they won't pick you if you don't them.

## *September 3*

## Why Are They Called Black-Eyed Susans?

Even for those not especially familiar with wildflower types, the black-eyed Susan is one of those flowers quite easily recognized—yellow petals surrounding that black (well, really dark brown) "eye" at the center.

Ray Allen, founder of American Meadows, explains that the flower's name comes from an Old English love poem of the same name, involving a sailor's love, Black-Eyed Susan, who comes aboard a ship to say goodbye to her Sweet William. He promises to stay safe on his journey and be true to her. It's assumed that English colonists applied this familiar moniker from the poem to the flower. Interestingly, gardeners who seed nonnative (but not invasive) Sweet William with the native common black-eyed Susan will find they will bloom together.

Black-eyed Susans are common across all fifty US states and Canada. The bloom's dark center holds up to five hundred individual flowers, each with a shallow nectar cup that means even tiny insect pollinators can drink easily.

## September 4
### Joe Pye: The Man, the Myth, the Legend, the Weed

Countless sources explain how the widespread Joe-Pye weed is named after a Native American herbalist who used a concoction from the plant to cure typhus, a nasty infectious disease now quite uncommon.

People have questioned how accurate the Joe Pye legend is. Did he even exist? Was he Native American? Some say his name derives from Native language for typhus. Others say he was actually a Caucasian snake-oil salesman. But a 2017 scholarly paper in the *Great Lakes Botanist* does a good job providing evidence that Joseph Shauquethqueat, known as Joe Pye, was a Mohican sachem (healer) who lived in Massachusetts and, later, New York.

The details of how he got his nickname and the typhus outbreak that may have made it stick may be lost, but Joe-Pye weed remains ubiquitous. The *Daily Advance* columnist Ted Manzer describes the plant as a "pasture nightmare but a hot perennial ornamental." There's no denying it's pretty, especially with butterflies gracing its blooms, but Manzer's "pasture nightmare" description comes from the fact that cattle avoid grazing it. He recalls his father continually fighting the plant, which grew so thick and large it could hide the livestock.[125]

Still, if you don't have cattle and you want to draw butterflies closer, a University of Vermont Extension presentation names Joe-Pye weed (there are several types, including spotted, hollow, and sweet-scented) among the top ten perennials that please pollinators. Butterflies, bees, wasps, flies, and moths all love the nectar. I've stood and watched the insect comings and goings on this plant, transfixed by the variety of visitors who share the feast.

Joe-Pye weed reminds us of the delights that can unfold via late bloomers—whether plants or other creatures, even us humans. It continues to show off its pink flowers even as the evenings start to carry a chill.

## September 5
### Is It a Slug? Is It a Moth? Why, it's a Slug Caterpillar Moth!

A fellow insect observer posted an online photo of what looked like a slug with a stinger. This was a head scratcher, but some knowledgeable soul quickly identified the type of creature, if not the exact species.

Butterflies and Moths of North America says there are about fifty species of slug caterpillar moths, more officially called *Limacodids*. Until now, I hadn't run into a moth name that includes "caterpillar." Typically, it's understood that caterpillar is the larval stage, no need to call that out. But, in this case, the caterpillars are distinctively odd. They are known to move like slugs; they have suckers instead of legs and feet. Also, they usually have stinging hairs (when they have hairs—some are naked!).

A lot of these creatures look very alien to me at both caterpillar and moth stages. If you have a chance, seek out a photo collection with an online search, or at iNaturalist. I learned that they are sometimes called cup moths because of the shape of their cocoons.

According to BugLady's column for the University of Wisconsin-Milwaukee, this species' eggs are so transparent that you can observe the larvae developing inside. She quotes from Dyar's *The Life-Histories of the New York Slug Caterpillars* (1899): "The appearance of the eggs is that of shining elliptical spots of moisture, rather than that of any ordinary lepidopterous egg."[126]

Slug caterpillar moth moms lay eggs on the undersurface of leaves, and when they hatch, the caterpillars go right to work eating, skeletonizing leaves from below, and eventually attacking the whole leaf as they grow. They are "generalist" eaters, not too picky about which plant to chow down on. The caterpillars' suckers make it easier to travel upside down.

*September 6*

## Shimmering Color in the Brush:
## Songbird "Trail Mix" and "Cheese Puffs"

I rifled through my mental filing cabinet as I looked at the blue berries pondside. Why did the word "silk" keep popping up? Silk, silky—oh yes, silky dogwood! I hadn't seen these friends in a year, and they were fruiting on schedule. The blue in the berries has a pleasing, gentle variegation with an opalescent touch, and gardening websites describe them as "porcelain blue." Silky dogwood is also sometimes called swamp dogwood, given its love for water. I only learned today that the "silky" refers to the hairs that cover the undersides of the leaves and the twigs—gray, turning purplish in spring and then reddish-brown in autumn. The pretty berries have distracted me from this namesake trait.

This plant has a cousin, red osier dogwood, which produces white to pale blue berries loved by songbirds. Basket weavers value its red, flexible branches.

And then there is the porcelain berry, oh-so-enchanting to the eye and also gobbled by our avian companions. Its mix of pastel colors reminds me of Easter eggs. Unfortunately, this plant is quite invasive—helped along by birds who are drawn to the bright berries. Comments on Sue Dingwell's column about them, "Unwanted and Unloved," at the Virginia Native Plant Society, point out that the nutrition porcelain berries provide for our native birds is inferior, likening them to the instant gratification but empty calories of cheese puffs in our human snacking world. It makes me sad that something so pretty is so reviled for crowding out all manner of native plants. The experts all seem to agree: it's got to go!

Both silky dogwood and red osier dogwood are native to Connecticut, and the high fat in their berries is important for those migratory birds who will be heading south all too soon, along with those birds who stick around as the cold encroaches.

## September 7

### Boneset Season

Driving along Route 9, I saw clusters of white wildflowers lining the adjacent woodlands. At highway speed, I couldn't be sure these were boneset blooms. But it is the right time of year—late summer to early fall.

Why the name boneset? Does this plant have some miraculous orthopedic indication? Encyclopedia.com says the Native American name for this plant (tribe not specified) translates into something like "malarial fever weed," and the Mohegan Medicine Woman Gladys Tantaquidgeon confirmed the use of its roots to treat chills and fever. In English, the moniker "boneset" ties into how it was used to treat "breakbone fever," the name for an influenza-like illness that caused severe bone pain. Sometimes it's called feverwort or sweat plant, and modern medical references deem its use risky, noting gastrointestinal symptoms and liver damage.

Bees have no problems with the stuff. Sweat bees, small carpenter bees, digger bees, and bumblebees all find the plant "moderately attractive," according to the Michigan State University Extension. In fact, the Lady Bird Johnson Wildflower Center's Plant Database says this plant is of special value to native bees.

People mix up boneset and white snakeroot, and I can see why. But boneset can get much taller than snakeroot, and it has longer, narrower leaves.

I love learning these facts, but mostly I treasure the quiet beauty of rather leggy wildflower clusters that appear later in the year—boneset as well as aster and white snakeroot come to mind. Their blooms don't steal the show like some of our larger, more colorful flowers, but they quietly brighten our landscapes as the days start to shorten.

## September 8

## It Killed Lincoln's Mom, Many Say

I think what I see scattered liberally along the woodland path is white snakeroot.

Botany requires precision and patience, and sometimes it frustrates me—the smaller wildflowers often look alike! But I'm trying to overcome my "plant blindness"—a term used by Matt Candeias at the In Defense of Plants podcast.

Saara Nafici's column at the Brooklyn Botanic Garden site seems to fit my find: "You barely notice the one- to four-foot-tall plant with toothy, dark green leaves until suddenly—poof! It's everywhere you turn, all abloom with fluffy white flowers."[127] The column shows a picture of telltale leaf markings left by a particular kind of fly larvae. I noticed that on these plants, too—circuitous trails adorning many leaves.

European settlers in the early 1800s let their livestock feed on this plant, not making the connection that the "milk sickness" that struck so many people was connected to cows grazing white snakeroot. Modern dairy practices make this illness, which reportedly killed Abraham Lincoln's mother, a rare occurrence.

A Shawnee medicine woman taught a frontier doctor about the plant's connection with illness, but Nafici says it was quite some time before enough doctors believed her to make a discernible difference in how many were stricken.

I find the plant beautiful. A 1911 description portrays its showy clusters as "profuse, soft, starry inflorescence of harmonious white."[128] I can't do better than that.

It's a danger for horses, as well as cows, and the humans drinking their milk. However, if you can imagine yourself a fly, a moth, or a bee for a moment, you can imagine feeling grateful for the nutrition offered by this late-season bloomer. As for the plant's common name, some Native American peoples, such as the Seminole and Cherokee, are reported to have used the root for snakebite medicines.

## *September 9*

### They Fit Perfectly: Bees in Jewelweed

I got it into my head that jewelweed is invasive. After all, it is everywhere in our yard! But the USDA tells me it is an "aggressive competitor," one of the few native plants that compete successfully against nonnative, and very invasive, garlic mustard. There is an ornamental jewelweed that is invasive, and that's all it took to confuse me on the issue. But even I, an amateur, can tell the two apart. The jewelweed I love to see out my kitchen window is orange. The invader is purple.

Bees fit perfectly into its spotted orange flowers. Yesterday, I came upon a bee's backside barely protruding from the cozy enclosure. He quickly backed out and duplicated his hasty visit at the flower next door. My eyes aren't always so good with rapid motion, so maybe that explains why I haven't picked up on this phenomenon yet: Apparently, bees emerge from the jewelweed flower with a white stripe down their backs, a mark left by the anthers in the snug-fitting bloom.

Mary Anne Borge at The Natural Web has gorgeous pictures of a host of bees pollinating jewelweed flowers—sweat bees, honeybees, bumblebees. Some visits were captured at pale jewelweed, a yellow variety. Her article reminds me that ruby-throated hummingbirds also enjoy the blooms, gathering nectar in late summer and early fall. And I learned that jewelweed can also reproduce by self-fertilizing—the flowers that do this don't open. No wonder they are so prolific!

How many times has the word "weed" appeared in today's entry? Paul Hetzler, in Adirondack Almanack, points out that the "weed" in this plant's name is unfortunate, lumping it in with invasive Japanese knotweed, knapweed, and the like. Quite the contrary. Hetzler notes, "It is nearly always welcome wherever it is found."[129] I'll miss watching the busy buzzing at these flowers once their season has passed.

## September 10

### Harvest Moon: Do We Want it to Shine On?

As I write this, the upcoming year's harvest moon is predicted to fall on September 10. Last year, it was a full ten days later. The harvest moon is the full moon closest to the autumn equinox, the day that starts autumn, when day and night are roughly equal in duration.

Deborah Byrd, writing for EarthSky, says "Nature is particularly cooperative in giving us dusk-till-dawn moonlight, for several evenings in a row, around the time of the harvest moon."[130]

Farmers, especially in times predating the benefits of electricity, have appreciated the harvest moon for the extra light it provides to allow tasks lingering into the evening. In Chinese culture, this moon is celebrated with a festival holiday and the eating of moon cakes.

When I was an emergency room nurse, my colleagues and I came to believe that things would get wilder when there was a full moon (not just the harvest moon—any full moon!). At LiveScience, Laura Poppick says pets seem more prone to injury with a full moon, and this might simply be explained by more time outside when the light is brighter. She also reports that antlion larvae dig larger holes when there is a full moon, even when they are in a darkened laboratory, no moon in sight. The list goes on, including lions killing more during the day—you get the idea.

There's that famous romantic song imploring the harvest moon to "shine on," but given these odd reports, maybe its relatively limited duration—appearing full for about three days—isn't a bad thing.

## September 11

### Pink Caterpillars and Noisy Ones

My friend Susan shared a photo of a dark pink caterpillar with magenta bands who was sitting on her verbena. Did I know what kind this was? I'm still not 100 percent sure—could it be a tobacco budworm moth caterpillar? I had a lovely time researching the question.

Tom Eisele of the Backyard Arthropod Project blog chronicled a pink caterpillar he found. It doesn't look the same as Susan's, but Eisele theorized that caterpillars changing color with foliage makes sense. It does appear that at least some caterpillars can change colors at will. Also, they can change colors over time, as they develop. Eisele also insisted that the pink caterpillar he brought home was purring. First, he felt a vibration, then he held the creature to his ear and heard it. Well, that's something I have never experienced, so of course, I had to look it up.

LiveScience writer Laura Geggel wrote a piece called, "Caterpillars Can Scream." That certainly got my attention. According to Geggel, "hawkmoth and sphinx moths . . . [produce] clicks, whistles and other sounds when attacked by hungry predators."[131] Yes, researchers have surrounded caterpillars with microphones and then poked them to simulate a predator. To me the "whistle" sounds like a very annoyed static. The mechanism the creature uses to make the sound is likened to how a teakettle whistles—air forced through a constricted space.

I found no other reports of caterpillars purring, but why not? How enlivening it is to not know and to try and find out.

## September 12

## Does that Bee Need a Crowbar?

I learned that bees must pry open bottle gentian flowers to get to the pollen. Only bumblebees can pollinate these blooms, since they are the only types of bees that have the size, and enough "brawn," to do the prying.

This is true for other flowers too. Heather Holm at Restoring the Landscape notes that it's the queen bumblebees who have the tongue length, size, and strength to pry open the petals on Dutchman's breeches. This happens in early spring. The queens, who have overwintered, fly low to the ground looking for good nesting sites. The nectar from Dutchman's breeches helps get their nesting phase underway. If smaller worker bees want nectar from these flowers, they must "cheat" by chewing holes through the petals to get to the sweet stuff. They are not strong enough, nor do they have long enough tongues, to get at it from the top. Wild white indigo is another case of bee strength and attributes meeting tight blossoms. If springtime is especially cool, flowers will open later and queen visits will occur more often, since the queens are stronger.

I was tickled years ago to learn that sometimes bees sleep in flowers. I wonder if they sleep more in these types of flowers, since they had to work harder to even get to the nectar.

## September 13

### Often Heard, Rarely Seen: Ovenbirds and Their Nests

Robert Frost has popped up in my research again. He wrote, in "The Oven Bird": "There is a singer everyone has heard, / Loud, a mid-summer and a mid-wood bird."[132] When I click into audio of ovenbird calls, I am reminded that their rapid, repeating crescendo of a song is often described as "teacher, teacher, teacher," and I sure I have heard this bird! But I'm not sure I've captured it in my binocular sights. Its stout body with streaked front is too distinctive to overlook.

We are well past the height of the most active singing season, which happens in May and June, and these birds do migrate—all the way to Florida and the Caribbean! But I wonder if I might finally find an ovenbird nest. Chris Wood at Connecticut Audubon points out that, "their nests are notoriously difficult to locate on purpose."[133]

I understand they are reminiscent of a Dutch oven, but I got confused as I searched around for images—do they build them from mud or from plant matter? It turns out there is also a South American ovenbird that builds a handsome mud hut. But our local ovenbirds build what All About Birds describes as "a domed nest of dead leaves, grasses, stems, bark, and hair," in thick leaf litter on the open forest floor. The inner cup is lined with deer or horsehair.

Like all ground nesting birds I know of, if the nest is occupied, the female, in an effort to create a distraction, will put on an "injured" act leading me off course if I get too close. What a treat it would be to find a nest like this, ideally long abandoned so as not to disturb the bird family.

## September 14

### Heady

Two weeks ago, I picked up on the scent of wild grapes, but the smallish fruits were not yet ripe. Now, as I scan the tangle of greenery, I am reminded not to rely so heavily on my sight. I close my eyes and take a deep whiff. Yes, there are grapes somewhere in here! I look again and spot a dark blue bunch that I'll have to stand on tiptoes to reach, and this year they are plumper than usual. I am lucky enough to grab them, and I pop a quick snack and fill a small bag with the prize. Sometimes, before I have even spotted it, the aroma clues me in as I walk toward a vine. I love this specific, heady scent that embodies the fleeting sweetness of late summer.

The slip skin is a bit chalky and mildly bitter, and the pulpy fruit has a few tiny, hard seeds, but the inner flavor is luscious to me, similar to what you'd get from a store-bought Concord grape.

In *Northern Woodlands*, Robbie Meyers writes that New England's wild grapes have been of increasing interest to northern winemakers. They have grafted a particularly hardy variety to a sweeter one, perfect for withstanding the harsh aspects of this climate while also adding something good for the palate.

## *September 15*

## The Stone Menagerie

We've named the garter snake that hangs out under our slate step Sylvester Jake. I haven't seen his/her face yet, but often an arc or the tail end of its length is hanging out of the crack between step and riser. I imagine SJ relishes the warmth transmitted by the heated stone. A couple yards to the left, the low stone wall has been home to God knows how many chipmunks over the years. Unoriginally, we have named each one Chippy.

These routine sightings, and the clearing of nearby land to reveal yet another stone wall, have made me wonder about the cohabitation of creatures in and around this ubiquitous outdoor New England decor. Joe Rankin wrote about this in *Northern Woodlands*.

Rankin explains that stone walls serve as "diverse microclimates and ecosystems and opportunities for creatures of all types."[134] The founder of the Stone Wall Initiative, interviewed for the piece, points out that the walls' structure and position relative to the ground help them to serve as both heat pumps and ventilators.

Cats and foxes walk the top; white-footed mice, salamanders, and chipmunks take advantage of the stones' shelter below. I've seen shed snakeskins woven around the stones. Many of these creatures wouldn't bother with the wall if there wasn't an abundance of insects there to feed them. Blanding's turtles, not native to Connecticut but with a pretty wide range including other New England states, migrate to stone walls, where they can find protection from predators and enjoy the comfort of prime, moist leaf litter.

When Robert Frost famously wrote, "Something there is that doesn't love a wall," it's clear he was talking about humans. But he was right that "Good fences make good neighbors."[135] We can interpret this in a welcoming way for the animal and insect friends hugging our stone walls.

## September 16

### The Perks of Untended Squash

Bird expert Melissa Mayntz, writing for The Spruce, reminded readers, "Birds do not have calendars."[136] Of course, this is tongue-in-cheek, a reminder that birds won't necessarily conform to what we would consider to be "fall migration." Their motivation to move south factors in light levels, temperature, climate, and food availability. Also, adult birds won't typically travel until their offspring are mature enough to travel, although parents and their broods don't necessarily migrate together.

Connecticut warblers are one type of bird that does seem to stick close to the expected autumn migration calendar, and they are also a desirable species to spot here. They are described by Tim Spahr, in a guest post for Shorebirder, as "extremely shy and wary."[137] Twice, though, Spahr mentions how these birds enjoy untended squash or pumpkins, so there's a good clue on where to start looking!

For the record, the Connecticut warbler doesn't breed in Connecticut and isn't especially common to the state. It can be challenging to identify, but my own amateur perspective is: wouldn't it be nice to spot a yellowish and greenish bird, maybe in a pumpkin patch? Could that be a Connecticut warbler? If so, it's amazing to know it will migrate all the way down to South America! If not, I'd still enjoy seeing the bird. I'm not sure I'd be able to distinguish the Connecticut variety from a common yellowthroat, a mourning warbler, or a Nashville warbler, especially since this bird tends to run away—literally—they spend a lot of time on the ground!—and vanish into the thicket.

Connecticut warblers are on the Yellow Watch List for declining bird populations. I didn't find much on how to help this species; specifically, the list says best management practices still need some work. For starters, they appreciate brush to hide in and plenty of water. And, maybe, grow some squash and neglect it after a while.

*September 17*

## The Gathering

Migration season is coming for many birds here in Connecticut, and quite a few species will begin to flock this time of year, prepping for their long journeys. Warblers, swallows, and northern flickers are among the types of birds that flock.

Connecticut nature writer Hal Borland was particularly impressed with northern flickers flocking, since they are especially solitary except for this time of year. He watched them chatting loudly together and seeming to play. He wrote, "There is general reluctance to grant birds such emotions as we know as human beings, but what would be more natural than that they, too, should enjoy September? . . . Who knows but that they discuss the summer's events and the trip ahead, in whatever way they can? In any case, the flickers are flocking, and they are obviously having a holiday."

*September 18*

## Clingy Climbers or Trees in Girdles

I've been reading up on vines, especially the woody ones. The more accurate name for woody vines is lianas. I often find them picturesque (well, except for the hairy-looking poison ivy), but of course, they can be damaging. When trees are girdled by these determined climbers, they can be deprived of water and nutrients.

How persistent vines are! They have many techniques for ascending their support of choice. Some, like poison ivy and trumpet creeper, have adhesive roots. Virginia creeper, which can look quite pretty with its scarlet leaves in the fall, uses tendrils with sticky pads at its tips to climb. Plants like grapes also have tendrils, but without the sticky parts. Those types are more about perfecting the art of coiling, and some nonadhesive tendril climbers use modified thorns to give them a leg up.

Other varieties, like wisterias, go bigger. No tendrils for them; they use their full stems to climb. And there is another way too. Plants like clematis use the stalks at the base of their leaves (petioles) to move towards the light.

The word on the street is that, with climate change, lianas will be ever more abundant. They do have some benefits, including helping creatures move from tree to tree, and providing fruit and pollen. Moderation seems to be key, but it's not clear the lianas embrace this principle. They are too busy embracing everything else they find!

## September 19

## Of Weevils and Walnuts

As I walked past a large black walnut tree one evening, I heard a few substantive kerplunks and one quite large nut whizzed just past my head. Has anyone, walking alone, been knocked out by a falling walnut? I bet some folks have at least stumbled away with a substantial, throbbing goose egg.

Under the tree, there were scores of discarded walnut shells. It amuses me to watch squirrels carry the rather cumbersome nuts to a favorite spot such as this, where they settle in and crack them open. This time of year, squirrels' faces bear telltale dark brown walnut stains.

We humans have used the black walnut in dyes and food colorings for eons. And the nut's scent is appealing, to me, reminiscent of a lemon with the smell of growing green things mixed in. There was a men's scent, Black Walnut, sold at the Banana Republic store chain, boasting a "woody, aromatic" fragrance.

If you noted the title, you may wonder what weevils have to do with all this. Well, last Sunday, Tom, Buddy, and I went up to White Memorial Conservation Center. We enjoyed a pizza while watching the marsh. Our attention was soon trained on a weevil wandering about, looking quite cute with his big eyes and snout. Weevils are infamous for laying their eggs in nuts and fruits. Interestingly, they are known to play dead when disturbed. They can, of course, wreak havoc for farmers, who I am sure are well over their cuteness (if they ever perceived it at all) and wish they would do more than just *play* dead.

I realize that even if I picked through photos of all the weevil species, I might still not be able to exactly identify what kind I found. But he (or she!) looks like he could be a nut weevil, and maybe some nut weevil offspring were in that very walnut that tried to give me a concussion.

*September 20*

# Ants Underground: A Tale of Impending Winter

I found myself wondering about the disappearance of ant hills over the winter. My working theory is that the portion of their homes we see—the mounds of sand with entrance holes—simply stop being maintained as the ants hibernate deeper down. These structures gradually come undone, and none of the hibernating ants give any thought to them. Steve Foster, writing for School of Bugs, says the ants purposely close the hole.

In the meantime, I wanted to know what's going on with the ants now. We humans in the Northeast are putting on our sweaters, and one evening I even popped the car heat on! Soon, the ants will have gone deeper underground and will together, sleepily and cozily, surround the queen. I am guessing they are still gathering food and fattening up for the lean winter, but I'll have to look more closely and see how active the entryways are.

Of course, there are so many ant species and they don't all behave the same. Most of us have the ant hill as our frame of reference, but Foster points out that some ants stay warm under tree bark, and some camp out under large rocks, which can hold heat and keep predators away. They might be drawn into our toasty homes, too, which means they can skip hibernation altogether—no need when they are so comfortable and surrounded by food! The same goes for tropical varieties—they stay active all year.

*September 21*

## Cosmopolitan Wonders: Fodder for Debate

My neighbor Susan and I have noticed BIG spiderwebs on and around our porches this year, more than I can remember from any other year. They are feet across, and often I find the builder right at the center, until she notices me and then scurries away behind the gutter downspout. I can't resist the reference to the kids' song about the "itsy bitsy spider" and the waterspout it climbs. Today's resident spider is about the size of my thumb above the knuckle, bigger if she stretches her legs out.

From what I can tell, we've got orb-weavers. That's incredibly vague, as there are thousands of species in this category worldwide. This spider family builds spiral, wheel-shaped webs, although it's not the only family with these web types. A different family with similar webs is known for its long jaws and yet another for making a different type of silk. Anyway, orb-weavers are known to be "cosmopolitan," which, in biogeographical terms, simply means they are found in all or most of the world.

It's incredible how much debate has gone on about the conspicuous center of these spiders' webs, called the stabilimentum. The original theory, that this feature strengthens the web, has pretty much been disproven. So, what's it for? To help camouflage the spider? To make her appear larger? To make the web visible to larger animals that might damage it? To attract prey by reflecting ultraviolet light? To attract the male? To help regulate excess silk? Some suggest that the purpose varies by species.

I went out to photograph my local stabilimentum and put my hand behind it for contrast. Our spider did not appreciate this gesture and hurriedly got away from me again—up the waterspout. (No rain in today's forecast. We know how that would turn out!)

# FALL

## September 22

### Connecticut Cactus

I reviewed a book, *Six Legs Walking*, about entomologist Elizabeth Bernays's life—how fascinating to peer down at the tiny lives of insects and learn so much.

One of Bernays's essays is about the prickly pear cacti near her Arizona home, and she relays how caterpillars saved the day when these plants had taken over huge swaths of Australia, destroying the lives and livelihoods of many a farmer. A hall in Queensland was named Cactoblastis Memorial Hall after the heroic chomping of the strategically introduced caterpillars. A movie called *The Conquest of the Prickly Pear* was made. There's much fanfare over there about the victory, complete with merchandise: plastic souvenir caterpillars.

Here in Connecticut, we don't seem to be in danger of a prickly pear invasion. In fact, many are surprised to learn about Connecticut's only native cactus, which is rare. It survives winter by drying out in the fall, mitigating the danger of freezing and the dangerous expansion that comes with it. The cactus is listed as a species of special concern here.

I have only seen this plant in Connecticut once, and I believe it was planted, not growing wild. It's something to hunt for, perhaps on Outer Island, part of our local National Wildlife Refuge. The yellow flowers in early summer would be a treat to come upon, and I am intrigued by the fact that the plants bear red, egg-shaped, edible fruits called tunas, said to taste like watermelon!

## September 23

### Weaving, Wowing, and a Little Imposing: The Yellow Garden Spider

Definitely not a favorite among those who get nervous around spiders, yellow garden spiders can't help but command attention with their bright yellow and black coloring with some orangey red on the legs, and impressive size. Those that really wow us are the females, who are three times larger than the males, sporting a body length up to one-and-one-tenth inch.

That doesn't sound huge, but the measurement doesn't include the generous helping of legs! Sometimes this spider is called the "writing spider" because of the "scribbled"—thicker, brighter, and more opaque—strands its web includes called the stabilimentum.

The spider I saw yesterday may not have had much longer to live. Females in this area die with the first hard frost after mating. Before that, she will have been "wooed" by her mate plucking on the strands of her web and deposited her egg sacs. In colder climates, the baby spiders will overwinter, emerging in spring—if they make it that long as the sacs are often parasitized.

There was a part of me that wanted to pick this spider up, feel her walk along my arm. I let her be, which was good for both me and her. First of all, it's usually the kindest policy to leave creatures how and where we find them. Also, I read today that they can bite if threatened, although inducing less pain than a bee sting. They do have venom, but its effects are intended for the unfortunates who land in the web, immobilizing them in preparation for suppertime.

## September 24
### Sticky Plant Propagation Schemes

Have you or your dog ever brought home a host of burrs? Did you know what plant they came from? There are so many sticky possibilities. Was it Virginia stickseed, also called beggar's lice, with prickles described as Velcro-like? Or maybe its cousin, nodding stickseed, also sporting sticky prickles? Maybe it was enchanter's nightshade; its tenacious seeds are drawn to socks like moths to a flame.

Burdock burrs are larger, with hooks on them. And then there are sandburs and cockleburs. Matt Candeias at the In Defense of Plants blog says cockleburs can thrive on stream banks, roadsides, or farm fields, altering their growing habits to take advantage of wherever they have landed. Also, cockleburs are quite toxic to humans and other mammals if ingested.

Candeias maintains that the cocklebur deserves some respect, though. It's had to become "clever" about preserving its seeds and assuring they get transported. The fact that it is an annual means it only gets one chance to germinate and propagate, so it produces two seeds that each work differently—one that germinates and another that can stay dormant for decades.

What lesson can we take away from burrs, other than the obvious and ultimate stick-to-itiveness—hang on, no matter what? Maybe it's this: the impulse to figure out how to adapt and maybe stay patient until the time is right.

## September 25
### Shine On

This weekend I had a prize find. I walked over to a scrubby area on the edge of a parking lot because I'd spotted a tall, yellow wildflower. Something hung from it, and I swear it looked metallic.

The rather dull gray of what turned out to be a walkingstick insect must have been catching the light just right. Later, when I researched this phenomenon, the only metallic walkingstick insect mentioned was a brilliant blue one in Madagascar, so that sure wasn't my bug. But it got me thinking.

I've seen quite a few metallic insects. I bet many readers have seen shiny gold, green, and bronze varieties of beetles, as I have. I haven't yet been lucky enough to come across a monarch chrysalis in the wild (only at a butterfly museum), but some of them positively glow, like a fine piece of jewelry. There are other metallic chrysalises that shimmer even more, like the variegated fritillary, native to many regions in the US, and the mirror-like common crow found in Australia.

Why the shimmer? Is it simply beauty for beauty's sake? Nancy Miorelli at Ask an Entomologist explains that both pigment and structure can figure into the "how" of insects or chrysalises appearing metallic. For the "why," the jury is still out. Theories include camouflage—looking like water or reflecting the surrounding visuals—and warning or startling predators. Whatever the reason, these brilliant gems are a pleasure to witness.

## September 26
### Hawk Warning Alarm System

At one point, our neighbor through the trees had chickens. I thought that pursuit had gone by the wayside, but what was that persistent, rhythmic clucking I heard? It sounded chicken-ish but went on too long. Also, the sound, while cluck-ish, had the quality of two wooden blocks being hit together with the committed air of a professional percussionist. "Maybe it's a squirrel?" I said to Tom. I know they have quite the vocal repertoire.

I get partial credit. By "squirrel," I meant a gray squirrel, one of the backyard friends we can count on seeing daily. But chipmunks are sometimes referred to as "striped squirrels." Others sometimes call them "ground squirrels," although there is in fact a creature called a ground squirrel that's a relative, and they live out West.

Lang Elliot, who studied animal behavior and ecology and did his thesis on the social behavior and foraging ecology of the eastern chipmunk, has a website called Music of Nature. Here he explains that "chipmunks respond to hawk fly-bys with a special 'aerial predator alarm call' . . . a hollow, resonant cluck . . . cluck . . . cluck . . . cluck . . . cluck . . . that is unmistakable."[138]

One of his audio examples is a whole chorus of chipmunks clucking. This doesn't mean they all saw the hawk. One started the clucking; the others joined in, in solidarity. Elliott thinks this ruckus discourages the hunting hawk, who will move on when it's clear he's been spotted. If he were to swoop down, the alerted chipmunks are ready for action, wound tight as springs, ready to leap out of sight at the first sign of trouble. Take that, hawk!

## September 27

### Puff Piece

Early autumn, for several years running, we've found sizeable puff mushrooms in our yard.

If you spent substantial time outside as a kid, chances are that at some point you ran across an old puff mushroom and had fun stomping on it, watching the "smoke" rise with each kick. The "smoke" is a wealth of spores—trillions of them!

Well before that smoky, late stage of the mushroom's life, some puffballs grow giant, their size and shape often likened to soccer balls. If you can definitively identify giant puffball mushrooms at this stage, you have the makings of a good meal. But caution must lead: if you were to harvest what you thought might be a smaller puffball, you might in fact have a deathcap or destroying angel mushroom—both potentially deadly. There is also the specter of the pigskin poison puffball to consider!

We have been fortunate to be able to positively identify some finds, and to me the mushroom tastes and has a mouth feel like tofu—neutral, but it takes on the flavor of your sauce.

In a *Northern Woodlands* piece, Madeline Bodin points out what should have been obvious, but I somehow hadn't thought through—these mushrooms love the sun! They frequent grassy fields and cemetery lawns. It's quite a tickle to stumble on one. The biggest viable one I've found so far has been about the size of large cantaloupe. They do not have a distinct stem. One warning sign for foragers to watch for: any color at all on the inside.

Some say fox and deer love to eat giant puffballs. That would be a bonus find—a grazing mammal and a puffball in one swoop.

## September 28

### Snot Gobbles of Autumn

Walking past a yew hedge today, I had a strong sense memory of holding and smelling and squishing the berries as a small girl. I played "kitchen" and used them to make my mud pies more tempting.

They had an appealing scent and a peculiar, mucus-like squishiness. I'm not the only one who picked up on this tactile detail; some call the berry a "snot gobble."

The fleshy part of the berries can be eaten, but the hard stone in the middle is toxic! Instructions I found at Nature's Restaurant convinced me I'll never try one. Here's an excerpt:

"Don't even think about eating the green ones—only eat one berry at a time. Do not put more than one at a time in your mouth, as this only increases the chances you will slip up and eat a seed. Use your tongue, not teeth, to remove the flesh from the berry, then before swallowing the flesh of the fruit, get the seed out of your mouth . . . If you were to bite on the seed, crack it and then accidentally swallow it—you're in trouble."[139]

That's way too much work and worry for me. Of note, the "berry" isn't really a berry, but rather an aril, an enticing appendage that draws wildlife. On YouTube, Roger Griffith says smaller birds have been seen eating just the fleshy part, or even the seed once they remove its coating. Rodents, according to Griffith, have been known to make winter stores of the seeds. He conjectures that the toxic coat falls away by the time they eat them. Some other creatures, like the UK's badgers, seem to be able to eat the arils, pit and all, with impunity.

## September 29

### Prehistoric Pretender, Friend to Scientists (and Potentially Nerve-Wracking Pet)

Walkingstick insects have been pretending to be plants for an incredibly long time. Dan Vergano at National Geographic reported on fossils, showing that these creatures disguised themselves as leaves starting some 126 million years ago, before there were even flowering plants.

I found myself wondering if these insects might have been used for study, since, unlike so many other insects, they can hold so still! Yes—a 2016 *New York Times* article by James Gorman says they are popular research subjects, as well as pets. They are low maintenance, they can't fly off, and their slow pace allows great opportunities for observation.

Something I hadn't thought of before: distressed walkingstick pet owners are sometimes unable to tell if their pets are dead or just playing dead, as their lifeless-looking stick imitations can go on for hours. I guess it is just a waiting game. If your pet is still alive, it will eventually need to move if it wants to eat.

## September 30

### The Singing Marsh

A friend shared a video from our local Pratt Cove. A slew of red-winged blackbirds—could there be thousands?—fill the air with chatting song, like a convention abuzz with excited attendees.

Why have these birds descended en masse into the marsh? Highly nutritive wild rice beckons, and they are busy feasting to fatten up for migration. Come spring, they will be among the first birds to come back from their "vacation" in the South.

I found a 1971 book by the US Fish and Wildlife Service—*Blackbirds and the Southern Rice Crop*. The book contains a lot of lamenting about blackbirds who are drawn to planted rice marshes rather than natural rice marshes. Wild Birds Unlimited confirms this is still going on today: "Large flocks of red-winged and other blackbirds can cause wide-scale damage to sunflower, corn and rice crops. The control measures used to reduce this crop damage are now the major source of adult mortality in red-winged blackbirds."[140] A USDA site lists a slew of schemes for scaring blackbirds away from crops—exploders, helium balloons, radio-controlled planes, scarecrows, pyrotechnics, and recorded distress calls. The worst solution, of course, is avicide—chemicals to kills them off.

Fortunately for our local red wings, no one around Pratt Cove seems to mind if they have a days-long food fest. I worry about how they will fare on their long trip south. My heart will lift when I first hear their buzzy calls in the spring.

## *October 1*

### When Will First Frost Be?

As the nights grow chillier, we wonder which morning we will wake to a sheen of frost on the porch, the plants, the car windshield. Gardeners worry about frost sneaking up and killing their prized specimens.

Predicting frost can be likened to predicting when a woman will go into labor. We have all this technology, but there remains some mystery as to exactly when it will happen. The *Farmer's Almanac* has been calculating all kinds of weather metrics since 1792. Adrienne LaFrance, in an article for the *Atlantic*, suggests that the magazine must have seemed akin to how we view a smartphone today—handheld and chock-full of information and entertainment.

These days, we can simply plug our zip code into an online engine and be given estimated first and last frost dates. As I write this, I'm told to expect the first fall frost in fourteen days.

I like Hal Borland's take on frost: "No garden should endure, with all its dividends and demands, more than about six months a year. The other six months one should be allowed to rest and dream and get rid of the calluses." First frost gives permission for just such a respite. But I don't think many gardeners would rise up to enthusiastically join Borland as he proclaims, "Hail the frost! Hail the blackened vine!" in anticipation of putting away the hoe for a while.

## October 2

### Why So Smart?

I've seen smartweed my whole life but only recently learned the name to go with the plant's "face." It's a type of buckwheat, and the variety I see most seems to be long-bristled smartweed, also known as Oriental lady's thumb.

I assumed this must be a particularly intelligent plant, but quickly found out it is so named because it smarts, or has a stinging quality. The plant's juices can make your eyes run, and the leaves and stems are edible and likened to the experience of hot peppers—best as a condiment used sparingly!

The Native American Ethnobotany Database says Lakota, Sioux, and Paiute peoples used the plant in food, with young shoots eaten as a relish in the spring by the Sioux. Green Deane at the Eat the Weeds site claims that putting a crushed bunch of the stuff in a small body of water will bring the fish to the top, as it interferes with oxygen intake. This is not something I've tried, nor do I plan to! Some people get dermatitis from handling smartweed. Not me—I have happy memories of sliding my thumb and forefinger along its tiny purple blooms to strip the plant as a child.

Ranger Greg's blog at the Museum of Life + Science reminds me of how even the humblest of weeds serves a purpose, pointing out that many tiny creatures use patches of this stuff for shelter or as a place to wait in ambush for prey.

## October 3

### The Katydid's "Swan" Song

Katydids have a distinctive song, and the consensus about it is bittersweet. It is quintessential summer, but it also portends the end of our longer, warmer days. They sing starting in August, and in the *Williamsport Sun-Gazette* (2017), Bill Bower interprets their song to transmit, "frost is coming" or "six more weeks," rather than "Katy did, Katy didn't!"

One katydid sat on my zinnia for twenty-four hours, until I finally touched it (was it dead?) and it hopped away. Was it having a prolonged feast, or could it have been laying eggs in the stem? I'll have to take a closer look. Maybe it was simply slowing down as the nights get cooler.

The frost will kill our current adult katydids, so if you still hear them singing, it really is their swan song. Both the males and the females can produce sound.

I was surprised to learn there are several types of katydids in Connecticut. One is just named katydid, but then there are the true katydid, the common meadow katydid, the eastern shieldback katydid, fork-tailed bush katydid, and more.

## *October 4*

## Return of the American Chestnut (or Patience is a Virtue)

I was pleased to attend a talk and forest walk led by Tom Wessels, a terrestrial ecologist. He is known for being able to "read" the forest and has a whole book about this, aptly titled *Reading the Forested Landscape*.

Wessels touched on the American chestnut blight, first found at the Bronx Zoo around the turn of the last century. An imported chestnut variety from East Asia carried the culprit. Planters didn't know that powerful parasitic fungal forces were at work, and within thirty or forty years, American chestnuts were nearly obliterated in the US.

There is some hope. Wessels has seen five stands of American chestnut that display some resistance to the blight. They are reproducing! Although these reproducers may die, Wessels explains that since they do have some degree of resistance and they must cross-pollinate to make viable nuts, each generation should be more resistant. He is confident that, eventually, the American chestnut will have a renaissance. This could take hundreds (or even thousands!) of years.

In the meantime, there's been some success with genetic engineering toward a stable American chestnut variety, but some in the conservation community express concern about the unknown impact of genetically modified trees. Wessels seems to favor patience over this modification— holding out for the natural return of the super robust specimen that used to be everywhere and fed wildlife and humans alike.

American chestnuts are stump sprouters. Wessels pointed out a wisp of a chestnut tree at the edge of the woods road; this likely came up from root systems more than a century old. Like beech leaves, toothy American chestnut leaves are marcescent, hanging onto the tree through winter.

I'll be keeping an eye out for these yellow specimens on my winter walks, warmed by the hope Wessels held out for future generations.

## October 5

## Birches Walking

In his book, *New England's Roadside Ecology*, Tom Wessels says paper birches are the most northerly growing hardwood in North America. Their white bark helps reflect winter sunlight, avoiding the expansion and contraction that trees with darker barks undergo, sometimes causing them to split open. Their peeling means they shed lichens and algae that would darken the bark. And the bark is rich in oils, which create a vapor barrier against below-freezing temperatures. Wessels calls birch bark "the original Gore-Tex™ waterproof fabric. Water can go into the lenticels, but it can't come out."

These handsome white trees were all around our Vermont summer cabin. I treasured the "scrolls" I coaxed from them. According to ArborDay, white-tailed deer scarf down paper birch leaves in the fall and snowshoe hares eat the tree's seedlings and saplings. Porcupines consume the inner bark. Both rodents and birds eat the seeds, and quite a range of cavity-nesting birds choose the paper birch. Yellow-bellied sapsuckers favor this tree as well. Hummingbirds and red squirrels love the sweet treat in sapsucker-created sapwells.

I thought that during his talk, Wessels said paper birches are moving north. Now, reading up further, I am not sure I heard that right. But many trees are moving north. Joanna Stancil at the USDA says yellow birches from the eastern US might cross into Canada by the early 2100s. Northern white cedar, American basswood, sugar maple, black ash, and bigtooth aspen trees are also heading north. She explains that tree seeds that make their way north, whether by wind or animal transport, are reaching once-frigid areas that have now warmed, making them suitable places to take root.

I find this both discouraging and heartening. I hate that this warming world means that trees will "walk off" and find more comfortable homes. But I marvel at their survival instinct and adaptability.

## *October 6*

### Turtle Shells: Growth, Evolution, and Who Eats Them

I ran a book event at Northwest Park in Windsor, Connecticut, yesterday—a gem of a place. The focus was on stillness and quiet observation in nature. It seemed fitting that Terry, the educator there, brought a turtle shell. Turtles are adept at stillness, as their cold-blooded physiology requires long periods basking in the sun. During the coldest months, they are mostly underwater and quite slow, although not hibernating. Their shells help them with the buildup of lactic acid that results from lack of oxygen.

The shell wasn't a pretty specimen. Terry first thought she had found the old sole of someone's shoe, but when she picked it up, she could see it was a remnant of an old box turtle shell.

I hadn't thought much about it before, but turtle shells, made of keratin and bone, take much longer to decompose than the rest of their bodies. There's not a ton of easily accessible information on this, but at least two sources estimate that the shells hang around for about fifty years. I did find out that there is a caterpillar called *Ceratophaga vicinella* that feeds on the keratin plates of dead gopher tortoises in south Florida. It makes me wonder if this might occur in other turtles, too, and perhaps hasn't been studied yet.

The turtle shell is a curious thing. The creature is fused within it—ribs included—and it grows as the turtle grows, just like our vertebrae grow with us. Its bony plates, called scutes, shed or peel away to accommodate growth.

Turtles didn't always have shells, though. Fossils have proven this. While there's an obvious evolutionary advantage to the protection offered by the shell, scientists think the earliest beginning of shell formation had more to do with the need to dig effectively.

## *October 7*

### Sunchoke Season, and Jerusalem Explained

Sunchokes bloom relatively late in New England. I learned this because Gavin just returned from a fall foraging intensive at Maine Primitive Skills School. There was a lot of digging involved, and a bounty of root vegetables shared at the final feast.

The "sun" in sunchoke refers to this plant's sunflower family. You might have heard the plants called Jerusalem artichokes too. Dale Carson, in *Indian Country Today* (2018), says "Jerusalem" is thought to be a contraction of the Italian word *girasol*, meaning "turning to the sun." The Chef's Garden blog says the term may refer to "New Jerusalem," a name Puritans used for America.

I haven't ever harvested sunchoke, though I hope Gavin will show me how to ID the plant and how best to dig up its roots. The Nomad Seed Project says identifying this plant is more challenging than it might seem, since there are several wild perennial sunflowers that look similar.

For those who know what they are doing, the reward is a knobby-looking root that looks similar to ginger. The Cooking Channel says sunchokes act like potatoes in the kitchen. But this site, and many others, includes a warning about this vegetable's tendency to cause gas. They are sometimes affectionately known as fartichokes, but the problem seems to happen more when they are consumed raw.

## *October 8*

## Geese Departing—It's Complicated

Do Canada geese still fly south for the winter? In an article for *National Geographic*, Brian Handwerk answers this question in the affirmative, but with a caveat—"it's complicated."

If you live in the US or Canada, you likely have looked up around this time of year to see their trademark migratory V-formations. You no doubt were drawn to look up in response to their honking vocalizations.

It's a bittersweet moment, saying goodbye to the geese. Their retreating formations are beautiful to witness, but it means the cold is encroaching. Then again, we know they will be back come spring.

Here's the rub, though: There's a healthy contingent of Canada geese who hang around all year. I often see them well into winter beside a quarry that filled up with water years ago. They sit on the bank, facing the water, wearing an air of ownership. I wondered if I was seeing an effect of climate change—milder winters meaning no need to migrate. But Handwerk says that even around the 1600s, it was known that some of these geese never migrated. And these days, our cities and suburbs have great appeal—lots of food, lots of office parks with large lawns, and typically not too much worry about hunters.

Then again, Handwerk says some birds who haven't migrated in generations may suddenly head toward the Arctic. They will eat and molt there. It may be because they've lost a nest, so they have no goslings keeping them home. An expert Handwerk interviewed pointed out that the same birds hissing at you in the office park may end up in the Arctic or sub-Arctic— "as wild a place as a Canada goose can go."

To many of us, they look rather mundane. But they are a testament to the wild in all of us, to the potential for wide-ranging adventures.

## *October 9*

## Autumn Means Fluff, and Fluff has Saved Lives

Technically, the "fluff" inside milkweed pods is called floss, and in autumn the pods split and release the strands of lightweight floss—seeds attached—into the wind.

At a mini-retreat I ran, one participant described a small piece of fluff that had descended close to her. Then, she looked up. The sky was a veritable superhighway of fluff!

Milkweed floss has had an interesting role in human history. During WWII, kapok, the typical filling for life jackets, became inaccessible. There was a great effort in America to have children collect bags of milkweed pods so the floss could be used as a replacement.

These days, so many are tuned into milkweed for a quite different reason; monarch butterflies need these plants for nourishment so their caterpillars can mature. I am heartened by seeing milkweed around more than I used to in recent years. People are letting it be when it pops up on its own and planting stands of it to help the butterflies along. Many sites provide instructions for harvesting the seeds, with the hope that milkweed can yet again help save young lives. Salvation in nature comes in many forms, and we humans can help with some of the saving.

*October 10*

## Tree Blood in the Cemetery

At Cypress Cemetery, one tall tree stood out—a spruce, I think. I spent more time looking at the four wide "compartments" around the base of the trunk than up at the branches.

In the first compartment, I noticed a tiny set of animal bones and wondered if they had once been in an owl pellet, ejected from high up. I didn't find any fresh pellets, but I noticed bone remnants in the other compartments too. Then I noticed thick globs of resin. They felt oily and tacky, and they smelled so "piney," for lack of a better word. This got me wondering—how is tree resin different from sap? Why do trees make these big globs?

Prabhat S. at Differencebetween says, "Sap is really the sugar that is found in the xylem and phloem cells in trees. Resin is a liquid . . . stored in the outer cells of trees. When a tree is cut or when a branch is cut, resin oozes out and clogs the broken area just like the blood clotting in wounds."[141] So resin is tree "blood" or maybe tree "platelets."

The US Forest Service says we humans have found countless uses for resin—as incense, as a sealing agent in ship building, for varnishes. Resin is added to beer. Rosin, used on stringed instrument bows, is made from— you guessed it—resin. And, of course, amber is fossilized resin, valued for its beauty but also a trove of data. Scientists have studied the DNA of organisms—plant leaves and tissues, flies, mosquitoes, beetles—preserved in amber.

So much arising from those "globs" on the ground!

*October 11*

## Feet Like Grappling Hooks, A Noise Like Distant Thunder

On vacation in the town of Saugerties in the Catskills, I looked up at a historic building's chimney, and a chimney swift was looking down at me.

How many more were within? Home and business owners who find they have a nest must be patient. These birds are federally protected; the birds and their nests cannot be removed.

Eventually, the babies will be raised and the birds will migrate to South America. But chimney occupancy is not just about breeding. Nonbreeding swifts huddle together in chimneys during migration and will roost in chimneys together during the summer. The homeowners will have to get a chimney cap installed if they don't want returning swifts next year.

I like to think people would be sympathetic to swifts, with or without a federal mandate. This sympathy is a good thing since they have been in decline since the 1960s. Once, these birds nested in hollow trees, but they turned to chimneys when there were fewer and fewer trees left standing. And they can't "hang out" just anywhere. The Connecticut Department of Energy and Enrivonmental Protection (DEEP) likens their feet to grappling hooks, so they can't perch easily on horizontal tree limbs as other birds do. Rough chimney walls are a perfect surface to which they can cling. The DEEP site has a nice writeup about how the town hall's chimneys in Willimantic, Connecticut, are a friendly host to swifts; they have hosted hundreds per night.

Connecticut Audubon's Birdcraft Center posted a piece about the chimney swift tower there, a memorial built to honor the organization's founder, Mabel Wright. She wrote, in her book *Birdcraft* (1895), "The whirling of the wings as the bird leaves the chimney makes a noise like distant thunder." Fortunately, many have built chimney swift towers to help these birds out.

*October 12*

---

## Round and (Not Yet) Bald

On the edge of Fort Saybrook Monument Park, I saw the second thing in the area dedicated to botanist Donald Swan. It sounds like he was brilliant and beloved—a professor, president of the Connecticut Botanical Society, and someone who devoted himself to chronicling the state's grandest trees.

The first memorial was a bench, closer to the beach. When I ran across the second one, I didn't see it at first. I was mesmerized by the tight, round cones on a conifer—not something you see every day in Connecticut! Eventually, I saw the marker at the base of the tree; this bald cypress was dedicated to Swan as well.

The tree's needles are soft, lush, and abundant, and it's hard to imagine that this deciduous conifer sheds its needles as it gets colder. Before that, they will turn yellow, russet red, or orange.

Bald cypresses love wet places, so this specimen's placement near a marsh, one that was seeping out onto the lawn a bit, was perfect. However, it's typically a much more southern plant. Project Noah says these trees are only occasionally found as far north as Connecticut.

This tree has many uses "in the wild," as opposed to under our saw blades, where these trees have often landed due to their prized, rot-resistant heartwood. Countless creatures eat the seeds. Floodwaters carry spare seeds along, allowing a chance for new cypresses to take root. On the other hand, the bald cypress is known to help soak up floodwaters and prevent erosion. It also traps pollutants and bald cypress swamps play host to frogs, salamanders, and toads during breeding season. You might find raptors enjoying the tree at its top end.

I bet the botanist would have been proud of this fine tree planted in his name. I plan to visit it through the seasons. In wintertime, I bet it will be hard to imagine these trees returning to their fullness.

## *October 13*

## Creature of the Brackish: Soon to Submerge

I spent many hours at the Stewart B. McKinney National Wildlife Refuge's Salt Meadow Unit yesterday, a lovely place so close to home. I didn't spot any northern diamondback terrapins, but the location got me thinking. These turtles are the only North American turtles that live in brackish water, according to the Connecticut DEEP page. How do their bodies handle all the salt? This species has a special gland near the eyes that excretes it.

They are a state species of special concern. Early in the last century, terrapins were a popular gourmet meal. Harvesting was unregulated, and lobster pots, crab pots, and motorboats didn't help the terrapins' cause. Pollution is a constant threat. I learned that in the Great Meadows Marsh Unit in Stratford—another part of the Refuge—there's a plan to restore the habitat, which has been contaminated by hazardous waste. The diamondback terrapin will benefit from the cleanup, as will the salt-marsh sparrow and other species that favor brackish environs.

As winter approaches, the terrapins will submerge themselves in the mud of tidal creeks to hibernate. I like to think of them tucked in, hoping they will be safe and emerge rested in the spring, ready for a comeback.

*October 14*

## Forest "Eggs": A Stinky Proposition

Gavin pulled a globular mass the size of an egg off some rotting wood nestled in the leaf litter. It seemed to have a "root," but it didn't look like any plant we'd ever seen or even heard of! We were compelled to poke at it and pry it open. The outer sac, once split, gave way to a slimy jelly. Under that, we saw a greenish core.

The "root" was, in fact, a cord-like mycelial (mushroom networking) strand. And the egg-like slime ball eventually triggered a dormant memory for Gavin, pulled up from his reading about fungi. He had found a stinkhorn egg—also called a witch's egg—a stinkhorn mushroom in an early stage. The stink that gives this mushroom its name is much less pronounced at the egg stage, according to First Nature.

There are many stinkhorn varieties, so the best I can do is guess as to which we found. Because the egg was whitish to yellowish, I think we found a young common stinkhorn, in Latin the *Phallus impudicus*, translated as "shameless" and "penis-like." I read that Darwin's granddaughter hated this phallic family of mushrooms so much that she was on a constant crusade to destroy them. Project Noah says she burned stinkhorns in secret to protect "the purity of thought among her female servants."

I heard the eggs are edible, but I found few recipes for them. Project Noah says the inner layer can be eaten raw. The eggs are eaten in France and Germany, sometimes raw, sometimes pickled or worked into sausages. Then again, Alan Bergo at the Forager Chef blog likens their taste to "old dust," and it can't even be masked by a strong pickling liquid; the liquid took on the overpowering taste and smell of the egg.

I won't be chasing down a chance to eat a stinkhorn egg, but it will be fun hunting for them as I walk through the woods.

*October 15*

## Inky Caps: Secrets in the Gooey Mess

Some inky cap mushrooms reproduce in an unusual way; they digest their own caps, rendering the caps and gills into black goo. The goo holds spores that are carried on the wind.

The common name is more than just a visual description. The goo has been used as an ink throughout history. In his blog, environmental artist Peter Ward describes the ink as having "a beautiful dark brown and textured quality . . . liable to fade if exposed to direct sunlight like many plant-based dyes."[142] Before they digest themselves and create that potential for ink, they are whitish, elongated fungi.

The inky cap mushroom family holds another surprise. One type, the shaggy mane, is able, given enough moisture, to grow with such force that it can push its way up through asphalt.

## October 16

## Nothing Gold Can Stay

Robert Frost coined the title of today's entry. This phrase both titles and wraps up his short poem on transience. We here in New England are constantly reminded of transience, of yesterday's summer and tomorrow's winter as we watch the slo-mo fireworks of foliage peaking in reds and golds, then drifting to the ground, cheerful, crisp piles giving way to blown, brown leaf litter.

I drove through long corridors of gold foliage on back roads to UConn yesterday. The gold I saw was likely hickories, maybe some aspens and poplars too. The color is from carotenoids, and it only comes out of hiding once chlorophyll production stops, helping the tree prepare for winter.

When I took Buddy out in the wee hours today, another gold popped out at me in the moonlight from the wide, lush mums in our front bed. *Chrysanthemum* translates to "gold flower," although now they come in many colors—endless cultivars. The website Mums says they used to look a lot more like daisies. I was interested to learn that these blooms are considered "death flowers" in Belgium and Austria. Maybe this arose from the fact that they are one of the longest lasting cut flowers, something that would stay pretty at the graveside for a long time. For me, mums bring memories of fall walks at Jones Beach. There's not much foliage at Long Island's Atlantic beaches, but the landscapers of a particular path from parking lot to boardwalk cram it with fluffy spreads of color.

No "death flower" for me; I prefer the Chinese association of the chrysanthemum with longevity. Nothing gold can stay, but it is something to relish while we have it. I might brew some chrysanthemum tea this morning. Then I can drink some autumn while I work.

## *October 17*

### Virginia Creeper and the Sphinx Moth Who Loves It

Virginia creeper may sound "creepy," but many extol its praises, using words like "carefree" and "forgiving" to describe how little care and maintenance are required in exchange for its spectacular crimson display each fall.

This plant's eagerness to spread has some wondering whether it could be invasive. It is not. Virginia creeper is native to eastern and central North America, and south to Mexico. That said, it can obscure whatever host plant it has decided to climb, and it's hard to get rid of once it's at that stage. It can even cross from tree to tree if the trees are close enough. Birds and other wildlife enjoy the vine's deep blue berries, but they are toxic to us humans and our canine companions.

One creature especially loves the Virginia creeper. Virginia creeper sphinx moth moms lay their eggs on the underside of this woody vine's leaves. When the eggs hatch, the new caterpillars eat their own eggshells, then move on to the leaves. Once fully grown, they spin loose cocoons on fallen leaves on the ground. Here in Connecticut, we have probably just passed the time for the year's second and final brood. The moths will live ten to thirty days, and they feed in a hummingbird-like manner—hovering over the plant. Both the larvae and the adult moths are not super picky; larvae will also eat grape leaves, for example, and adults will sip from several types of flowers.

It's amazing to think about how many tiny creatures live alongside us, often never spotted.

## *October 18*

### Barred Homebodies and the Harriet Tubman Link

Into Birds blogger Renee Hewitt says barred owls don't typically travel far. This observation sparked her feelings of compatibility with these owls. While sticking close to home during the pandemic, she had these mysterious and majestic birds to keep her company.

My sister's family has been watching a barred owl on their Vermont property for some months—a reliable companion. This afternoon, they watched it doze off. When it flies, they are blown away by its wingspan.

Most of us know that an owl represents wisdom. They are associated with the Greek goddess Athena or her counterpart Minerva in Roman lore. Other legends frame the owl as an unlucky or ominous omen. The website Native Languages says Aztec and Mayan religions viewed owls as companions of the gods of death. But the owl seems to have played a positive role for underground railroad conductor Harriet Tubman.

A piece by Allison Keyes at National Audubon Society talks about Tubman using owl calls to communicate covertly with refugees in her charge, and her calls included the barred owl's well-known "Who cooks for you? Who cooks for YOU all?" Keyes's article recounts how a ranger at the Harriet Tubman Underground Railroad State Park shares a poem by Robert Hayden, "Runagate, Runagate," with visitors. The poem mentions Tubman and her owl calls.

I like this thought from Bonita Portzline at the *Gettysburg Times* (2020): "Mimicking birds to alert and lead was a tool that helped her to challenge the moral arc of the universe. Harriet Tubman and the owl's voice helped to bend it toward the just and right."[143]

## October 19

## Lovely Snowberries, But Fish May Not Agree

The map at Native Plants PNW says the common snowberry is found just about everywhere in North America. I'm not sure if the shrub I saw on my trip to Colorado was the common variety, the western variety, the mountain variety, or one of several other types, but I do know I haven't spotted it close to home.

I seem to have "berry radar" lately, taken in by the beauty of shimmering and multi-toned blue silky dogwood berries, the "Easter egg" color palette of porcelain berries (why do some invasives have to be so pretty?), and now these plump, white snowberries that look a bit like vanilla yogurt raisins.

It always seems a natural question: can I eat these? Well, one of the snowberry's nicknames—corpse berry—gives pause. However, the Native American Ethnobotany Database says some tribes, such as the Algonquin, Chippewa, and Sioux, consumed parts of the plant fresh or dried, or in a beverage. Several bird species, including robins and thrushes, eat them, as do bears.

Erna Gunther's book *Ethnobotany of Western Washington* says, per the Green River tribe—also known as the Skopamish and part of the Muckleshoot nation in Washington—"when these berries are plentiful, there will be many dog salmon."[144] It is said that tribes would put large quantities of snowberries into waterways to stupefy or kill the fish.

Sphinx moth larvae eat the leaves of this plant. In fact, snowberries have their "own" snowberry clearwing moth that eats the leaves when in caterpillar form. The adults look a bit like bumblebees, with fuzzy, golden-yellow bodies sporting black and yellow bands.

## *October 20*

## Caching In

Creatures are filling their larders. Nature writer Mary Holland reports on white-footed mice and deer mice using abandoned birds' nests to store food. She shares a photo of an abandoned northern cardinal nest filled with rose hips in her excellent, photo-filled book *Naturally Curious Day by Day*.

Squirrels are busy burying nuts, hickories and acorns mostly. Edwin Way Teale wrote about watching a squirrel unearth buried hickory nuts, reburying them elsewhere. Was it seeking a safer hiding place? Was it pilfering nuts from another squirrel's cache?

At the Atlas Obscura site, Kelsey Kennedy reports on a study in *Royal Society Open Science*. Researchers found that while fox squirrel habits surrounding nuts appear to be random, on closer observation it's apparent they sometimes use a system to organize nuts by size as well as type. Kennedy likened this to how we humans put our groceries away with predictable arrangements so we know where to look each time. (Fox squirrels are found in the Eastern and Central US, but not New England.)

Eastern chipmunks, of course, have a different approach. They fill their cheeks to bursting so they can carry food back home. The Georgia Department of Natural Resources reports that chipmunks can fit thirty-two beechnuts, seven acorns, or up to seventy sunflower seeds in those cheeks.

## October 21

### Sticky, Silky, Crazy Strong

This morning I was surprised by how big a cobweb in a neglected corner had grown. I grabbed a towel to brush it away and was impressed with the stickiness of the stuff. That got me wondering about the amorphous cobwebs inside and the often elaborately designed spiderwebs outside.

Science ABC says "cobweb" can simply mean "old [and typically long-abandoned] spiderweb," but there is a spider family called *Theridiidae* that is known as "cobweb spiders." If you've seen their webs, you know they're not exactly works of art. They are known to be disorganized. The stickiness is due to droplets that will snare insects passing by, and of course, that stickiness grabs dust too.

It's not clear why some spiders create art and others just slap up a sheet of unimpressive-looking stickiness. But it does appear it's not just about looks. Some orb-weavers are said to create a tighter weave to catch flies, and a stronger and stickier web to catch crickets. They do this in response to the prey that are most prominent nearby. Then again, there is the seemingly less inspired trashline orb-weaver, who wraps up garbage, including excrement and spare prey parts, in a straight line. This helps hide the spider and her egg sacs, so you could argue it's especially clever—less work and they can hide in plain sight.

Whatever the aesthetic, spider silk is highly prized for its strength (superior to steel) and flexibility, and attempting to reproduce those qualities has stymied scientists. There's a long history of spiderwebs being used for bandages, and scientists have experimented with using golden orb-weaver silk to make a foundational mesh on which to grow new skin, helping in healing serious wounds.

## October 22

### Witch Hazel Shooting Gallery

One of my favorite parts of Geoffrey A. Hammerson's book *Connecticut Wildlife* is Chapter 22: "A Naturalist's Calendar." For each day of the year, Hammerson shares a cross-section of observations he's made over the years. He recounts bringing witch hazel seedpods into his office around this time of year, with the delight of watching the seeds shoot out after a day.

The Wild Seed Project recommends October as the ideal month for collecting witch hazel seedpods—so important to gather them before they decide to explode! If you can get them inside a paper bag before that, the seeds will be contained.

Witch hazel adds unique and welcome color in these parts as it is such a late bloomer. But there are many other plants that engage in "shooting," from sphagnum moss to jewelweed to wisteria.

*October 23*

## Inside a Hornets' Nest

I once carried a large hornets' nest, no doubt blown down by a recent storm, from a field back to my car. It was bigger than a basketball and, of course, well past the time when there would be any danger. With most wasps and hornets, it's only the mated queen who overwinters, often under bark or in some tiny rock crevice, maybe even a burrow.

I might have made a pretty penny with my find. It may sound odd, but you can go online and buy abandoned nests. Hornets' nests can be deterrents to new hornets setting up shop, and there are plenty of fake versions to buy. Many like the aesthetics of the nests; others relish taking them apart.

My big find sat on a shelf above my desk. One day, I watched a spider climb out. In *Connecticut Wildlife*, Geoffrey A. Hammerson inventoried the contents of a bald-faced hornet's nest he dissected: one sleepy adult hornet, one dead one, quite a few dead larvae and pupae, a small spider, and a yellow moth.

It's possible the yellow moth wasn't simply taking shelter. Caterpillars of a particular kind of moth, *Chalcoela iphitalis*, or sooty-winged chalcoela, eat the larvae of various kinds of wasps. These moths can overtake paper wasp nests. In a column for the *Columbus Dispatch*, naturalist Jim McCormac points out that adult paper wasps often feed on moth caterpillars, labeling this moth invasion, "a particularly apropos form of revenge."[145]

*October 24*

## Forest Gems: Slug Feasts and Acid Trips?

Walking at Chatfield Hollow State Park, I was delighted to spot a cluster of *Amanita* mushrooms. My best guess was that these were *Amanita gemmata*, *gemmata* meaning "gemmed," but a newsletter reader corrected me; she was pretty sure they were *Amanita muscaria*, or fly agaric, which are usually bright red with white "dots"—the quintessential "toadstool" often seen in fairy tale illustrations. The specimen I photographed was a glowing orange dotted with white. Mushroom ID can be tricky!

*A. gemmata* and *muscaria* both come with dire warnings. An unfortunate human who decides to eat *A. gemmata* will start appearing intoxicated or have visual hallucinations three minutes to three hours later. Severe gastrointestinal distress, agitation, slow heartbeat, and sometimes coma, convulsions, and death can follow. Similarly, *A. muscaria* are infamous especially for their central nervous system effects, with a risk of death in severe cases.

*A. gemmata* are found in mixed hardwood-conifer forests or pure pine stands. They are in mycorrhizal relationships with several kinds of pines and often live near Norway spruces. The relationship is mutually beneficial; the tree gives the fungus some carbon, and the fungus provides nutrients and protection from disease. *A. muscaria* has symbiotic relationships with many trees, including pine, oak, spruce, fir, birch, and cedar.

Who else can benefit from *Amanita* nutrients? Slugs eat some *Amanitas*. Quite little is known about the mushroom eating habits of slugs. Do they help spread spores? How do their systems manage some highly toxic varieties? Why are they repelled by some fungus types?

The toxin in several *Amanita* types is a metabolite of ibotenic acid. Are there some slugs on the forest floor recovering from "acid trips" from their mushroom nibbles? *Amanita*, so captivating to behold, can remind us of the many mysteries still unsolved about lives beyond the human realm.

*October 25*

## Down of a Thistle: Autumn Floating Toward Winter

Is it too early in the year to quote Clement C. Moore's poem "A Visit from St. Nicholas"? Maybe, but it popped into my head yesterday as I walked past a host of fluffy plants. Moore describes the reindeer in his oft-quoted poem as flying easily, with the implication that it was a silent exercise too: "And away they all flew, like the down of a thistle."[146]

I wonder how many kids today, perhaps hearing the poem on Christmas Eve, can readily call up a mental picture of a thistle. But in 1823, when Moore's poem was first published in a Troy, New York newspaper, we were a much more agricultural society. Kids then were likely more familiar with the thistle, whose seeds can travel far on the fluff the plant makes and wreak havoc by inserting themselves enthusiastically into planted crops. It creates a problem for grazing cattle too; they avoid it because of the thorns. I don't know if it's still true today, but a 2013 article about a serious thistle problem for Missouri farmers cited a law that says, "landowners must control all thistles each year to prevent them from going to seed."

Thistle seeds can travel up to a half mile. Impressively, another down-making plant, a giant type of dandelion called salsify or goat's beard, is said to travel across mountain ranges out West. A host of other plants spread this way, including fleabanes, clematis, milkweed, and cattails, and the use of the fluff isn't limited to seed dispersal. We humans have used cattail fluff for stuffing and insulation, and as a cotton ball in wounds. Songbirds line their nests with it.

How many types of fluffy plants or their airborne seeds can you spot on your autumn walks?

## October 26

## Slug Eggs

They look like small crystal balls to me, or translucent pearls—quite pretty! Typically, they are found in garden debris or under logs.

If you search "slug eggs," you find determined gardeners on the warpath. Slugs can mean garden destruction. But I like Mary Holland's viewpoint better—look for them under rotting logs, which protect them from freezing as well as from drying out. On her Naturally Curious site, Holland cautions: "remember to place the log back exactly as you found it."[147]

But before you do, look at that cluster of about thirty eggs. It really does resemble a bit of jewelry, about an inch around.

BBC Earth posted a video of slug eggs hatching inside a wall. The embryos are spinning impatiently in their orbs, not looking very different from early human embryos. It only takes about four weeks for the eggs to hatch, and I found it adorable to see the little eye stalks tentatively poke out and, milliseconds later, the newly minted slugs gliding away from the egg mass. The new slugs were translucent too. I'm not sure if that's true for all baby slugs, but I did learn that some slugs can change color because of food they've consumed as well as exposure to light and moisture.

*October 27*

## City Lichens and Macabre Lichens that Walk

Matt Candeias at the In Defense of Plants podcast interviewed Jessica Allen, a lichenologist who clearly chose the right profession. She is over-the-moon excited about anything to do with lichens, with the sort of enthusiasm that's contagious.

When you study lichens, you end up learning about other creatures who interact with them and also about the health of our environment. Lichens are extremely sensitive to air pollution. Allen says they seem more "stressed" in cities, but still, there are many to be found in urban spaces. She wrote a book about northeastern urban lichens.

Allen lit up when talking about lacewing insects, or more specifically, their larvae. I read up a bit more, focusing on green lacewings, which are widespread across the continent. (There are 1300 lacewing types worldwide!) In the larval stage, green lacewings pile plant litter, dead insect debris, and lichens on their backs, which protect them from predators like ants. Also, biologist Thomas Eisner found, by "undressing" some lacewing larvae, that the naked insects had a lot of trouble infiltrating aphid colonies without their outfits.

The larvae eat like there is no tomorrow, feeding on any small insect they find, with a special penchant for aphids. They are sometimes called aphid lions or trash bugs. They truly can look like a little bit of lichen that has decided to take a walk.

*October 28*

## Late October, but Hearing Spring

I am fully aware that November is just around the corner, and when I walked Buddy this morning, I wore a hooded jacked to keep the cool drizzle at bay. But when I sat at my desk a little later, I heard spring—that is, my personal audio icon of spring. The song of the white-throated sparrow recalls screen windows and burgeoning daffodils. For whatever reason, I haven't heard a white-throated sparrow around here in a while. This bird has one of the handful of songs that I can identify for sure: "Poor Sam Peabody, Peabody, Peabody."

A quick look at the migration map on All About Birds told me that while these birds are found in the Northeast all year, those that breed here tend to leave in autumn, and they are replaced by wintering birds who were busy breeding farther north this spring! I wonder if that gap in hearing my favorite bird song had anything to do with this "changing of the guard."

Getting your feeders ready? Project Feederwatch says these birds like cracked corn and black oil sunflower seeds.

*October 29*

## Gliding Through Our Treetops (or Attics?): The Northern and Southern Contingents

I know flying squirrels are exceedingly adorable. I know they stretch out their arms to help their extra flaps of skin go taut, helping them glide from tree to tree. I watched one launch flights in my bedroom after it "visited" from the attic, and we chased it around. They can shift direction with the help of their rudder-like tails.

But when I looked them up at CT.gov, I learned a new fact: Connecticut has two types of flying squirrels—the southern and the northern varieties. The southern variety, surprisingly, is much more common here in Connecticut and has gray-brown fur on top and sides with white fur along its "undercarriage." The northern variety has the same, except it is a bit darker and redder, overall. Both types eat a similar diet—seeds, nuts or berries, fungi, insects, small animals.

It is their especially big, dark eyes that make them cute and also help them see at night. I guess their nocturnal activity helps explain why I've never seen one in nature. But they are known to glide to the forest floor to get their food, mostly at dusk. They've got a great vantage point, of course, so I'm sure they avoid launching if they spot a human walking below. Still, I'd love to come upon one as it floats down from its spot high in the canopy.

And the canopy must be just right: generally close, but also with enough open space below so that gliding is unimpeded! As winter approaches, our houses look more and more attractive to these creatures. Sometimes they will share a nest, huddling for warmth.

## October 30

### Is Tennessee the Buckeye State?

If you know what the states' nicknames are, you'll know that the answer to today's title is no. Tennessee is the Volunteer State, a nod to its many soldiers who fought the British in the War of 1812. Ohio is the Buckeye State, owing to the buckeye trees that once covered the land. Buckeye nuts are so named because they resemble the eye of a male deer, an association modern supermarket-goers might not readily make, but it made sense that practiced hunters put the two visuals together.

During my writing residency on an old orchard property in eastern Tennessee, I saw an abundance of buckeyes. Not the nut—the butterfly! The common buckeye was a welcome sight. Its brown, orange, and black color scheme with dots of purple drew me, although they are quite jumpy in response to nearby movement. I never did manage a good photo!

Those of us in the northern states and Canada can also see this elusive color show flitting about, but for breeding, these butterflies often prefer to be down south. Buckeyes in the north will soon be heading back down for the winter—if they haven't left already. In the meantime, they will enjoy late-season asters especially.

The first part of the Latin name *Junonia coenia* makes sense. *Junonia* means "peacock," and the butterfly has false eyes like the peacock's tail.

Butterflies often get increasingly beautiful as they go through their stages, especially in cases where the chrysalis is a veritable work of museum-quality art. The most stunning stage is that of old age, for most!

I wish we would perceive humans in the same way—breathtakingly beautiful as they near the end of the road, having gone through all of the trials and tribulations of life.

## October 31

### The Merry Crabapple

Chelsea Green Publishing's blog says, "A crabapple tree will merrily produce crabapples with zero maintenance."[148] This is my kind of horticulture, and the truth of this statement is borne out by the random crabapple trees I've been running across. One was in a tangle of leggy weeds behind a supermarket, sporting many fruits with subdued, Bosc pear-like color. Another, with rosy apples, looked like it had lived in its streetside spot forever, churning out an enthusiastic number of tart offspring.

The blog refers to these fruits' "surprisingly sweet secret," so I had to read on. Typically, a few tiny bites are all I can muster. Some say their name is shorthand for their sourness. The trick to turning these apples into something more palatable starts with a taste. If they are sour but still taste like an apple and are crisp, there may be hope. If you spit the flesh out immediately because it's so acrid, move on!

Crabapply jelly seems to be the go-to recipe, although the blog also suggests jazzing up your applesauce by adding some of these renegades, or juicing and fermenting to make cider vinegar. The jelly involves a nearly half proportion of sugar.

The Yale Nature Walk site says people crossbred some crabapple varieties to create the much more palatable apples we eat today. And, as with many berries and fruits that are not tasty in raw form to humans, an array of birds and mammals—deer, rabbits, woodchucks, voles, foxes, etc.—have no problem digging into crabapples. Songbirds appreciate the cover of the foliage as well as the fruit.

## November 1

### Farming the Forest

I went to a local talk once in which the elderly, and seemingly quite knowledgeable, speaker discussed how Native Americans in our local Connecticut woodlands had "farmed the forest." The practices he described were more than just foraging. Trees were not razed to make room for crops, but the indigenous people would more gently encourage certain foods, like berries or nuts, to grow in a particular area, keeping the surrounding woods intact.

David J. Tenenbaum's piece on the University of Wisconsin's The Why Files site quotes professor Nancy Turner, who has spent years studying indigenous agriculture in British Columbia. She says, "They used perennial cultivation. 'Keep it living' was part of their philosophy, and it shows the way they valued other life. A lot of perennial plants were being cultivated, but outsiders saw this as random plucking." She also noted that streams were "gardened"—tended and cleaned—for salmon, with eggs being transplanted to new channels when the stream changed course.[149]

There is a modern practice of forest farming too—cultivating crops beneath the shade of taller trees—typically for supplemental income. Harvests include medicinal herbs, mushrooms, native ornamentals, moss, various fruits and berries, nuts, ramps, and decorative plants. A botanical supplement called "wild simulated goldenseal" looks quite promising for the pocketbook. Dr. Jeanine Davis's article for the NC State Extension service says a forest farmer can make over $10,000 per half acre of this plant—if they can wait five years to harvest!

# November 2

## Nurses in Nature or Trees on Stilts

I've been reading *New England's Roadside Ecology* by Tom Wessels. Nurse logs come up quite a bit in his book, and he says white pine is the only Connecticut tree species that makes a good nurse log.

In his blog on nurse logs at Nature's Depths, neuroscientist John Palka explains that decaying wood is a good substrate for growth, aided by the moisture held in that space. A seed that lands on a fallen tree that will serve as a nurse log can find a comfortable crack in which to start germinating, and the space left by the fallen tree allows for a decent dose of sunshine.

Have you ever spotted a tree that looks like its roots are standing on tiptoe, above ground? This is referred to as being on stilts. When the nurse log fully decays, the tree that grew on it is left standing high, sometimes with an impressive measure of empty space between the stilts.

Science is finding more and more instances of trees sharing resources, and in this case, the nurse log is serving a great purpose after death.

The unfailing generosity of trees is something we humans can look to. With their much broader experience of time and quiet absorption of and contribution to the earth, surely trees have something to teach us.

## November 3

### Monarchs in Mexico and the Many Milkweeds that Helped

Journey North, a migration tracking website, has been reporting on the monarchs. On October 10, large numbers were seen streaming across Kansas and Oklahoma. On October 17, large roosts were seen in Mexico.

It's lovely to read about, but it doesn't take away from the fact that the monarch population has significantly declined. I have hopes that more folks planting milkweed may help, just as bluebird nesting boxes in the 1960s and 70s made a difference. The birds had lost many of their natural nesting opportunities.

Quite a few people think of the monarchs' favored milkweed as a single plant, but there are host milkweeds for egg laying and other varieties that provide nectar. The US Forest Service lists twenty-four beneficial types of milkweed plants for monarch butterflies in eastern North America alone.

Those who study botany perform a real service and can help us sort out what type of milkweed to plant. For example, tropical milkweeds that can grow year-round in mild climates also carry the risk of facilitating monarch infection with a debilitating parasite. Planting milkweed native to your region is crucial.

In Mexico, monarchs traditionally return at the time of the corn harvest. The indigenous Purépecha Indians tracked their fall arrival and coined the name *parákata*, for "harvester butterfly." Their arrival coinciding with the Day of the Dead holiday is connected to the folklore that they are the souls of ancestors returning for a visit.

## November 4

### Did They Jump for Joy at the First Snow?

We had some "real" snow this week. Not high volume, but in New England, when it first "sticks"—coats the grass and the cars—that is a harbinger of the season's change.

Snow has its appeal, but it doesn't make me jump for joy because it can impede my outdoor adventures a bit. But for snow fleas and snow flies, a snow day is an ideal day.

Most of the time, when we are out and about, snow flies and snow fleas are laying super low. They exist in the unseen microworld that flourishes in leaf litter. A piece by Gwen Pearson in *Wired* says snow fleas, which are springtails that can leap up to 100 times their body length, "help make more soil by snarfing up fungal spores, insect poop, and other debris."[150]

I've written about snow fleas before, but snow flies are a new one on me. They also like leaf litter and, contrary to their common name, are flightless. Both the fleas and the flies mate during cool weather. They thrive on the surface of snow and, of course, become much easier to spot against the white backdrop.

The University of Washington is asking for citizen science helpers, mountaineers or backcountry skiers in the state who can collect some snow flies for study. They are trying to determine how these creatures' brains and muscles are adapted to work in below freezing temperatures.

Pearson claims that snow fleas are quite adorable up close. With the next snowfall, I want to go out with my hand lens, ready to magnify what looks like scattered, jumping pepper on the snow.

## *November 5*

### Bobcat with a View

Tracker/guide/photographer and sometime philosopher Paul Rezendes's book *The Wild Within: Adventures in Nature and Animal Teachings* starts with Rezendes leading students on a bobcat tracking expedition. To immerse themselves in the path and experience of the animal, they crouch and crawl through brush and scramble clumsily along harsh ridges that the bobcat would have navigated with lithe and silent steps.

Here's the part that got me: "I've found more bobcat lays than I can remember, and almost every one had a scenic view."[151] He describes lays as "motel rooms" that bobcats have scattered through their territories. Rather than denning after hunting, they will rest in these places.

I know the bobcat's "room with a view" might not be chosen for aesthetic reasons. Perhaps the view coincides with harder to get to, safer spots, and of course, it has the advantage of letting the cat survey all manner of comings and goings. Still, the idea of the bobcat gazing down on a pleasing landscape grabs me. The lay Rezendes described was in a small, scooped out quasi-cave in a cliff face. It looked southward, over the hills and dense woodlands of northcentral Massachusetts. He could see reservoir waters in the distance. This snug spot had been chosen carefully by the cat.

Local papers and social media often report bobcat sightings. Roughly four thousand sightings have been reported in Connecticut this year. With winter coming, the cats won't hibernate or migrate. They will be out during the day more often as they change their habits to match the daytime activity of their prey in winter.

## November 6

## Bedtime for Land Beavers: Groundhogs Down Under

On my last full day of writing residency in Tennessee, I emerged from my trailer to spot a groundhog in the middle distance, trundling around on the lawn by the barn and getting his fill of grass. I had my binoculars, so I placed myself on a hill and spied on my rodent neighbor. The groundhog showed no alarm, and something about his pace was very relaxing. He'd munch on some grass for a while, stop briefly as if listening for any sign of danger, and then continue moseying around his spot. Gradually, he walked out of my visual range, I suspect to a burrow below the barn.

It's around the time that groundhog hibernation starts in Connecticut. Their burrows are well designed, angling uphill at first to prevent flooding and including a designated latrine area that will be sealed off when full.

I'm not sure why it never occurred to me before that groundhogs look like beavers. I was tickled to learn they are sometimes called "land beavers." The nickname "whistle pigs" refers to the high-pitched noise they make to signal danger. And most of us know the term "woodchuck," although it has nothing to do with wood—or chucking it. Partnership with Native Americans says it possibly derives from the Algonquian word for the creatures: *wuchak*. There may be connections with Narragansett and Cree words, as well.

I've never craned my neck upward to search for groundhogs, but I will have to start. I was surprised to learn they sometimes climb trees!

# November 7
## Beaver Pantries

I checked the daily log in *Connecticut Wildlife* by Geoffrey A. Hammerson. One November day, Hammerson logged what he saw in a beaver food cache—eastern hemlock, mountain laurel, and yellow birch, with a striped maple topping it all off.

A cache that feeds a colony can contain up to about 2500 pounds of bark, leaves, and twigs, with the larger logs used to weigh down the pile, according to naturalist Mary Holland.

In an article for the *American Midland Naturalist*, Peter E. Busher reports on "cafeteria-style feeding experiments" in western Massachusetts. Beavers seemed to especially like caching witch hazel branches. They seemed to prefer red maple for an immediate snack or for construction purposes at first, only storing these types of branches as it got colder. Busher concludes that in early autumn, the beavers are more discerning, but they get less picky later in the caching period, even including pine, which they didn't favor earlier, in their stores.[152]

When the pond ices over, beavers will be able to get to their underwater cache and have plenty to eat this winter.

# November 8
## Curious Spiders and Bees: They Are Watching Us

Today a Facebook friend posted a picture of a golden jumping spider, quite magnified in the shot, and made a joke about selling the house to get away from it. While she is an insect lover and could appreciate the pretty iridescent color sported by her visitor, she still felt freaked out by the eight spiky legs. Imagine if she knew it was watching her intently, even curious about her!

I read a Q and A on the Oregon State University Extension Service's site. "Was this jumping spider stalking me?" The inquirer recounts an experience of trying to remove a spider from his steering wheel, only to have it climb right back up to the same spot and appear to be staring him down. The expert explained that jumping spiders use their sharp vision to study prey, and this makes them appear to be curious. Also, there's a type of jumping spider called *Phidippus audax*—the name translates as "audacious" or "daring." So, in other words, size difference notwithstanding, they will have no problem getting up in your face.

Reading this made me think about the carpenter bees I've watched around our garage. On so many occasions, they have come up to me after I've left my car and hovered close to my face for a while. I've always had the impression they were curious about me. It turns out, they are! Winton Ray at the Cincinnati Zoo blog explains that male carpenter bees are vigilant about their territory and will intensively investigate anything in their proximity. No need to worry about this intensity, unless perhaps you are another male carpenter bee.

## November 9
### Nests De- and Re-constructed

Vermont's Otter Creek Audubon Society came to the school where my sister works and treated the kids to some nest education and creation. The kids relished pulling abandoned nests apart to see what they might find: fishing line, yarn, human hair, horse hair, bug carcasses, live bugs, and seeds. Then they were tasked with planning and building nests of their own.

I bet this assignment created newfound appreciation for birds' skills, persistence, and ingenuity. What materials to gather? Are they soft enough and safe for baby birds? How to hold the nest together? Where is the best place for the nest? What kind of decor might be available, and what purpose might it serve?

Research suggests that nest decor isn't a random happening. One study of rock sparrows found that feather decorations seemed to serve as a status symbol and may have drawn females to the nest. Another study of black kites in Spain found that these raptors were using plastic, and not just any plastic—it had to be white!—to intimidate other birds. It's thought that the birds who choose the plastic are displaying bravado, purposely drawing attention to their nests because they are "all that"— confident and strong enough to fend off other birds who might covet what their conspicuous abodes have to offer.

## November 10

### Trees Growing on Trees

Today I stopped to scrutinize a wide, gnarly, deciduous tree at Fountain Hill Cemetery. I'm not sure what type of tree it is or even how much life is left in it, but I noticed several small conifers growing out of crevices higher up.

How had they gotten there? Had their seeds simply blown over, or did some pine nut-loving birds drop them? The minitrees growing on the much bigger and older tree are scrawny but well defined. I wonder how big they will get.

Plants that grow on other plants without parasitizing them are called epiphytes. At the Our City Forest blog, Chad Machinski explains, "These plants only use the tree as a support system and take no nutrients from the tree itself. They instead rely on rainwater to carry nutrients down tree bark or on collections of soil and detritus in the crotches of branches."[153]

Finding a fully developed tree growing atop another is quite rare. Online you can find photos of a tree in Italy called Bialbero di Casorzo; it is a full cherry tree growing out of a mulberry tree.

More often than trees growing on trees, epiphytes are other kinds of plants, and they seem better suited and more varied in areas outside New England. Take the Spanish moss (technically a bromeliad) down south, leather leaf ferns in redwood forests, and orchids and bromeliads in rain forests.

I've not yet seen a redwood forest up close, and I think once the universal awe at the sheer size of the trees passed, I might be even more fascinated by the many other kinds of trees growing on these giants. They include cascara, Sitka spruce, Douglas fir, western hemlock, and California bay laurel. Epiphytes in redwood forests make it possible for an array of terrestrial animals to live in the canopy.

## November 11

### Who Lives in Moss?

As color gradually fades from the landscape, I love that moss hangs on through it all, offering bright, lush spots on what becomes a much more monotone world.

The simple structure of moss belies its multifaceted functions: it breaks down rocks and soil and absorbs moisture in the landscape. It is often a pioneer, a first "settler" of rocky land. We humans appreciate its vivid greens, but a host of creatures survives and thrives because of moss.

Within moss, creatures find pockets of air, plentiful water, insulation, and protection. Dominant aquatic moss-dwelling invertebrate groups include nematodes, tardigrades, and bdelloid rotifers. All of them are nearly microscopic. All are equipped to dehydrate when water is scarce and then "come alive" again when water returns. The tiniest inhabitants are not alone, though; there are plenty of air breathing and more easily seen spiders, worms, and insects living in or under moss. Scientists have techniques for extracting both aquatic and air-breathing creatures from moss. It would be a neat exercise to see what comes crawling out!

Many sources suggest that we humans consider moss lawns to replace our typical grass. One happy side effect is the wealth of lightning bugs likely to result! These insects especially favor moss. Birds, amphibians, and reptiles will be happy about the "buffet" of smaller creatures living in and under the moss; several types of birds will use it to line their nests. The air will be cleaner, and erosion will be staved off. Sounds like an intriguing proposition.

## November 12

### Yellow Shoes in the Woods

A walk in the woods around this time might have you coming home with gold-dusted sneakers. The spiky projections at the center of ground pine, a clubmoss (not actually a moss), are primed to explode, ejecting their bright yellow spores. The spores will ride the wind and thus propagate the species. Connecticut boasts a host of clubmosses—mountain firmoss, shining firmoss, inundated bog clubmoss, blue clubmoss, and so on.

According to William Needham's *Hiker's Notebook* blog, reproduction is painstakingly slow, in that the plant lies dormant for up to seven years and can take up to fifteen years to reach sexual maturity. The spores have unique properties with tons of applications. They are famous for having been used in flash photography and magic tricks since they ignite in a flash. A property that minimizes friction makes them useful in everything from body powders to skin-soothing medicines to latex condom coatings.

Foxtail clubmoss is endangered in Connecticut, and fir clubmoss is a species of special concern; it may even have left the state entirely. Years ago, these plants were harvested for Christmas decor. That, combined with slow reproduction, has spelled danger for these plants.

## November 13

### Foxes in Winter, Gekkering to Come

I was surprised to look out my kitchen window and see snow yesterday morning. Not enough to turn the fallen leaves white, but enough to remind me that winter is indeed coming, a bit sooner than expected. Last evening, as I drove home after dark, a fox crossed the road before me.

Megan McCarthy McPhaul's article in *Northern Woodlands* reminds me that foxes become much more active as the cold comes on—no hibernation for these creatures. They travel farther; they are busy day and night. Breeding will start about mid-January, and there will be pups (or kits or cubs—according to your preferred name for fox babies) starting in early spring.

Before breeding, though, foxes have little interest in dens, preferring to be outside hunting and foraging. I loved the mental picture sparked by a description on a wildlife control website of foxes sleeping beneath a fresh coating of snow. Luxurious tails are crucial protection in the cold, a plush wrap to burrow into for warmth.

If you are ever lucky enough to hear a fox "chuckling," that sound is called a gekker. The online Animal Facts Encyclopedia says "a litter of kits play-fighting will roll around gekkering for hours at a time. And a vixen defending her den will gekker an intruder right out of her territory."[154]

## November 14

### Leggy and Hungry

They startle with their "hairy," skittering look, although what we are seeing isn't hair—it's fifteen pairs of legs running fast!

Kiersten Hickman at Family Handyman says people often want to kill this houseguest. But the house centipede quickly and efficiently grabs roaches, silverfish, termites, moths, bedbugs, and flies with its many legs and eats them up.

These insects are born with eight legs, and the count continues to grow into adulthood. Their progressively longer legs from front to back helps them avoid tangling when they run fast. Their speed? Equivalent to us humans running 42 mph!

And then, of course, there are millipedes. How to tell centipedes and millipedes apart? You might figure, from their names' prefixes, that it's the numbers of legs that are the best clue. Millipedes can have up to 750 legs, while centipedes can have more than 350 legs. But who can even begin to count them as the insect runs away or curls up into a tight ball? Centipedes will run away immediately once uncovered, while millipedes will roll up and stay motionless.

Also, generally, millipedes move more slowly. They eat different things too. While centipedes go after small insects, millipedes eat decaying plant matter.

Centipedes are more likely to be spotted in our homes, where they are going after bugs. On occasion, a millipede might come inside, too, since they seek protected places in cold weather. They are spotted indoors in early spring as they come out of their winter hiding places.

## *November 15*

## Birds in Hedges: Have You Heard Their "Conventions"?

During my whirlwind day, I stopped to pause, look around, and breathe the outside air—albeit in a parking lot. Soon I heard chattering and chirping from a multitude of birds. Where were they? I scanned the trees, which looked bare. Then, I realized their songs were emanating from a row of boxwoods. I could not see one of the birds!

I like the question Cathleen Kenna's article in *Today's Farm* asks: "Are your hedges fit for birds and bees?" *Today's Farm* is an Irish publication, so not all the creatures the article names are found in Connecticut hedges. But, oh, the menagerie that can inhabit a hedge: "The dense base of the hedge is home to small birds such as robins and small mammals including hedgehogs [oh, how I wish for local hedgehogs] and shrews [we have those!]. In hard weather, this may be the only unfrozen foraging ground."[155] Kenna frames hedges as "networks for nature," with birds, bats, and bees sticking close to them rather than lingering in open spaces.

Rachel Freeman Long, writing at *Green Blog*, offered a summary of a California study that involved counting birds in hedgerows over time. Researchers counted 2,203 birds from winter into spring and discovered that farms with hedgerows drew forty-one species, while control areas (weedy edges of farm fields) only drew twenty-two. Also, three times as many birds used hedgerows in wintertime compared with spring—I am sure they appreciate the cozy surround and hiding place!

One person posted a video of a hedgerow, "Sunset Birdsong at the Bottom of My Garden," and decided to add, "Stop Ripping Up Hedges Please!" The video offered a pleasing variety of birdsong. Another melodious hedge video chirped on for a full thirty minutes. Consider playing this kind of audio treat from time to time, especially if you are stuck inside for a while.

## *November 16*

## Gull Skills: Cracking the Case

Yesterday my friend Crystal and I stood on a Long Island beach and watched as a gull picked up a conch shell, flew high above the beach, and dropped it, descending quickly to eat the now-exposed meat.

Scientists have studied these behaviors. Both studies I found showed that younger gulls weren't as adept at productive shell dropping. The youngest ones would sometimes peck ineffectively at a shell on the ground. Or they would figure out the "fly high and drop it" approach, but end up dropping the shell into the water. Oops! When they did drop the shells on the beach, they tended to need to repeat the act more times before the shell opened. They watch their elders and, between observation and trial and error, they eventually figure it out.

In the *Christian Science Monitor*, Doug Struck wrote about damage from this gull behavior. A car shop told a car owner about his hood's deep dent (for which he had blamed his kids!): "This looks a clam dent." If you live in a seaside area with a dense gull population, this is not too uncommon. And a school in a Massachusetts shore town had to close for three days due to serious roof leaks. The cause? Gulls incessantly dropping shells on its already compromised roof. Another family was plagued by the daily dawn cacophony of gulls dropping clams and mussels on their metal roof! At least one entrepreneur has founded a business aimed at controlling these kinds of behaviors.

And there's the poop too. The article says folks in Gloucester, Massachusetts sometimes call the results of frequent gull droppings "a Gloucester paint job."

At the beach, though, it's good entertainment and quite a sight to watch the gulls pick their meal, soar high, execute their "food prep," and come back down to feast.

## November 17

### Misnomer and Medicine: The Juniper Berry

On a chilly cemetery walk, the vivid color of juniper berries jumped out at me. I was reminded that the "berries" are in fact seed cones. According to Mother Nature Network, quite a few birds eat the seeds, but more so in wintertime, after tastier foods have become scarce. Bobwhites, turkeys, bluebirds, thrushes, thrashers, mockingbirds, catbirds, warblers, grosbeaks, jays, sapsuckers, other woodpeckers, and waxwings eat juniper berries.

Humans have used juniper as an herbal remedy for indigestion and lung ailments, among many other things. An indigenous (Gitxsan) term for the plant translates to "boughs of the supernatural," seemingly in tribute to the plant's perceived powers. I was surprised to find this plant listed on drugs.com. (The site warns of toxicity, so it's not a good idea to consume juniper without advice from a well-versed expert.)

And there's gin, which some view as "medicine" of a sort. To be called gin, this drink must have a predominant juniper flavor. The berries were first added to better the taste of an otherwise quite bitter beverage.

Quite a few paint companies have some variation of the color "Juniper Berry." The several I found all mimicked young juniper berries, which are green. I prefer the arresting blue of the older berries, scattered like a cobalt constellation across the bush.

Take a moment: where else in nature, besides the sky, can you see constellations?

## November 18

### Nature at . . . the Empire State Building?

Helen Macdonald's essay, "High-Rise," in *Vesper Flights*, made me wonder about what contingent of next year's northerly spring bird migration will fly over the Empire State Building and how I might manage a nighttime trip there.

This isn't the first time I've heard an account of nighttime birdwatching at this monolith. Alison Davis, a treasured workshop facilitator at Edwin Way Teale's Trail Wood, once treated her group to a read-aloud account of the same experience by Teale. What a great idea he had, I thought.

Macdonald's essay is rich with astounding facts. Falcons will store their kills on high-rise ledges, just as they would do on a cliffside. An astounding number of insects and spiders are flying, at any given time, in the air above us and, yes, above the Empire State Building. Macdonald's piece estimates at least seven-and-a-half million of these creatures pass over a square mile of city in a month, the spiders hanging onto electrostatically charged silk.

This huge biomass is travel food for birds, who, above the iconic building, are not even at their greatest altitude. As MacDonald puts it, "even the tallest buildings dip into only the shallows of the sky." Then, after she points her binoculars straight up, into the darkness: "Birds invisible to the naked eye swim into view, and there are birds above them, and birds higher still."[156]

It's lovely to imagine nights like those described by Teale and Macdonald. There is a difficult side to this phenomenon, too, addressed by NYC Audubon's Lights Out New York program, which encourages high-rise owners to shut off their lights at night. This can prevent the deaths of birds who become disoriented among the tall, bright buildings. Maybe more eloquent descriptions of what is going on—so high up there—will help bring more people around to doing the right thing.

## *November 19*

## Spotted or Striped? Wintergreen's Welcome Winter Color

During a hike with my Master Naturalist class, we all gathered around some spotted wintergreen plants in the woods. It was yet another case of me scratching my head over the name. Each long, green leaf had a clearly delineated white stripe. Why was it called "spotted?"

Spotted wintergreen is the common name that stuck, at least around here. But I'm not the only one for whom the stripe was the obvious choice. Other nicknames include striped wintergreen or striped prince's pine. The "spotted" comes in because it looks mottled, at times.

The scientific name, *Chimaphila*, means "lover of winter." We tend to notice this low plant more when many other taller plants have lost their leaves. Wintergreen hangs onto its leaves and their green color all winter.

The "wintergreen" part of the name has a pretty obvious connotation, although the Perennial Nursery Company is quick to point out that spotted wintergreen is not a "true" wintergreen plant, not even a relative. "Wintergreen" was once used more commonly, while "evergreen" is the term today for plants that hold onto their green color through the cold. True wintergreens are aromatic shrubs—they smell minty and produce red berries. In fact, Ari Rockland-Miller at the *Mushroom Forager* blog calls wintergreen shrub berries his favorite "January breath mint and trailside snack."[157]

I like these poetic sentences from Edwin Way Teale about spotted wintergreen: "And so it will continue all through the winter months. Whenever we brush the snow aside we will find buried beneath this color of summer days."

## November 20

### Opossums: Many Defenses, and Don't forget the "O"

Gavin spotted two opossums along Route 80—one scampering in a roadside ditch, one running across the road. I think I saw a dead one too. Opossum roadkill is not an uncommon sight; they frequent roads at night so are often in harm's way.

People often say "possum" interchangeably with "opossum." But there is, in fact, a completely different animal called a possum in Australia, New Guinea, Indonesia, and other Pacific places. These animals act similarly but look quite different.

Opossums lack what we call a distinguished palette. Alaina Knochel's writeup at Penn State's Virtual Nature Trail says, "Depending upon availability and opportunity an opossum will eat insects and other invertebrates, fruits, small mammals, birds, bird eggs, carcasses, garbage, and even other opossums." It's no wonder the next sentence is: "An opossum will very rarely starve"![158]

They are also flexible about where they live. They may take over an abandoned burrow of another animal, live in a hollow log, or reside beneath a house. They move around a lot to avoid predators.

These creatures rarely get rabies; this may have to do with their low body temperature. They are North America's only marsupial, and they are nonaggressive. Besides playing dead, they throw predators off with excessive drooling, widening their mouths in a threatening manner (called "alligator mouth") and releasing a green, smelly fluid from you-don't-want-to-know-where.

I think the not-so-cuddly look of these animals can give them a bad rap. Maybe this info from National Geographic's *Photo Ark* can soften that impression: Their newborns, tiny as honeybees, develop in their mom's pouch; as they mature they ride on her back while she hunts. Less than half of each litter survives. Oh, and they climb trees and sometimes nest in tree holes. I've only seen them roadside. It will be a banner day when I find one looking down from a tree.

## *November 21*

### Long Runways: The Heavy Truth about Common Loons

Continuing my read of *The Wild Within* by tracker and photographer Paul Rezendes, I was surprised to learn that common loons have solid bones. I've often been struck how "light as a feather" many birds are, and I assumed this had to do with the fact that they have hollow bones.

I learned today, though, that this is a variable trait. The number of hollow bones varies by species, and they are more common in large birds that glide and soar than in diving birds. Even flightless birds can have hollow bones, although they might not reap the same benefit from them as birds that fly.

Rosie Costain, a volunteer at Montana Natural History Center, explains that hollow bones are pneumatized, with air sacs attached: "Essentially, their lungs extend throughout their bones"[159] and help birds take in more oxygen. Also, hollow bones don't make birds lighter. In fact, Costain says bird bones are heavier than those of creatures of a similar size, owing to their dense composition.

Penguin and puffin bones are also solid. Rezendes notes that the solid bones and comparatively small wings of the common loon contribute to the fact that loons need a long "runway" for takeoff.

I also learned that the sounds often associated with loons, sometimes described as "crazy laughs," are called tremolos. The wails they make are longer and more mournful sounding.

These birds are often associated with northern waters, but they are medium distance migrants, according to All About Birds. Those from eastern Canada come down to our Atlantic coast, typically starting in October.

## November 22

### Intrepid, Tiny Masters of Disguise: Saw-Whet Owls

This week in 2020, a saw-whet owl, later dubbed Rockefeller, was rescued from the Rockefeller Center Christmas tree that had been hauled downstate. The public took a shine to this hitchhiker, and he was released after some recovery time at Ravensbeard Wildlife Center. Most people expressed sympathy tinged with delight, while others were angry that this owl had to be traumatized because of a holiday tradition.

A commercial venture surrounding the owl surfaced immediately. The National Bobblehead Hall of Fame and Museum unveiled a Rockefeller bobblehead. It's good to hear that a portion of the sales went to the Ravensbeard Center.

The most common theory for the name "saw-whet" is that this owl's sound mimics that of a saw being whetted. When I listen to the audio, I hear what sounds like a kid practicing staccato, high-pitched notes on a recorder. There's another theory about the name that seems to make more sense: "Chouette" is the word for the owl in France and some parts of Canada, with the Anglicized, phonetic version becoming "saw-whet."

Most of the time, this bird is silent, and without sound as a clue, it is nearly impossible to spot in the wild. Writing for the Maryland Department of Natural Resources, John Taylor comments that the saw-whet "disappears simply by not moving." Its coloring simply blends into the forest. Hence, a photo of the bird can appear to be a random shot of some conifer branches.

While saw-whets weigh in at around three to five ounces, it's clear these birds pack a lot of power. They are equipped to cross vast bodies of water. One landed on a fishing vessel seventy miles from shore. While undeniably adorable, they are far from dainty. All About Birds reports how quickly the nest devolves into chaos, filling up with feces, pellets, and rotting prey parts after the fastidious mom flies away. These accessories are not included with the bobblehead.

## November 23
### Caterpillars, Sweaters, Cedar

I don't think I've ever seen a clothes moth. They are buff-colored and about the size of a grain of rice.

We had a cedar closet in my childhood home. The cool, dark room smelled good. But Mom didn't trust that cedar alone would stave off the sweater- and blanket-eating moths we kept hearing about. For good measure, she scattered a host of moth balls around the room.

Mom was right about not trusting the closet's powers. Cedar oil can repel moths when used in high concentrations, as in a cedar chest with a nice, tight lid, but a whole closet may lose its "magic" against hungry insects. I didn't know then that it is the larvae (caterpillars) of the *Tineidae* moth family, or fungus moths—not so affectionately known as clothes moths—who do the chewing. Under normal, outdoor circumstances, they eat—you guessed it—fungi, as well as lichens and dead organic material.

They also like keratin, a fiber found in feathers and hair, nesting materials in the wild. But if they find their way into our homes, our sweaters will do. In a moist environment, sweaters can hold onto some fungi. And the caterpillars have some costly tastes because the animal-fiber origins of silk, wool, cashmere, angora, leather, and fur have a special appeal. The female moth can typically lay forty or fifty eggs on an item of clothing.

Mom was misguided about using a liberal handful or two of naphthalene mothballs. Both people and pets can be harmed by their fumes, and kids and dogs have been known to ingest them, to toxic effect.

## November 24
### Unnoticed Pantry: Doorweed, Gooseweed, Birdweed

Today, as I walked the mile to town, I looked at the many plants and their seedpods, fruits, or berries, many of which were scrubby species I couldn't name. But I could see groups of birds flitting in and out of the bushes that looked bare at first glance, still getting their fill though summer is long gone.

I try to read Edwin Way Teale's *A Walk Through the Year* every day. Today's entry started out talking about a plant of many names. Its scientific name is *Polygonum aviculare*, but Teale called it doorweed, common knotweed, gooseweed, and birdweed, among other things. Teale's description especially supported the birdweed moniker. He wrote about tree sparrows and juncos working the low, matted plant to get at tiny seeds, and the pleasure of watching them forage.

How many other small, humble-looking plants—things we walk past and walk over—are sustaining the birds that stay here in the North all through winter? I'll be viewing even the most bedraggled-looking patches with new appreciation this season. To help the neighborhood birds along, I've put out the feeder, too, happy to think about them finding sustenance here as the natural food supply dwindles or is covered by snow.

A heated birdbath may be in order too. I've read that water can be difficult for birds to find later in the season. At the National Wildlife Federation, Laura Tangley explains, "Even in places with abundant snow and ice, it costs birds precious calories and body heat to melt frozen water."[160]

## *November 25*

## The Long Sleep: Mason Bees Wait for Spring

My neighbor Susan has a mason bee house, an attractive amalgamation of stacked "straws" made of either cardboard or bamboo.

Mason bees rarely sting, and Judy Beaudette at the Ecological Landscape Alliance says encouraging wild bees can help counter declines in honeybee colonies. Chris McLaughlin at Fine Gardening says mason bees will pollinate nearly anything, but they especially like stone fruit trees, including plums, cherries, and peaches.

I was surprised to learn that mason bees are only active for about eight to ten weeks in spring. They hibernate for about ten months of the year.

Unlike bees who colonize, each female mason bee functions independently. She might lay eggs in naturally occurring tunnels such as hollow plant stems or passages created by wood-borer beetles. Or she might find a human-made mason bee abode an attractive place to shelter her offspring. She leaves food in the tunnel for her future babies and uses mud to seal off a chamber for each egg. She plugs each tunnel's entrance too. With this task complete, she dies.

When larvae hatch, they eat the food so thoughtfully left by mom. A bit later, they spin a cocoon and stay resting in the chamber. The magic number is fifty-five degrees. When the young adult bee registers that temperature consistently, it will emerge and begin its intense pollination season.

Entomologist Kim Stoner says we have sixteen types in Connecticut, and about 140–150 species of mason bees are native to North America.

## November 26

# The Bog Down in the Valley—Oh!

(Today's title is a lyric from an Irish folksong I used to sing to Gavin called the "The Rattlin' Bog." Rattlin' means "splendid" or "super," so that seems fitting for the Plymouth area's impressive bog views!)

Thanksgiving Day found our family on an unexpected road trip to Plymouth, Massachusetts, to stand with Native peoples on the National Day of Mourning.

Before we got to Plymouth, my eyes opened wide. A road leading into the city was peppered with cranberry bogs! Their deep red-purple shone across the subdued autumn landscape. This was a new sight for me.

The New England Historical Society points out that "If the Pilgrims served cranberries at the earliest Thanksgiving, they would have used them as a sweetener or a flavoring ingredient, not as a dish."[161] They explain that a Massachusetts man, Henry Hall, later figured out how to spread sand over cranberry plants, which made them thrive, then later flood the bogs, causing the berries to float up for easy picking.

Cranberries, in the same genus as blueberries, are native to New England. Writing for the National Wildlife Federation, Janet Marinelli says folks think they can't grow cranberries because they don't have a bog handy, but while these plants do like moisture, they don't need bogs to grow.

If you seek cranberries in the wild, writer and forager Josh Fecteau says the fruits like to hide quite low to the ground among the leafy stems. Janet at One Acre Farm says ripening begins in September, but you get sweeter berries if you delay harvesting until October or November. You might have some competition; reportedly, some birds like them, although they are not a favorite due to their tart quality. The UMass Cranberry Station says deer wandering into commercial bogs may eat up to four barrels over a season.

## November 27

### Spotting Spots: A Soft Porch Mystery

In a rather random pattern over the years—in terms of season—we've had the pleasure of finding soft, spotted balls dozing in corners atop our porch pillars. These are Carolina wrens. So many porches are graced with these visits. I searched "bird sleeping on porch" and found myriad snapshots just like ours of the tiny visitor.

Ornithologist David Sibley wrote about the "mystery spots" so visible on the sleeping wrens. What purpose do they serve? Normally the spotted rump feathers lay below the wings, but when the birds fluff them up, they can cover the wings. An initial notation of his, based on reader photos, said that showing spots was a display behavior while the bird was singing, which "means something important to other Carolina wrens." Later, Sibley noted the birds are "fluffed up to conserve heat" and still mused about the spots—are they camouflage? If so, why don't more birds have these markings?

Sibley supported a reader's theory that the white spots, which "glow" even in poor light, are "a great indicator of the position of the territorial owner to the intruder (or mate, or whomever)." But years later, as the online conversation on this mystery continued, Sibley mused, "Maybe there is no obvious reason for the spots?"[162]

For me, they exist to endear the bird to me even more. I'd still treasure a less distinctive-looking ball of fluff, but somehow the spots contribute to an extra large feeling of affection for this minute porch guest.

## November 28

### Pink Hanging On: A Rare Native Brightens the Landscape

Walking around East Haddam, my friend Pam and I were drawn to a fluffy-looking, tall pink plant. It had an exotic, cloud-like look.

Pink muhly grass is native to New England, but rare in these parts. I haven't been by the plant since, but by now its pink may have faded to a straw or silvery color. It will stay that way for winter. Birds enjoy the shelter of the grass, sometimes including its dead stems in their nests. Sparrows and finches like its seeds.

This perennial grass, sometimes called hairgrass, favors southeastern states and is, sadly, endangered in Connecticut. Around here, it favors dry, rocky woodlands and openings along trap rock ridges.

The first part of pink muhly grass's scientific name, *Muhlenbergia capillaris*, refers to a very productive man. Gotthilf Muhlenberg was a botanist, chemist, mineralogist, and Lutheran pastor. *A Daily Gardener* blog posted a quote from his journal: "It is winter, and there is little to do . . . Toward spring I should go out and [put together] a chronology of the trees; how they come out, the flowers, how they appear . . . I should especially [take note of] the flowers and fruit."[163]

As cold sets in and pink muhly grass loses its magical pink cloud look, maybe we can make plans like Muhlenberg did—perhaps at not such a grand scale—to pay attention to what we see and when, to catalog color, regeneration, and growth, and also learn how we can conserve and protect our local creature cousins—flora and fauna alike.

## *November 29*

### Squirrel Connoisseurs: Way Beyond Nut Gathering

*Bangor Daily News* published an intriguing piece by Aislinn Sarnacki—"Squirrels Prepare for Winter by Hanging Mushrooms in Trees to Dry."[164]

I received this with a skeptical eye. But Sarnacki's article is convincing. She, too, had been skeptical. At first, she saw a naturalist group member's Facebook post showing photos of mushrooms reportedly left out to dry by an American red squirrel. She remained skeptical even as she found blog posts about this behavior, aware that misinformation has a way of racing around the Internet.

Then she found more reliable sources, like the Society of Northwestern Vertebrate Biology and even a 1924 edition of the *Journal of Mammalogy*, reporting the same thing. In the 1924 article, William Everett Cram reported watching red squirrels carefully laying out harvested mushrooms in forked branches. They left them to dry for about a week and then stored them. Sarnacki also reports investigating a heavily mushroomed, heavily squirreled area of her local landscape and finding several instances of mushrooms and mushroom chunks balanced on tree stumps and crooks of branches.

We humans tend to become incredulous when we learn this sort of thing. Could it be true? Do these rodents have this level of forethought? While we must be careful to look for good evidence, I think the assumption that "only humans could figure this out" is a frequent mistake. Just because animals can't speak or write doesn't mean they lack intelligence and forethought. And who among us has not witnessed clever, persistent squirrels conquering just about every bird feeder model?

We are overrun with gray squirrels around here; red squirrels tend to reside much farther north. Still, whether home or off to northern parts, I'll be watching. Will I see, with my own eyes, industrious mushroom-hunting squirrels and their "dehydration stations"?

## *November 30*

## When Squash Were Wild

Our Thanksgiving table included a buttered and syruped honeynut squash, a relatively new cultivar that looks like a butternut, shrunken down.

Squash became a diet staple for early American colonists who, initially unimpressed with the vegetable, grew to appreciate its utility during long winters. They learned about this food from Native peoples, according to Dale Carson, a writer of Abenaki descent.

I got to wondering about when squash was first cultivated. Many of us, from the limited education we got about Native culture in school, learned about the Three Sisters planting method. In a Native Voices column for PBS, Navajo journalist Andi Murphy explains, "They're planted in a symbiotic triad where beans are planted at the base of the corn stalks. The stalks offer climbing bean vines support as they reach for sunlight from the earth. The beans, in turn, pump beneficial nitrogen back into the soil, fertilizing the corn and squash, while the squash's broad, spiny leaves protect the bean plants from predatory animals."[165] Murphy writes beautifully about her own memories of and perspective on these three vegetables, which she calls "a trifecta of agricultural sustainability."

Digging far back, archaeology expert K. Kris Hirst's piece at ThoughtCo remarks that wild squash was quite bitter and could be toxic. Apparently, mastodons did fine with it; their body mass could handle the toxins. Around the time they died out, squash domestication began—ten thousand years ago! Humans selected traits surrounding edibility, but they may have had another motive, too: gourds made for handy containers when scooped out. Squash were also used to create fishing weights.

The inedible Ozark gourd, likely an ancestor to our modern, edible squash, can still be found in eastern woodlands. The gourds look remarkably like eggs and are used in crafts. People who kept chickens used to place these gourds in hen nests to encourage the hens to lay more and to stay on the nest until their new chicks hatched.

## December 1

## Porcupine Love

We have fewer porcupines in Connecticut than in Vermont, where we visited with family for the Thanksgiving weekend. That got me thinking: what are winters like for porcupines?

Between September and December, love is in the air for these critters. I was astonished to learn that female porcupines are only fertile for eight to twelve hours one day per year! Males battle for the privilege of mating with females, with some bizarre rites. The male who wins will guard the female and stimulate her biological receptiveness by dripping urine onto her. The female will literally scream at the male if she is not interested, whle also shaking off the urine and running away. When she is receptive, she must curve her tail over her quills to avoid severe injury to the male.

Porcupine pregnancies are up to seven months long, and the babies— only one or two per litter—are called porcupettes. Females spend eleven months of every year either pregnant or nursing! Quills are soft at birth— great news for the mother! The babies can forage within days of being born, carrying on the porcupine tradition of gnawing on all sorts of plants.

In rough weather, such as during snow storms here in New England, these pointy creatures are quite often in their dens, sometimes sharing the space, although they otherwise tend to be solitary. They don't hibernate; quills have the added benefit of providing insulation.

## Among the Fastest

I am still enjoying Helen Macdonald's essay collection *Vesper Flights*. In her piece "Hares," she notes that hares "are our fastest land animal."[166] I assume she was writing about England, from where she hails. But that got me thinking: how fast do hares rate in the US? North American Nature, a site authored by mammalogist Bryan Harding, clocks hares at up to 40 mph. The North American pronghorn is at the top of the speed list—up to 96 mph! But it was a hare that got Harding researching who the fastest land mammals are on this continent, and he was amazed by the pace at which hares bounded across fields.

Hares don't burrow. They simply live out in the open, keeping simple nests on the ground. The depressions they make on the ground are called forms. Given the exposed nests, it's good that the young are born pretty much ready to be independent.

Like rabbits, hares eat and then retreat to cover. I wonder if that's what shot out from under our rhododendron the other morning. Predawn, Buddy flushed something fast out of the bush.

In Connecticut we have snowshoe hares, although I have only seen a couple. They're also called varying hares because of their changing coat color—white in winter to match the snow; brown the rest of the year to better match the landscape.

European hares—or brown hares—were introduced to the US from Europe as a game animal, and they are quite common around the Hudson Valley in New York. The females are known to box when they are unwilling to mate with persistent males.

*December 3*

## Bejeweled December

It's easy to take color for granted in spring and summer. My mom liked to quote the Rodgers and Hammerstein song "June Is Bustin' Out All Over," which waxes enthusiastic over buds of all kinds, Virginia creepers, and morning glories thriving at start of summer.

Hal Borland notes, "it wasn't an outdoor poet who coined the phrase 'bleak

December.'" He advises us to notice how the green in hemlocks, pines, amd clubmosses seems twice as bright now. He calls creeping partridgeberry fruits "dewdrop sized rubies" and describes the "bloodstone fruit" of the sumac, and the coral and carnelian "bangles" found on bittersweet. He praises topaz and ruby colors on the barberry bushes. . .his list goes on!

And, finally, his succinct wisdom: "December wasn't meant to be June." As found in Ecclesiastes in the Bible and later the song "Turn, Turn, Turn" by the Byrds: "To everything there is a season."

## December 4

## Easy December Living for Bald Eagles

Here in Connecticut, it's in December that thoughts turn toward vacations in tropical climes. Winter is not in its full harshness yet, but it's time to start the scraping and shoveling, and to keep an eye out for black ice on walkways and roads. Shorter days assert their presence with ever more generous helpings of darkness.

For bald eagles in Maine and Canada, however, our state to the south provides relief—open waters—translation: fish!—as opposed to ice! The DEEP site reports that up to a hundred eagles winter in Connecticut, starting in December. Breeding starts next month, with eggs by February or March. Our local Winter Wildlife Eagle Cruises with RiverQuest are chilly but fascinating affairs, with many pairs of binoculars trained over the water, spotting eagles as well as swans, grebes, mergansers, gulls, etc.

I have yet to witness firsthand the courtship display in which the male and female bald eagles spiral down towards the earth together, talons intertwined. I love Patricia Edmonds's *National Geographic* headline: "For Amorous Bald Eagles, a 'Death Spiral' is a Hot Time."

## December 5

## Silent Stealthy Squeezers

A Cooper's hawk perched on our deck railing, looking stately and fierce. No other birds were in sight and for good reason. These raptors are known for their determined approach to hunting, and they mostly eat birds, particularly favoring European starlings, mourning doves, American robins, jays, and other medium-sized birds. They swoop through vegetation to get to their avian prey, although not without incurring physical damage; one of the facts listed by All About Birds is that 23 percent of Cooper's hawk skeletons studied had healed-over fractures in their chest bones.

Dogged persistence isn't simply a fluke of personality; it is necessary for survival. These birds need to take in about seventy grams of food each day—the equivalent of seven black-capped chickadees! It makes sense that they prefer larger birds as only one robin is needed to provide the same amount of food as those seven chickadees.

Cooper's hawk talons must be super strong. Their kills are made by repeated squeezing of their unlucky prey. They have been seen drowning their supper too. As is the way in the natural world, they also serve as prey, to great horned owls, red-tailed hawks, and northern goshawks. And, earlier last century, Cooper's hawks were common victims of human hunting, with hunters snagging up to 40 percent of all first-year birds. They were also victims of DDT. But the Cooper's hawk population has had an uptick in recent years.

## December 6

## Woodchucks and Squatters

I wondered about someone's observation of a woodchuck gathering leaves this time of year. Searching for information about it, I was reminded that burrow maintenance is one of this creature's essential chores. They need a soft landing place for hibernation, typically October to March, and also for lining the nest when babies are born in spring.

A nature writer for PennLive, Marcus Schneck, explains that while woodchucks' heart rate, body temperature, and breathing rate drop dramatically for their "long winter's nap," hibernation isn't simply one long, uninterrupted sleep. Sometimes they have short periods of wakefulness. I wonder if during these periods they look for fresh "bed linens."

Woodchuck burrows are multi-chambered, including latrine areas, and have multiple entrances. When it gets quite cold, the woodchuck is likely sleeping in a lower chamber. But cottontail rabbits, skunks, and red foxes, driven by the chill, may "squat" in an upper chamber of the woodchuck burrow.

## December 7

### Stump Blossoms

We see things differently once the colder season arrives. Gone are nearly all blossoms, though some berries linger on. Gone are some birds, too, off to seek a richer food supply until spring returns. The shapes of many trees become more striking now that their branches are bare, and abandoned birds' nests suddenly "appear" on those branches. Some were within our easy reach this past spring but hidden by thick layers of leaves.

At Chatfield Hollow, I found myself looking down at mosses covering stones, at rows of small orange mushrooms along fallen trunks, at the mosaic of leaves my sneakers were swishing through. I leaned in to look at the hand-sized, white rosette gracing a tree stump, its kin cascading off the edge like a miniwaterfall, wondering what kind of mushroom I had here. Could it be a Berkeley's polypore, also known as a "stump blossom?"

They are so nicknamed because, no surprise, they like decaying stumps. They can also be parasitic, eating away at living trees and causing "butt rot" at their bases. I was surprised to learn they are edible when still young, adding a "meaty" element to meals when braised, according to Drew Wiberg at Mushroom Benefits.

I'd like to see a stump blossom when it first emerges from the ground. It's said to look like knobby, irregular fingers, which expand and morph over time into overlapping "shelves."

## December 8

### Feast for the Eyes, Feast for the Birds

I walked Chatfield Hollow's boardwalk through a red maple swamp, navigating patches of ice. The swamp's color is subdued in winter, but I could see clusters of winterberry holly. Landscaping enthusiasts in New England wax poetic about the bright winter beauty of this plant—until the birds consume all the berries!

So many beautiful blooms and berries have come and gone by this time of year. (I liked the Hollow's signage: the plants are "not dead but resting, waiting for spring.") But starting in November, winterberry gets its time to shine. Before that, this plant bordering woods and fields can go completely unnoticed.

Exploring Birds says the eastern bluebird and the cedar waxwing favor these berries. Robins, catbirds, and mockingbirds also enjoy this crimson feast.

A note for gardeners: the berry-making plant is female, but she needs the berry-less males nearby. So, it's important to keep nonproducing winterberry plants around!

## December 9

## Even Winter Has Blossoms: A New Flower to Find

It's been cold and my work life has been incredibly busy. During times like these, the next best thing to getting out in nature is reading about it. I am grateful for the piles of books scattered throughout the house, but for smaller bites, I love posts like those from our local wildlife refuge. The place and the posts are such a treat, and the refuge's Salt Meadow Unit is especially meaningful because Gavin completed his Eagle Scout project there not long ago.

This week the Refuge's Facebook post featured seaside goldenrod. Have I walked by it on winter beaches and simply not fully attended to it? It looks vaguely familiar, but now I want a good tramp along the coast to look for it.

The post referred readers to Elise Leduc's blog, *Seashore to Forest Floor*, which gives a bit more detail on the plant. The author starts out: "Winter doesn't mean the end of wildflower identification. Many plants retain easily identifiable seedpods and other features."[167] While this goldenrod's yellow has long since faded for the season, the fluffy-looking dried flower is easy to spot. The wind will take the fluff, dispersing seed as it goes. It will be fun to watch for the yellow to return as winter retreats.

## December 10

## Ostrich Ferns in Winter

*Northern Woodlands* has a great "This Week in the Woods" feature online with photos and blurbs about what can be found each week of the year. One such find for the second week of December is the ostrich fern's brown fertile fronds, recommended "if you're feeling a bit depressed by the long nights and lack of outside color." It's not that viewing these rather brittle-looking spikes will suddenly bring about some illusion of spring. In fact, folks seeing these dark brown fronds often assume they are dead. Rather, it's the idea that you can find them now so you can map their location for later!

In spring this is where the new fiddleheads can be harvested, if you are inclined to enjoy dining on them. (As with all foraged foods, caution is of utmost importance. It's reported that thousands get food poisoning each year from improperly stored or prepared fiddleheads.)

I don't find the brown fronds unsightly. Writer Phran Novelli at CBS Philly likens them to "feathers stuck in the snow."[168] I agree.

## December 11

### Starlings: Here Because of the Bard

The other morning I looked up to see five European starlings alight on a telephone wire. The winter white spots on their bellies were prominent. Although breeding season is long gone, I still saw a bit of iridescence glimmering above.

Shakespeare enthusiasts brought this species over from Europe in the 1890s. Their goal was to have every bird mentioned in a Shakespeare work be represented here. The starling only got one mention, in *Henry IV, Part I*. The explosion of starlings (at least two hundred billion) in the US descends from just ten birds that the enthusiasts introduced.

Many, but not all, of this species move south with the cold. These birds are known to be great mimics of other birds and of other things too. BirdNote audio of a starling includes the bird making a red-tailed hawk noise, then a killdeer, then a quail, then a phone ringing. The theory is that this attracts the females. Well, quite a few human females are drawn to musicians—so I can kind of relate.

I've been hearing a red-tailed around lately (or maybe not!). Maybe this mimicry explains why I can never spot the hawk!

## December 12

### Architecture to the Fore

Yesterday I saw a host of silvery, furry catkins on the now-bare magnolia tree. Nestled among them was an impressively woven bird nest complete with a layer of mud mortar. I marveled: I could have reached through the leaves and touched this finely crafted nest when the weather was warm, but it was so well hidden by foliage.

On more walks this week, I peered at shapely brown husks that housed blossoms in the spring, and both Tom and I recognized the natural "Christmas ornament" look of the sweetgum pods we passed under. Tom brought a sycamore seed pod home.

Online craft sites are gaga about seedpods, hawking dried lotus pods, cotton bolls, acorn caps, sweetgum and sycamore balls, water chestnut seeds, etc. They are, after all, quite striking, with an astonishing array of shapes and textures.

This time of year, we get to see structure—not just seedpods and nests—but how the tree branches frame the sky and what their essential shapes are beneath all the "clothes" worn in spring and summer.

In *Wise Living* magazine, Hannah Stephenson writes about the beauty of structural plants in the garden—the pleasure of a spiky teasel head, naturally dried hydrangea blooms, feathery ornamental grasses, twisted corkscrew hazelnut limbs.

Catkins (flowering spikes) alone are a winter treat, all the more noticeable on bare shrubs and trees. Search for images of catkins in winter to see some stunning displays.

## December 13

### Far from Pretty, Full of Eco-Stories

Once or twice a day, a wet-sounding "plop" hits the forest floor beneath an owl who has regurgitated a packet of fur and bones twelve to twenty hours after a meal. All birds of prey make pellets—the indigestible "leftovers" from a bird or small mammal they have eaten.

The *Washington Post* published Christopher Ingraham's fascinating article about entrepreneurs who collect and sell these bone-laden leavings to schools, museums, and research labs. There I learned that barn owls are special because they have weak digestive systems and tend to swallow prey whole, meaning that skeletons are typically expelled nearly intact.

Expert pellet harvesters get so they can tell the region a pellet came from—they are looser when they come from the moist Pacific Northwest, for example. Drier pellets, from warmer parts of California, are harder to dissect but boast a better mix of prey. Sometimes wool-eating moths get into the merchandise and ruin business for the people who bake the pellets to sterilize them and ship them to customers. While most customers are science-focused, sometimes they want the tiny bones for jewelry or witchcraft purposes.

Owl pellets are, of course, a reminder of the brutality of nature, predators efficiently and mercilessly scooping up the smaller and more vulnerable. But for the nature/science geek, they are a source of rapt fascination, an unsightly container for intriguing stories. I was also reminded that the pellets themselves are mini-ecosystems—here clothes moths, as well as carpet beetles and fungi, find shelter. Clothes moth larvae often mature into adults within the pellets.

## December 14

## The Bitter and the Sweet of Bittersweet

On an autumn day years ago, I put a berry-laden bittersweet branch into my pack, with some berries still green. I forgot about it until much later that day, and when I pulled it out the berries had fully ripened into a stunning red and yellow collection.

I appreciate bittersweet's beauty and how it brightens our chilly days, but now I know that gorgeous branch was Asiatic bittersweet, an invasive that can unfortunately smother native vegetation. It spreads by underground roots and, once it has killed the surrounding growth, can become a monoculture. Its seeds can linger in birds' guts for weeks, which means they can be redeposited quite far away from where the birds dined.

Asiatic bittersweet often makes its way into holiday décor, but experts warn against this. Birds will eat the berries off those handsome door wreaths and disperse them.

Fortunately, we have a native version of the plant, American bittersweet. Its fruits are orange when ripe and only appear at the tips of the branchlets, while the Asiatic version can grow fruits all along its stems. Differentiating the two "cousins" can be challenging. The USDA warns: "beware mislabeled nursery stock"—so it sounds like even experts get it wrong sometimes. The native version is, unfortunately, a species of special concern in Connecticut.

Some say a poem by Percy Bysshe Shelley, titled "Passion,"[169] was referring to bittersweet (although it could have been yet another bittersweet variety, known as woody nightshade). This would be fitting, since the berries are, indeed, toxic to us humans (whatever the variety). Here's the start:

> Fair are thy berries to the dazzled sight,
>   Fair is thy chequered stalk of mingling hues,
> And yet thou dost conceal
> A deadly poison there
> Uniting good and ill.

## December 15

### Christmas Fleas

Full disclosure: As far as I know there's no such thing as Christmas fleas. But I like my nickname for these minute but hardy arthropods. (Actually, hexapods, a subset of that family, closer to a crustacean than an insect). Look at any quintessential, placid, snow-blanketed scene on a Christmas card, and it's fun to imagine that somewhere on the snow, too small to be captured by the artist, is a virtual dance party put on by snow fleas.

Snow fleas are not technically fleas, and they are often referred to as springtails. They live in and on organic materials, commonly leaf litter, and come out on top of the snow on warmer days, searching for food. Tiny as they are, they play a role in decomposition, an essential part of nature's life cycle.

Not surprisingly, given their name, snow fleas can jump great distances, using an appendage to launch themselves skyward. And, this sounds nearly impossible, but Sy Montgomery's book *The Curious Naturalist* reports that sometimes they emerge in voluminous numbers, stopping trains in Switzerland because their squashed bodies make the rails slippery. Sometimes they are mistaken for a powdery chemical spill on a highway.

Mostly, though, they are just tiny, entertaining specks that look like random dirt on the snow—until you realize the "dirt" is leaping about. They don't bite; they don't parasitize. So let the dance party continue.

## December 16

## (Sort of) Red-Bellied, Well-Fed, and Warm(er)

Snow is coming—lots of it. This motivates me to fill the feeders. I've watched birds visit it even during heavy wind and snowfall. Red-bellied woodpeckers bring delightful color, and they especially love the suet.

In a column for the *Day*, Bill Hobbs says these birds used to be a rare sight in Connecticut, as recently as fifty years ago. Now, areas with relatively densely spaced houses and plant life mean warm microclimates that suit the birds. They enjoy our feeders, for sure, but also hammer acorns, berries, and insects into tree bark, creating a pantry they can visit later.

I am not the only one a bit stymied by the name "red-bellied." Their bellies aren't red when compared with the markings on their heads. Actually, the National Audubon Society advises birdwatchers not to look toward the belly to identify these birds, commenting that whoever first named these birds must have had a wry sense of humor! Their belly's "red" is simply a subdued blush on the lower abdomen.

## December 17

## Wild Colors and Shapes: The Magical Surprise of Slime Molds

The tree stump I admired at Fountain Hill Cemetery hosted a potpourri of organisms—bracket fungi, a wealth of moss, and a surprisingly bright, long line of pink slime mold, with each segment little bigger than a pinhead. I think this marvel might have been *Lycogala*, or wolf's milk. They used to be classified as fungi, but slime molds are now in their own category. They are amoebas that often have multiple nuclei.

I haven't thought much about amoebas since middle school science class, but these highly colorful creatures can steal the show with their outrageous colors and shapes. Writing for the Connecticut Agricultural Experiment Station, Dr. Sharon M. Douglas notes another lovely feature: Often, they will appear to "magically" sprout overnight. People can get alarmed by this, but these organisms do no harm. Eventually, they dry up, take on a powdery quality, and "disappear." Also, they are misnamed. They are not molds. Like mushrooms, they multiply via spores.

Put simply, amoebas fuse and multiply, eventually making the fruiting bodies we can see with the naked eye. Lacy M. Johnson's article in *Orion*, "What Slime Knows," describes a vast, seemingly endless array of slime molds. They can look like sponges; hard calcium deposits; a host of tiny, bright stalks; iridescent beads; tufts of cotton candy; and dog vomit. They are found on every continent. They can go dormant for centuries, maybe even millennia, and "come to life" again when conditions are favorable.

Johnson's article makes me think: We humans have assumed a hierarchy of intelligence, but in nature we see all kinds of intelligence. These molds, despite the lack of an identified brain or any sense of vision or smell, are seemingly able to keep time and learn patterns. They can even solve mazes!

*December 18*

## Grace Under Ice: How Trees Endure

Yesterday's weather closed the schools and had me scraping sheets of ice off my car, which shattered into piles of chunky diamonds. Ice deepened the winter color of the trees and drew a dazzling outline around every facet of their branched beauty.

A lot of us think less about trees than we do about creatures who are mobile. Michael Gambino, curator of the Friends of Edith Read Wildlife Sanctuary, wrote how trees survive winter, commenting, "They are always there, silent and uncomplaining through heat and sleet and gloom of night."[170]

How do trees endure winter weather? Leaves drop after the trees create a seal against water vapor loss. Evergreens get to keep their needles because their thick sap won't freeze like the sap in deciduous trees. Also, their smaller, waxy "leaves" are less likely to be a source of water loss.

Bark plays an essential role, of course, and I learned that protection against sun in winter is of great importance. It's the cycle of heating as well as cooling and the resulting expansion and contraction that creates the risk for freezing and cracking.

The Morton Arboretum lists a host of injuries that can befall trees in winter, including two I never thought much about. The first is salt damage to trees near de-iced pavement. Trees take a hit from flying salt as well as from exposure through their roots. And girdling caused by mice and rabbits feeding on bark when other food is scarce is another threat. Gardeners protect landscaped trees from would-be chewers with screen wire or hardware cloth.

Next time I admire a tree's winter-wrapped beauty, I'll admire its tenacity even more!

## *December 19*

### Black Bear Cubs Coming Soon

While black bear mating season happened back in the summer, the resulting embryos didn't implant and start to develop until the mother settled into her den. The cubs are typically born mid-January to early February.

In the den, the mother licks the cubs and keeps them warm against her belly. We've all heard of fat, sleeping bears in their dens who filled up with nutrition before hibernation. But it's impressive that bear moms can make plenty of milk from what they have stored in their bodies for hibernation. A nursing bear mother can lose more than a third of her body weight. In case you were wondering, bear milk tastes sweet, like condensed milk, according to bear researcher LaVern Beier.

Cubs are just eight to twelve ounces when born but balloon to eighty pounds by the end of their first year. Bear moms train and protect the cubs for about seventeen months and then must physically chase them away as they again become ready for mating. But a mother's bond is strong; she may allow them to stay in parts of her territory for longer, simply avoiding them but also ejecting nonfamily bears that encroach on the area. Male offspring tend to move along, while females tend to stick closer to their original home.

*December 20*

## Bird Breath: Visible "Music"

Tomorrow's entry in Edwin Way Teale's beloved almanac, *A Walk Through the Year*, has Teale musing about condensed water vapor. On a cold day, he watches his breath draft away "like a small cloud of steam" and recalls seeing this happen with dogs and cows. He remembers watching mallards and pintails close to shore, making tiny white puffs. But he wonders aloud about smaller birds; with all his time observing birds, he never saw a "breath cloud," so to speak, come from a smaller bird. He concludes that "the quantity of moist air expelled by the lungs of these birds is insufficient to make an observable amount of vapor." Technically, what we see coming from birds' mouths (and our own) on cold days is condensed water droplets that arise right after the warm gas from our lungs hits the air.

Teale didn't have the benefit of Internet searches, and photographic technologies have skyrocketed since his era. I've seen enough credible photographs of birds "blowing smoke" to be sure that this can be seen with many birds, even smaller ones. Birds captured "smoking" on camera include sparrows, cardinals, robins, red-winged blackbirds, and a blue tit, along with bigger varieties like ravens, swans, and great blue herons. I got excited when I thought one of the photos even showed a hummingbird making smoke rings, but it turned out he was just carrying a piece of cattail fluff, and of course, in our area hummingbirds migrate south in cold weather!

It's pleasant, and perhaps a bit Disneyesque, to imagine that each individual puff of vapor is a bird's musical note written on the air. If we caught these puffs, would we have a symphony in a jar?

# Endnotes

1. https://portal.ct.gov/DEEP/Wildlife/Fact-Sheets/Least-Tern
2. https://www.gardenguides.com/13404795-why-spray-fruit-trees-with-water-before-a-freeze.html
3. E. O. Wilson, "A Biologist's Manifesto for Preserving Life on Earth," *Sierra Magazine* (January/February 2017).
4. Jamie Murphy, "Environment: The Quiet Apocalypse," *Time Magazine* (October 13, 1986).
5. https://extension.unh.edu/blog/2018/02/american-larch-stick-mud
6. https://www.pgc.pa.gov/Education/WildlifeNotesIndex/Pages/SnowshoeHare.aspx
7. Editors of *EarthSky*, "Fifty years of data show spring and fall bird migrations changing," *EarthSky* (February 25, 2020).
8. "Some Keep the Sabbath Going to Church" was first published in 1864 in *The Round Table*.
9. http://www.naturegeezer.com/2007/01/hoop-poles.html
10. Chandler S. Richmond, *Beyond the Spring: Cordelia Stanwood of Birdsacre* (Latona Press, 1978).
11. https://nautil.us/what-pigeons-teach-us-about-love-4241
12. https://www.theday.com/columns/20190302/recalling-when-bobwhites-flourished-here
13. https://www.npr.org/sections/krulwich/2014/08/02/337094266/guess-who-s-been-waiting-in-the-lobby-for-a-hundred-million-years
14. https://www.projectnoah.org/spottings/8719518
15. https://www.earthlawcenter.org/blog-entries/2018/9/daylighting-la-bievre-river-in-paris-france
16. https://www.ctaudubon.org/2019/01/mew-gull-2
17. https://www.democratandchronicle.com/story/news/2019/04/07/stink-bugs-back-what-to-know/3394265002
18. https://www.courant.com/news/connecticut/hc-xpm-2002-10-19-0210190301-story.html
19. https://www.dupageforest.org/blog/natures-valentines
20. https://matt-candeias.squarespace.com/?offset=1430744937832
21. https://treehut.co/blogs/news/what-is-burl-wood-its-weirder-than-you-think
22. https://northernwoodlands.org/pdf/TOS__Burls.pdf
23. https://ctwoodlands.org/wp-content/uploads/2022/10/Woodlands-Winter-2021-min.pdf
24. https://www.pixiespocket.com/2017/12/foraging-rose-hips.html
25. https://menunkatuck.org/a-touch-of-the-tropics-in-connecticuts-woods
26. http://the3foragers.blogspot.com/2014/04/connecticut-ramps.html
27. https://www.allaboutbirds.org/guide/Red-winged__Blackbird/lifehistory
28. "My November Guest" was published in 1913 in *A Boy's Will*, the first published volume of Robert Frost's poetry.
29. Charles Stannard, "A Look Back at the Flood of '82," *Hartford Courant* (June 5, 2002).
30. https://www.audubon.org/news/when-youre-bird-world-always-looks-psychedelic
31. https://www.lauraerickson.com/radio/program/9343/chickadee-color
32. http://bobarnebeck.com/muskrats.htm
33. https://www.collectorsweekly.com/articles/the-craze-for-traditional-native-american-baskets
34. https://biocitizen.org/how-do-spring-peepers-know-when-to-start-singing
35. Steve Bender, "The Only Good Place For a Weeping Willow," *Southern Living* (May 9, 2022).
36. https://www.offthegridnews.com/how-to-2/its-the-quirky-medicinal-tree-that-pharmaceutical-companies-use
37. https://www.nwf.org/Educational-Resources/Wildlife-Guide/Plants-and-Fungi/Quaking-Aspen
38. https://www.nps.gov/brca/learn/nature/quakingaspen.htm
39. https://treesforlife.org.uk/into-the-forest/habitats-and-ecology/ecology/plant-galls
40. https://www.allaboutbirds.org/news/what-can-i-do-about-a-bird-that-sings-all-night-long-outside-my-window
41. https://bwdmagazine.com/learn/house-finch

42. https://www.researchgate.net/publication/345692797__Sex__shells__and__weaponry__coercive__reproductive__tactics__in__the__Painted__Turtle__Chrysemys__picta

43. https://old.post-gazette.com/pg/11086/1135078-358.stm

44. https://celebrateurbanbirds.org/learn/birds/focal-species/northern-cardinal

45. https://bwdmagazine.com/learn/house-finch

46. https://www.northlandtackle.com/leeches-vs-minnows-vs-nightcrawlers

47. Charles Darwin, *On the Origin of Species* (London: John Murray, 1859).

48. https://www.audubon.org/news/how-orioles-build-those-incredible-hanging-nests

49. Daniel M. Brooks, "Birds Caught in Spider Webs: A Synthesis of Patterns," *The Wilson Journal of Ornithology* 124 (2012).

50. David Taft, "Evil, Invasive, Delicious," *The New York Times* (May 11, 2017).

51. https://www.allaboutbirds.org/guide/Mute__Swan/sounds#:~:text=theMLarchive.-,Calls,hissingwhenthreatenedordisturbed

52. https://portal.ct.gov/DEEP/Wildlife/Fact-Sheets/Mute-Swan

53. https://daily.jstor.org/mute-swans-harmful-invasive-species

54. https://www.homestratosphere.com/types-of-ranunculus

55. https://www.hobbyfarms.com/3-myths-about-moles

56. https://www.popsci.com/star-nosed-moles

57. https://anitasanchez.com/2012/10/25/basal-rosettes-life-in-the-flat-lane

58. https://indiananativeplants.org/wp-content/uploads/GW__Hepatica.doc#:~:text=TheancientDoctrineofSignatures,ownusesfortheHepatica

59. https://www.bbg.org/gardening/article/box__turtles

60. Jay Griffiths, "Dwelling on Earth," *Emergence Magazine* (October 3, 2019).

61. Ruth Smith, "Stop to See—But Don't Smell—The Trillium," *Berkshire Eagle* (May 7, 2014).

62. http://st-eni.eniscuola.net/en/2016/06/27/the-numbers-of-nature-the-fibonacci-sequence

63. http://st-eni.eniscuola.net/en/2015/12/17/the-perfection-of-the-snail

64. http://www.hort.cornell.edu/bjorkman/lab/arboretum/trees/burning__bush.html

65. https://www.allaboutbirds.org/guide/Double-crested__Cormorant

66. https://www.fieldandstream.com/how-to-find-clean-and-cook-fiddlehead-ferns

67. https://www.sermoncentral.com/sermon-illustrations/61203/cecil-b-demille-toldthis-wonderful-experience-by-sermon-central

68. https://www.allaboutbirds.org/guide/Veery/sounds

69. https://www.dnr.state.mn.us/invasives/aquaticanimals/banded-mystery-snail/index.html

70. https://emergencemagazine.org/essay/eleven-ways

71. https://www.nytimes.com/1978/06/29/archives/gardening-mountain-laurel-blooms-in-the-densest-shade-some-sources.html

72. https://artofeating.com/shagbark-hickory-nuts

73. https://naturewalk.yale.edu/trees/fagaceae/fagus-sylvatica/weeping-beech-13

74. https://www.sciencedaily.com/releases/2020/05/200512205552.htm

75. https://www.frontiersin.org/articles/10.3389/fpls.2020.569811/full

76. https://link.springer.com/article/10.1007/BF01092548

77. https://natureedmonton.wordpress.com/2013/08/03/sedges-have-edges

78. https://uwm.edu/field-station/two-long-horned-borers

79. The link to this article is no longer available.

80. Carl Sagan, *The Dragons of Eden: Speculations on the Evolution of Human Intelligence* (Ballantine, 1989).

81. https://www.newstribune.com/news/2018/apr/11/Findingmountain-mints

82. https://petkeen.com/fox-cubs-growing-up

83. https://www.wildlifeonline.me.uk/animals/article/red-fox-diet-hunting-strategies-behaviour

84. https://www.gardensalive.com/product/wineberriesthe-forbidden-fruit

85. Ibid.

86. https://www.allaboutbirds.org/guide/Belted__Kingfisher/lifehistory

87. https://www.nytimes.com/2002/07/21/nyregion/july-is-a-glorious-month-to-horseflies-too.html

88. The BugLady, "Northern Walkingstick (Family *Diapheromeridae*)," University of Wisconsin—Milwaukee (October 28, 2008); https://uwm.edu/field-station/northern-walkingstick

89. bear.org | https://vimeo.com/125647077
90. Bob Duchesne, "9 Things You Probably Don't Know about Maine's Wild Blueberries," *Bangor Daily News* (July 18, 2022).
91. https://www.audubon.org/news/is-swallow-or-swift
92. https://theweek.com/articles/447605/how-learned-love-evillooking-earwig
93. http://www.westernny.com/beaver.html
94. https://www.nationalgeographic.com/animals/article/beavers-climate-change-conservation-news
95. https://blogs.illinois.edu/view/7362/566620
96. https://en.wikipedia.org/wiki/Aleuria__aurantia#Description
97. https://www.fs.usda.gov/wildflowers/beauty/mycotrophic/monotropa__uniflora.shtml
98. https://www.wimberglandscaping.com/ReadArticle.aspx?e=24
99. https://archives.weru.org/awanadjo-almanack/2021/07/awanadjo-almanack-7-16-21-fireweed
100. https://www.youtube.com/watch?v=mTGCDMgl4Q4
101. https://vimeo.com/83472406
102. https://www.maine.gov/dacf/php/gotpests/bugs/leafhopper.htm
103. https://www.nepm.org/2019-04-11/one-mans-quest-to-protect-a-rare-kind-of-hazelnut-tree#stream/0
104. Francis Higginson, *New England's Plantation; Or, A Short and True Description of the Commodities and Discommodities of that Country*, (T.C. and R.C., 1680).
105. G. E. Hutchinson, "Homage to Santa Rosalia or Why Are There So Many Kinds of Animals?" *The American Naturalist* (1959).
106. Jake Buehler, "Praying Mantises Hunt and Eat Fish, in a First," *National Geographic* (September 20, 2018).
107. http://bugeric.blogspot.com/2012/10/wasp-wednesday-four-toothed-mason-wasp.html
108. http://www.helpabee.org/specialists-vs-generalists.html
109. https://www.post-gazette.com/life/outdoors/2007/12/30/Wildlife-Making-a-difference-for-Carolina-wrens/stories/200712300243
110. https://bugguide.net/node/view/9013
111. https://www.jstor.org/stable/24987358
112. https://www.mvtimes.com/2016/10/19/tree-crickets
113. https://foragerchef.com/the-horn-of-death-black-trumpet-mushrooms
114. https://www.nytimes.com/2002/02/27/dining/out-of-darkness-bright-new-flavor.html
115. Edwin Way Teale, *Journey into Summer: A Naturalist's Record of a 19,000-Mile Journey Through the North American Summer* (New York: Dodd, Mead, 1960).
116. https://monarchbutterflylifecycle.com/blogs/raise/how-to-raise-eastern-tiger-swallowtails?__pos=5&__sid=d0e6d847f&__ss=r
117. https://www.nytimes.com/2016/06/12/nyregion/studying-the-tiger-swallowtail-a-familiar-sight-flitting-in-the-city.html
118. https://www.youtube.com/watch?v=bdNcsvuILQk
119. https://www.popsci.com/story/blogs/ask-us-anything/crow-raven-aggressive-behavior
120. https://baynature.org/2020/10/29/flying-in-for-the-crow-funeral
121. http://ianadamsphotography.com/news/drill-baby-drill-the-ins-and-outs-of-ichneumon-wasps
122. Erik Ofgang, "There Are No Mountain Lions in Connecticut, So Why Do We Keep Seeing Them?" *CTInsider* (October 24, 2019).
123. https://www.indefenseofplants.com/blog/2017/5/3/invasion-of-the-earthworms?rq=earthworms
124. This poem is in the public domain and easily found online.
125. https://www.dailyadvance.com/features/columnists/joe-pye-weed-is-a-pasture-nightmare-but-a-hot-perennial-ornamental/article__6327db44-b926-5fb7-aa97-f8565e169e94.html
126. https://www.biodiversitylibrary.org/item/36372#page/258/mode/1up
127. https://www.bbg.org/news/weed__of__the__month__white__snakeroot
128. https://www.friendsofthewildflowergarden.org/pages/history/ebwriting/tribune80611.html
129. https://www.adirondackalmanack.com/2015/07/jewelweed-definitely-not-a-weed.html
130. https://earthsky.org/astronomy-essentials/harvest-moon-2
131. https://www.livescience.com/61868-caterpillar-sounds-mystery-solved.html

132. "The Oven Bird" appeared in Robert Frost's third poetry collection, *Mountain Interval*. It was published in 1916 by Henry Holt.

133. https://www.ctaudubon.org/2019/06/ovenbird

134. https://northernwoodlands.org/outside__story/article/stone-walls

135. "Mending Wall" appeared in *North of Boston*, Robert Frost's second poetry collection. It was published in 1914 by David Nutt.

136. https://www.thespruce.com/when-is-fall-migration-386049

137. https://www.shorebirder.com/2020/08/guest-post-by-tim-spahr-finding.html

138. https://musicofnature.com/the-clucking-munks

139. http://natures-restaurant-online.com/Yew.html

140. https://blasdell.wbu.com/red-winged-blackbirds

141. http://www.differencebetween.net/science/nature/difference-between-sap-and-resin

142. https://intim8ecology.wordpress.com/tag/mushroom

143. Bonita Portzline, "Nature's Comfort and Joy: Challenging Challenge," *Gettysburg Times* (June 26, 2020).

144. Erna Gunther, *Ethnobotany of Western Washington*, University of Washington (1973).

145. https://www.dispatch.com/story/lifestyle/home-garden/how-to/2017/02/19/wasp-eating-moth-fills-rare/22431440007

146. Clement C. Moore, "A Visit from Saint Nicholas," *Troy Sentinel* (December 23, 1823).

147. https://naturallycuriouswithmaryholland.wordpress.com/2012/10/26/snail-and-slug-eggs

148. https://www.chelseagreen.com/2022/surprisingly-sweet-crab-apples

149. https://whyfiles.org/2012/farming-native-american-style/index.html

150. https://www.wired.com/2014/01/snow-fleas

151. Paul Rezendes, *The Wild Within: Adventures in Nature and Animal Teachings*, BookSurge Publishing (May 19, 2009)

152. Peter E. Busher, "Food Caching Behavior Beavers (*Castor canadensis*): Selection and Use of Woody Species," *American Midland Naturalist* 135, no. 2 (April 1996).

153. https://www.ourcityforest.org/blog/2016/3/30/the-forest-within-the-forest-the-hidden-world-of-epiphytes-1

154. https://www.animalfactsencyclopedia.com/Fox-facts.html

155. https://www.teagasc.ie/media/website/publications/2019/Environment---Hedges-fit-for-birds-and-bees.pdf

156. Helen Macdonald, "High-Rise," *Vesper Flights*, Grove Press (2021).

157. https://www.themushroomforager.com/blog/2017/1/17/wintergreen-the-hardy-wild-breath-mint

158. The link to this article is no longer available.

159. https://www.montananaturalist.org/blog-post/avian-adaptations

160. https://blog.nwf.org/2014/12/dont-forget-water-for-birds-in-winter

161. https://www.newenglandhistoricalsociety.com/six-cranberry-bogs-throughout-new-england

162. https://www.sibleyguides.com/2011/03/carolina-wren-mystery-spots

163. https://thedailygardener.org/otb20200122

164. https://www.bangordailynews.com/2021/10/25/outdoors/squirrels-prepare-for-winter-by-hanging-mushrooms-in-trees-to-dry

165. https://www.pbs.org/native-america/blogs/native-voices/meet-the-three-sisters-who-sustain-native-america

166. Helen Macdonald, "Hares," *Vesper Flights*, Grove Press (2021).

167. https://www.seashoretoforestfloor.com/wildflower-wednesday-seaside-goldenrod

168. https://www.cbsnews.com/philadelphia/news/ostrich-ferns-offer-something-for-every-season

169. Percy Bysshe Shelley, "Passion," in *The Esdaile Notebook*, edited by Kenneth Neill Camerson (Alfred A. Knopf, 2000).

170. https://friendsofreadwildlifesanctuary.org/survival-adaptations-how-trees-cope-with-winter

# About the Author

KATHERINE HAUSWIRTH writes about nature, often with a spiritual bent. Her work has been published in *Whole Life Times, Spirituality & Health*, the *Christian Science Monitor, Still Point Arts Quarterly, Connecticut Woodlands, Pilgrimage, The Wayfarer*, and *Re-Imagining*. She has been a writer in residence at Trail Wood in Connecticut, Acadia National Park in Maine, and with the Orchard Keeper Writers Residency in Tennessee. Her essay collection, *The Book of Noticing: Collections and Connections on the Trail* (Homebound Publications, 2017), won honorable mention for general nonfiction in ASJA's 2018 contest; a piece from the book won a first prize in the Soul-Making Keats Literary Competition.

# SHANTI ARTS

## NATURE ▪ ART ▪ SPIRIT

Please visit us online
to browse our entire book catalog,
including poetry collections and fiction,
books on travel, nature, healing, art,
photography, and more.

Also take a look at our highly regarded art
and literary journal, *Still Point Arts Quarterly*,
which may be downloaded for free.

www.shantiarts.com